# company accounting and financial statements

# company accounting and financial statements

## 6th edition

**robert rodgers**

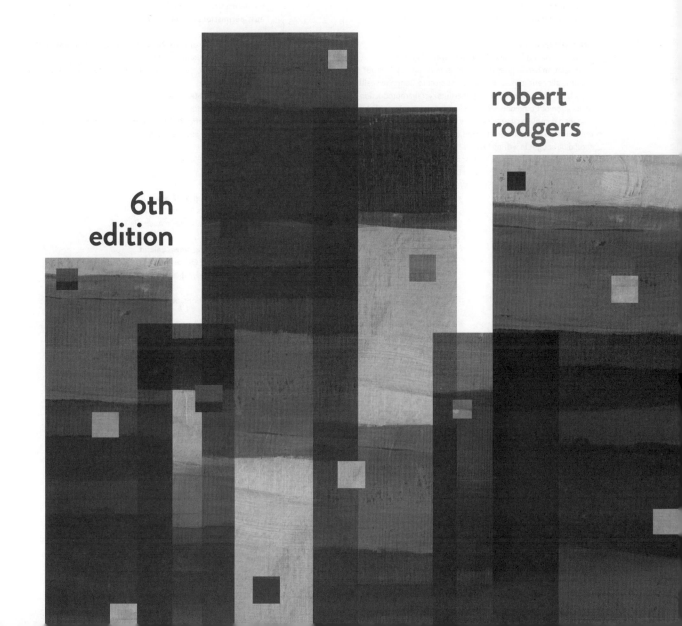

**Company Accounting and Financial Statements**
**6th Edition**
**Robert Rodgers**

Publishing manager: Dorothy Chiu
Publishing editor: Sophie Kalienicki
Developmental editor: James Forsyth/Stephanie Heriot
Senior project editor: Nathan Katz
Cover designer: Danielle Maccarone
Text designer: Pier Vido/Danielle Maccarone
Editor: Averil Lewis
Proofreader: Paul Smitz
Indexer: Russell Brooks
Permissions researcher: Wendy Duncan
Art direction: Danielle Maccarone
Cover: iStockphoto/© Qweek
Typeset by Cenveo Publishing Services

Any URLs contained in this publication were checked for currency during the production process. Note, however, that the publisher cannot vouch for the ongoing currency of URLs.

Third edition published in 2002
Fourth edition published in 2005
Fifth edition published in 2009
This sixth edition published in 2014

**Acknowledgements**
© Commonwealth of Australia sources within this text:
All legislation herein is reproduced by permission but does not purport to be the official or authorised version. It is subject to Commonwealth of Australia copyright. The *Copyright Act 1968* permits certain reproduction and publication of Commonwealth legislation. In particular, s.182A of the Act enables a complete copy to be made by or on behalf of a particular person. For reproduction or publication beyond that permitted by the Act, permission should be sought in writing from the Commonwealth available from the Australian Accounting Standards Board. Requests in the first instance should be addressed to the Administration Director, Australian Accounting Standards Board, PO Box 204, Collins Street West, Melbourne, Victoria, 8007.

For product information and technology assistance,
in Australia call **1300 790 853**;
in New Zealand call **0800 449 725**

For permission to use material from this text or product, please email
**aust.permissions@cengage.com**

**National Library of Australia Cataloguing-in-Publication Data**
Author: Rodgers, Robert, author.
Title: Company accounting and financial statements / Robert Rodgers.
Edition: 6 edition.
ISBN: 9780170238007 (paperback)
Notes: Includes index.
Subjects: Corporations--Accounting. Corporations--Accounting--Problems, exercises, etc. Financial statements. Financial statements--Problems, exercises, etc.
Dewey Number: 657.95

**Cengage Learning Australia**
Level 7, 80 Dorcas Street
South Melbourne, Victoria Australia 3205

**Cengage Learning New Zealand**
Unit 4B Rosedale Office Park
331 Rosedale Road, Albany, North Shore 0632, NZ

For learning solutions, visit **cengage.com.au**

Printed in China by RR Donnelley Asia Printing Solutions Limited.
2 3 4 5 6 7 18 17 16 15

# Brief Contents

# Contents

# Preface

*Company Accounting and Financial Statements* has been written to meet the performance criteria of the competency unit FNSACC504A Prepare Financial Reports for Corporate Entities in the Financial Services Training Package (FNS11).

The text enables learners to comprehend and apply a range of accounting and financial reporting issues facing Australian corporate entities to ensure the entity's compliance with the Australian Accounting Standards and the *Corporations Act 2001* (Cwlth).

The text has been written in a style that assists learners to meet the practical requirements of both the unit of competency and the Australian Accounting Standards in a timely and efficient manner by focusing on well-structured explanations and illustrations and avoiding unnecessary theoretical debate.

# Outcomes grid

## FNSACC504A Prepare financial reports for corporate entities

| Element | | Performance criteria | Text chapter |
|---|---|---|---|
| 1 | Compile data | Data is systematically coded, classified and checked for accuracy and reliability in accordance with organisational policies, procedures and accounting standards | 1, 2, 3, 4, 5, 6, 7, 8, 9, 10 |
| | | Conversion and consolidation procedures are used to compile data in accordance with organisational policies and procedures | 2, 3, 4, 5, 6, 7, 8, 9, 10 |
| | | Valuations in compliance with relevant accounting standards are recorded | 2, 3, 4, 5, 6, 7, 8, 9, 10 |
| | | Effects of taxation are identified and recorded | 6, 8, 9, 10 |
| 2 | Prepare reports | Charts, diagrams and supporting data are presented in an appropriate format | 8, 9, 10 |
| | | Structure and format of reports are clear and conform to statutory requirements and organisational procedures | 8, 9, 10 |
| | | Statements and data are error free, comprehensive and comply with statutory requirements and organisational procedures | 8, 9, 10 |

# Resources guide

## FOR THE STUDENT

As you read this text you will find a wealth of features in every chapter to help you understand and enjoy your studies of *Company Accounting and Financial Statements*.

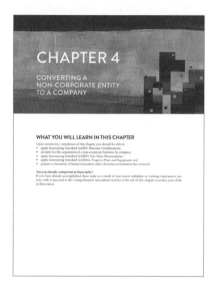

**Learning objectives** are listed at the start of each chapter to give you a clear sense of what the chapter will cover.

**Worked examples**, presented as Illustrations, clearly demonstrate theory in practice so you can easily visualise concepts.

**In-chapter questions** enable you to test your comprehension of key concepts as you work your way through each chapter.

**Comprehensive assessment activities** at the end of each chapter will enable you to consolidate chapter concepts.

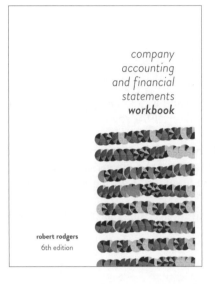

The workbook for this new 6th edition of *Company Accounting and Financial Statements* is specifically structured to work in combination with the revised table of contents, and provides consistent and professionally presented solution templates for each chapter.

*Visit www.cengagebrain.com.au and search for this book.*

**Online quizzes** provide additional practice of chapter concepts.

# FOR THE INSTRUCTOR

**Cengage Learning is pleased to provide you with a selection of in-text and online supplements to help you lecture in accounting.**

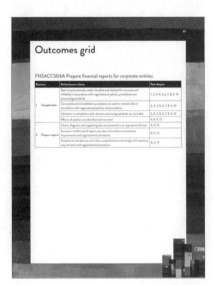

The Outcomes grid at the start of the text clearly maps text content to FNSACC504A *Prepare Financial Reports for Corporate Entities* in compliance with the TAFE performance criteria.

**Instructors Manual** with Solutions.

**PowerPoint Presentations** have been prepared to cover the main points of the chapters, and can be edited to suit your course. Use these slides to enhance your lectures and reinforce key principles.

A **Testbank** of questions covering the learning objectives and key topics has been prepared for your use. These are available in Word format and can be downloaded directly into your own learning management system.

Additional chapters of **advanced material** are also provided as a resource.

*Please contact your Cengage Learning sales representative or visit www.cengage.com.au.*

# About the author

*Robert Rodgers*

Robert Rodgers is a qualified accountant, has a full teaching qualification and is qualified to assess and train in the workplace. He has applied his professional skills in the TAFE sector since 1976, specialising in the delivery and assessment of accounting courses at the vocational level.

Robert has a thorough understanding of the operations and intricacies of the Financial Services Training Package through his involvement in the development and implementation of the Financial Services Training Package (Accounting) in Victoria, and understands the need to provide quality learning materials that suit learners and educators in a challenging learning environment.

He has also produced numerous published and unpublished training and learning materials and assessment tools for use in the vocational training sector nationwide.

# Acknowledgements

Cengage Learning extends our appreciation to Paul De Lange, Professor of Accounting at RMIT University, Melbourne, Australia. Professor Paul De Lange was instrumental in the establishment of this title and has been a valued co-author and contributor for the previous five editions. Cengage Learning thanks Paul De Lange for his involvement and for his contribution to the success of *Company Accounting and Financial Statements*.

Cengage Learning would also like to thank the following people for their helpful reviewing and insightful comments during the development of this edition:

- Lee Homewood – Swinburne
- Sue Fisher – TAFE NSW
- Antonia Wood – TAFE NSW
- David Crebbin – Victoria University
- Heather Talbot – TAFE SA
- Karen Nicita – NSW Department of Education & Training
- Inal Duman – Brisbane North Institute of TAFE.

Every effort has been made to trace and acknowledge copyright. However, if any infringement has occurred, the publishers tender their apologies and invite the copyright holders to contact them.

# CHAPTER 1

## INTRODUCTION TO CORPORATE ENTITIES

## WHAT YOU WILL LEARN IN THIS CHAPTER

Upon satisfactory completion of this chapter you should be able to:
- identify a corporate entity;
- differentiate between a corporate reporting entity and a non-reporting corporate entity;
- differentiate between the main types of companies under the *Corporations Act 2001* (Cwlth);
- describe the procedures required to register a company;
- record the issue of shares to establish a company and its costs of establishment;
- describe the roles of financial regulators; and
- list the records required by the Corporations Act.

**Are you already competent at these tasks?**
If you have already accomplished these tasks as a result of your recent workplace or training experiences you may wish to proceed to the Comprehensive Assessment Activity at the end of this chapter to assess your skills in these areas.

## 1.1 INTRODUCTION

When a business is commenced its owner(s) must consider a range of issues, including the business structure and name, rules and regulations relating to the business operation and taxation issues, including the Goods and Services Tax (GST) and income tax.

Business structures include non-incorporated and incorporated entities. Non-incorporated structures include sole trader or partnership forms of ownership, while incorporated businesses include company forms of ownership.

This chapter examines the nature and establishment of an incorporated entity and the conditions that make it a corporate reporting entity.

## 1.2 WHAT IS A REPORTING ENTITY?

Accounting in Australia is guided by the Australian Accounting Standards developed by the Australian Accounting Standards Board (AASB). The Board has adopted a Framework for the Preparation and Presentation of Financial Statements which sets out the concepts that underlie the preparation and presentation of financial statements for external users.

The Framework refers to the Statement of Accounting Concepts 1 (SAC 1) which explores the concept of a reporting entity and its requirement to prepare general purpose financial reports for dependent external users.

SAC 1 states the following in respect of 'reporting entities' and 'general purpose financial reports'.[1]

> (Para 40) Reporting entities are all entities (including economic entities) in respect of which it is reasonable to expect the existence of users dependent on general purpose financial reports for information which will be useful to them for making and evaluating decisions about the allocation of scarce resources.

> (Para 41) Reporting entities shall prepare general purpose financial reports. Such reports shall be prepared in accordance with Statements of Accounting Concepts and Accounting Standards.

Consequently any organisation that has users who are dependent on its financial reports for information is deemed to be a reporting entity and must therefore provide financial reports that comply with the Australian Accounting Standards.

SAC 1 (Para 19) discusses the identification and existence of a 'Dependent User' and in Paras 20–22 provides the following factors that may give rise to a dependent user.

**1  Separation of management from economic interest**

Where an organisation is owned (economic interest) and managed by different people the owners may not be in a position to obtain financial information readily as they do not manage or control the organisation. Thus the owners may be viewed as dependent on the organisation, resulting in the organisation being a reporting entity.

The separation of management and economic interest can occur in a company form of ownership where the owners of a company (shareholders) hand the management of the company to independent directors.

Where the ownership and the management of the business are not separated, as may be the case for a sole trader or a partnership, then dependency does not arise – hence the business is not a reporting entity.

**2  Economic, political importance or influence**

An entity may be considered important economically and politically (or socially) as it has an impact on the wellbeing of external parties who may be dependent on the entity for information.

Where entities possess a greater economic, political or social importance there is a greater likelihood of the existence of dependent users seeking information on the entity, hence the entity is a reporting entity and must produce compliant financial reports.

Organisations falling under this category may include those which enjoy dominant positions in markets (such as banks, mining interests, supermarkets and petrol producers) and those which impact on a society politically or socially (such as hospitals, child care providers and environmentally sensitive organisations).

---

1  http://www.aasb.gov.au/admin/file/content102/c3/SAC1_8-90_2001V.pdf, p.15.

### 3   Financial characteristics

Financial characteristics may include the size of an entity based on the value of its assets or sales turnover, the number of employees or the amount of its loans.

The larger the size of the entity and its control of resources the more likely it is that there will exist external users dependent on general purpose financial reports for financial information.

Where an organisation is dependent on funding or resourcing from governments such as schools, hospitals and aged care facilities the general public become dependent users and hence these entities become reporting entities.

When these factors are applied to an organisation and it can be determined that:

- there is no separation of ownership and management;
- the entity does not have a political or economic influence; and
- there are no significant financial characteristics,

then the organisation is considered a non-reporting entity as it does not have dependent users and may not be required to prepare financial statements pursuant to the Australian Accounting Standards.

## Question 1.1

Explain which of the following entities could be considered 'reporting entities' and should prepare 'general purpose financial reports'.

**a** Jay Trading is owned and controlled by Jason Jay. The business has 10 employees and manufactures components for the car industry.

**b** Sanyon Ltd, a public company with 5000 shareholders and five directors with branches in 10 countries, employing over 10 000 employees.

**c** PB Enterprises, a partnership owned and operated by Paul and Barry which operates a uranium mine in South Australia close to environmentally sensitive wetlands. The company has 20 employees and receives significant government funding.

**d** A public hospital.

## 1.3   CORPORATE ENTITIES

An individual or group of individuals may choose to organise themselves for business purposes as a registered company in accordance with the *Corporations Act 2001*. When a business is registered under the Corporations Act it becomes an incorporated company and the owner(s) are called shareholder(s).

A company is not a 'real person'; however, it is considered 'an artificial legal person' under the law. Consequently a company's power is exercised through agents (called directors) who are elected by the shareholders to operate and manage the company on their behalf.

When a company's ownership and control (shareholders and directors) are separated a dependency relationship can be identified. This will result in the company being a corporate reporting entity which must prepare general purpose financial reports.

The Corporations Act allows a company to exercise much the same powers as an individual person, it can sue and be sued and is permitted to raise finance by issuing shares and debentures.

Unlike a sole trader or partnership a company is unaffected by the death or bankruptcy of a shareholder and does not cease to exist when there is a change in ownership.

### Private and public companies

The Corporations Act provides for the registration of:

- proprietary (private) companies; and
- public companies.

To be registered as a company the entity must have a minimum of one member (shareholder). Proprietary companies (also referred to as private companies) are restricted to a maximum of 50 (non-employee) shareholders, while there is no restriction on the maximum number of shareholders for a public company.

Proprietary companies must also be classified as either 'small' or 'large'. The classification as to the size of the proprietary company is important, as small proprietary companies will generally have reduced financial reporting requirements (non-reporting entities) compared to large proprietary companies (reporting entities).

Public companies and large proprietary companies will generally have dependent users and must provide financial reports that comply with the accounting standards; hence they are classified as reporting entities.

A survey of Australian companies in 2011 indicated that there were 21 000 public companies and 180 000 proprietary companies, 4000 of which lodged financial statements as they were considered large proprietary companies.[2]

To be classified as a large proprietary company, the company must meet at least two of the following requirements.

1   whether the company has consolidated revenue exceeding $25 million;
2   whether the assets controlled by the company exceed $12.5 million; and
3   whether the company has 50 or more employees at the end of the financial year.

If the company can satisfy only one of these requirements it is considered to be a small proprietary company. The following table summarises the distinction between small and large proprietary companies.

| Requirement | Small proprietary company | Large proprietary company |
| --- | --- | --- |
| Value of consolidated revenue | less than $25m | greater than $25m |
| Value of gross controlled assets | less than $12.5m | greater than $12.5m |
| Number of employees | less than 50 | greater than 50 |

## Question 1.2

Explain how the Corporations Act distinguishes between a reporting entity and a non-reporting entity.

## Question 1.3

Why does the Corporations Act distinguish between a small and large proprietary company?

# 1.4   SHARE CAPITAL

Owners of a company are referred to as 'shareholders'. To become a shareholder of a company, a person or entity must obtain a share or shares issued by that company.

Most companies registered in Australia are companies limited by shares, where the liability of each shareholder is limited to the maximum value of the shares acquired by the shareholder at the time of allotment; for example, Ted purchased 10 000 $2.00 shares in a public company limited by shares, hence Ted's liability is $20 000.

In the event of company liquidation, shareholders are only liable to contribute any unpaid amounts owing on their shares; their personal assets are thereby protected; that is, the shareholders have limited liability. This can be contrasted to sole traders and partnerships where the owners have unlimited liability for the debts of their businesses.

When a company is registered under the *Corporations Act 2001* the names of the founding members (also known as subscribers) must be recorded on the application form along with the classification and quantity of shares they have agreed to take in the company. Classes of shares include:

---

2   Greg Tanzer, 'ASIC steps up action on lodging financials', *The Australian*, 25 May 2012.

## Ordinary shares

An ordinary share is the basic type of share and the most common. Ordinary shares generally provide a shareholder with full voting rights and the right to receive dividends. However, the rate of dividend depends on the profit performance of the company and the decisions of the directors in relation to the distribution of profits.

## Preference shares

Preference shares provide a shareholder preferential rights to a fixed rate of dividends before dividends to ordinary shareholders are declared. Preference shares may also have the following characteristics:

- **Participating or non-participating:** Participating preference shares entitle holders to participate with ordinary shareholders in dividends declared in excess of the fixed preferential dividend rate.
- **Cumulative and non-cumulative dividends:** Cumulative preference shares entitle holders who receive less than the fixed preferential dividend in any one year to receive the arrears of preferential dividend, plus the current year's preferential dividend in the following period, before the ordinary shareholders receive any dividend.
- **Repayment of capital:** Shareholders may be entitled to preferential rights in regard to return of capital when a company is wound up.

## Deferred or founder shares

Deferred or founder shares are usually issued to the initial subscribers or founders of the company named on the company's application for registration. These shares normally receive dividends after they have been paid to other classes of shareholders. By accepting deferred shares the founders are trying to make a statement that they believe in the future profitability of the company which may persuade others to invest in the company.

## 1.5 ADVANTAGES AND DISADVANTAGES OF FORMING A COMPANY

### The advantages of forming a company include:

#### Limited liability of shareholders

In a company limited by shares (both proprietary and public) the liability of shareholders for debts of the company is limited to any unpaid amounts owing on the shares. The shareholders (owners) are therefore protected against possible financial ruin if the company is unable to pay its debts.

#### Perpetual succession or continuity of existence

A company, unlike a sole trader or partnership, has perpetual succession as it does not dissolve on the death or retirement of an owner, or on the transfer of ownership, because the company is a separate legal entity with an independent existence from that of its owners.

#### Increased capital

A company offers the possibility of a greater number of owners of the business and therefore greater access to capital. It should be noted, however, that a proprietary company is prohibited from inviting the public to subscribe for shares or debentures in the company. A proprietary company is also prohibited from having more than 50 non-employee members.

#### Income tax

The income tax rate applied to companies may be lower than the personal income tax rates that are applied to the incomes of sole traders or partners. Companies currently incur an income tax rate of 30%, while individuals can pay up to 47.00%.

### Transferability of shares

Shareholders in public companies are able to transfer their ownership in a company by selling their shares. Shareholders in a proprietary company are restricted from transferring their shares to the public. This restriction usually means that shareholders can only transfer their shares to a person approved by the directors.

## The disadvantages of forming a company include:

### Separation of ownership and control

A company is owned by its shareholders; however, it is required by the Corporations Act to appoint directors who are responsible for the operation and management of the company. Founding shareholders of small proprietary companies may appoint themselves as directors, giving them both ownership and control of the company, in which case there is no separation of ownership and control. However, in larger proprietary companies and public companies shareholders will not have direct control over the company as they appoint independent directors.

### Difficulty of formation

In some cases the formation of a company may be quite involved and require the expertise of members of the legal and accounting professions. This may be particularly relevant where the shareholders require the drawing up of a specific and detailed company constitution.

### Cost of formation and registration

The costs of forming a company include business name registration fees, licences and legal costs of employing a solicitor or accountant to oversee the formation of the company. In addition an application must be lodged with the Australian Securities and Investments Commission (ASIC) and the relevant lodgement fees must be paid.

### Subject to regulations of the Corporations Act

A company incorporated under the Corporations Act must comply with the rules and regulations of the Act. These can be complex, and penalties may be imposed on the company's directors for contravention of sections of the Act.

## Question 1.4

Trigger and Sharon are contemplating converting their partnership business into a proprietary company limited by shares. Explain:

**a** how their personal liability will change; and

**b** why they will need to appoint company directors.

## 1.6   PROCEDURES FOR THE REGISTRATION OF A COMPANY

The procedure for the registration of a company limited by shares under the Corporations Act involves the following steps:

1 register the business name;
2 adopt the Replaceable Rules or prepare a constitution;
3 allot shares to founding members;
4 appoint director(s) and company secretary;
5 complete and lodge the application form; and
6 commence business on the granting of the Certificate of Registration.

The ASIC website http://www.asic.gov.au (homepage illustrated overleaf) provides an excellent resource for information relating to companies. This site explains the registration procedures, provides the appropriate forms, explains the legal requirements and shows the registration costs.

**Figure 1.1** Screenshot of ASIC's website

Source: ASIC, http://www.asic.gov.au.

# Step 1  Register the business name

The registration of a company involves registering the business name. The ASIC website provides a national centralised register for all Australian business name registrations. This site allows a prospective applicant to search the Business Names Register to determine if a company name has already been taken and cannot be used, to register a new business name and to make payment for its registration.

When registering a business name the following requirements must be met:
- a proprietary company shall have the word 'Proprietary' or the abbreviation 'Pty' as part of its name, inserted immediately before the word 'Limited' or before the abbreviation 'Ltd'; and
- a limited company shall have the word 'Limited' or the abbreviation 'Ltd' as part of and at the end of its name.

# Step 2  Adopt the Replaceable Rules or prepare a constitution

When establishing a company, the founding shareholders must establish the rules and procedures it will use to govern its internal management, such as appointing, remunerating and removing directors, calling and conducting meetings of directors and meetings of members (shareholders), issuing shares and paying dividends.

The Corporations Act allows a new company to be governed by the Replaceable Rules contained within the Act, by a constitution or by a combination of the Replaceable Rules and a constitution. Replaceable Rules apply to all companies with the exception of single shareholder/single director companies. The Replaceable Rules can be viewed on the ASIC website.

# Step 3  Allot shares to founding members

The founding members of the company, known as subscriber shareholders, will need to determine the type, number and value of each share that they each will take in the newly formed company.

# Step 4  Appoint director(s) and company secretary

In accordance with the Corporations Act, a proprietary company will need to appoint a director who will be responsible for the day-to-day operations of the company. A public company must appoint at least three directors. In addition, the company directors will need to appoint a company secretary who is responsible for ensuring that the company complies with its obligations under the law.

## Step 5 Complete and lodge the application form

The registration of a company with ASIC must be made by a person, with the application including the following contents:
- the type of company to be registered;
- the proposed company name;
- the name and address of each person who consents to be a member;
- the name and address of each person who consents to be a director or company secretary;
- the address of the proposed registered office and principal place of business; and
- for a company limited by shares, the type and number of shares that each member agrees to take and the amount that each member agrees to pay (or owe) on each share.

The application form (Form 201 Registration of a Company) can be downloaded from the ASIC website.

## Step 6 Commence business on the granting of the Certificate of Registration

If ASIC is satisfied with the application for registration of the company, it will register the company and issue the company with a Certificate of Registration.

The shares that are to be taken by the founding members named on the application form are deemed to be issued to the members on the date of registration of the company.

## Question 1.5

Wendy and Bill operate a partnership and have decided to convert to a company limited by shares. You are required to prepare a brief report that explains their options and the procedures that they will need to follow in order to obtain registration under the Corporations Act.

## 1.7 ACCOUNTING FOR SHARES ISSUED ON REGISTRATION

Both private and public companies are required to provide the name(s) of people who have agreed to become the founding members of the company when it is seeking registration. These people, referred to as 'subscribers', are recorded in the Register of Members as the first shareholders of the company.

As the subscribers have accepted shares in the company and signed the application for registration they have legal ownership of the shares and have an obligation to pay for the shares taken.

When accounting for shares issued to form a company two steps are required. These are:
1 issue the shares to the subscribers (on the date that the company was incorporated); and
2 issue receipts to the subscribers (upon payment for the shares).

 **Illustration**

Albert Park Ltd was registered as a public company limited by shares on 1 July. The application for registration of the company named three founding members who had agreed to take in a total of $375 000 in shares consisting of the following:
- 50 000 ordinary shares each at an issue price of $1.00 per share and
- 10 000 preference shares at an issue price of $2.50 each and
- 10 000 deferred shares at an issue price of $5.00 each.

Payment for the shares was required by 14 July.

The journal and general ledger entries recording these transactions would be as follows:

**1　Issue of shares to subscribers**

**General journal – Albert Park Ltd**

| Date | Details | Debit | Credit |
|---|---|---|---|
| | | $ | $ |
| 1 July | Subscribers | 375 000 | |
| | Share capital – ordinary shares | | 150 000 |
| | Share capital – preference shares | | 75 000 |
| | Share capital – deferred shares | | 150 000 |
| | *Issued shares to subscribers as per application for registration* | | |

**2　Receipt of subscribers' payments**

**General journal – Albert Park Ltd**

| Date | Details | Debit | Credit |
|---|---|---|---|
| | | $ | $ |
| 14 July | Bank | 375 000 | |
| | Subscribers | | 375 000 |
| | *Receipted money paid by subscribers* | | |

The company's statement of financial position after these transactions would be as follows:

**Albert Park Ltd**
**Statement of financial position**
**at 14 July**

| Shareholders' equity | $ |
|---|---|
| Share capital | |
| Ordinary shares (150 000 @ $1.00 each) | 150 000 |
| Preference shares (30 000 @ $2.50 each) | 75 000 |
| Deferred shares (30 000 @ $5.00 each) | 150 000 |
| Total shareholders' equity | 375 000 |
| Assets | |
| Bank | 375 000 |
| Total assets | 375 000 |

# Question 1.6

Castaway Ltd was incorporated on 1 July. The application for registration of the company listed five members who had each agreed to take 1000 ordinary shares at an issue price of $2.00 each. Subscribers were required to pay for the shares by 31 July. You are required to:

a　prepare journal entries to record the share transactions; and

b　prepare a statement of financial position as at 31 July.

## Question 1.7

Weffacol Suppliers Ltd was registered as a public company on 31 January. The four members whose names were listed on the registration papers had each agreed to take the following shares in the company, with payment to be made by 28 February:

- Ordinary shares: 100 000 each at an issue price of $0.50 each.
- Preference shares: 20 000 each at an issue price of $5.00 each.

You are required to:

a  prepare journal entries to record the share transactions; and
b  prepare a statement of financial position as at 28 February.

# 1.8  ACCOUNTING FOR COSTS OF ESTABLISHING A COMPANY

The formation of a company will involve costs associated with obtaining financial advice on establishing the business, legal advice in relation to company registration and adoption of a suitable constitution, and the costs of registration.

The payment of these establishment costs will give rise to an account specifically named to describe the costs associated with the formation of the company. These costs can be called formation costs, preliminary costs, establishment costs or set-up costs.

The journal entry to record the payment of costs of establishing a company is:

### General journal

| | | |
|---|---|---|
| Establishment costs (expense) | Debit | |
| GST paid (asset) | Debit | |
| Bank (asset) | | Credit |

## Illustration

Albert Park Ltd was registered as a public company on 1 July. The costs of forming the company included the following:

| | | |
|---|---|---|
| Accounting advice | $4 250 | (includes $386 GST) |
| Legal costs | $2 750 | (includes $250 GST) |
| Registration and other costs | $ 520 | (includes $48 GST) |
| Total establishment costs | $7 520 | (includes $684 GST) |

These costs would be recorded in the journal and general ledger as follows:

### General journal – Albert Park Ltd

| Date | Details | Debit | Credit |
|---|---|---|---|
| 2015 | | $ | $ |
| 1 July | Establishment costs | 6 836 | |
| | GST paid | 684 | |
| | Bank | | 7 520 |
| | *To record cost of establishing the company* | | |

## Question 1.8

You are required to record the following transactions in the general journal of Harris Pty Ltd.

- The company was incorporated on 18 May with five founding members agreeing to take 20 000 $1.00 ordinary shares each in the business making payment on 25 May.
- The business incurred $1980 (inclusive of GST) in establishment costs which were paid for on 18 May.

## 1.9 AUTHORITIES GOVERNING COMPANIES

Companies registered in Australia are closely monitored and scrutinised to ensure that they comply with their statutory obligations, operate in a fair and competitive market and report in accordance with the law. The following bodies are responsible for different aspects of corporate entities.

### Australian Securities and Investments Commission

ASIC is responsible for regulating the financial markets in Australia to ensure that investors have confidence in the market and that the market operates in accordance with the law.

The federal government appoints between three and eight people as members of ASIC, whose functions include:

- overall administration of matters relating to companies – these include registration formalities and the issue of certificates of registration, registration of business names, receipt and monitoring of companies' annual returns, and dealing with enquiries from the public about companies;
- investigation of companies suspected of non-compliance with the Corporations Act or accounting standards;
- formulation and issue of certain corporate reporting and compliance requirements in their ASIC releases; and
- the referral of matters to other statutory bodies, which include the Companies and Securities Advisory Panel and the Companies Auditors and Liquidators Disciplinary Board.

### Australian Securities Exchange

The Australian Securities Exchange (ASX) provides a market for the sale and purchase of securities, including company shares. Public companies wishing to raise finance can list their shares with the securities exchange, where they can be bought and sold by investors. The ASX, through its listing and trading rules, has implemented its responsibility under the Corporations Act for the appropriateness of stock (share) market activities.

Part of this responsibility entails the monitoring of companies and the transmission of information about them to existing and potential shareholders. The ASX maintains listing rules that govern certain aspects of share trading, company administration and compulsory reporting. The listing rules do not conflict with the Corporations Act or the accounting standards, but are complementary or additional to those authorities.

### Australian Accounting Standards Board

The Australian Accounting Standards Board (AASB) is responsible for the setting of accounting standards in Australia. The standards have been undergoing change to bring about their alignment with international accounting standards.

The AASB standards apply to all entities regulated by the Corporations Act, including public companies and large proprietary companies (reporting entities) as well as managed investment schemes such as unit trusts.[3]

Under the Corporations Act, AASB standards have the force of law, as:

- a company's directors must ensure that its financial statements comply with accounting standards;

---

3   Source http://www.aasb.gov.au

- auditors of companies are required to state whether the accounts have been made out in accordance with accounting standards; and
- there are substantial penalties for company directors' non-compliance.

The Accounting Standard AASB101: Presentation of Financial Statements specifies that a complete set of financial statements include:

a a statement of financial position as at the end of the period;

b a statement of comprehensive income for the period;

c a statement of changes in equity for the period;

d a statement of cash flows for the period; and

e notes, comprising a summary of significant accounting policies and other explanatory information.

The AASB website is an invaluable reference for keeping current with the Australian Accounting Standards and their developments.

## 1.10 COMPANY STATUTORY RECORDS

The Corporations Act requires companies to ensure that many of their records comply with the Act. These include:

### Minutes of general meetings and meetings of directors

A company must keep minute books recording such things as proceedings and resolutions at meetings of members and directors, the details of which must be recorded within one month of the meeting.

### Accounting records

A company must keep written financial records that:

a correctly record and explain its transactions, and

b enable true and fair financial statements to be prepared and audited.

An overview of the obligations for financial reports and audit, described in the Act, includes:

1 the preparation of financial reports, including financial statements, disclosures and notes, and directors' declaration;

2 the preparation of the directors' report;

3 the auditing of the financial report and obtaining the auditor's report;

4 the forwarding of the financial reports and auditor's report to members; and

5 the lodging of the financial report, directors' report and auditor's report with ASIC.

The Corporations Act requires that all reporting entities (public companies and large proprietary companies) prepare annual audited financial reports and directors' reports.

Small proprietary companies (non-reporting entities), do not have to prepare published annual financial reports in accordance with the Act unless requested to do so by their shareholders or ASIC, and they are exempt from having their accounts audited.

## Question 1.9

Wendy and Bill established a large proprietary company and were named as the company's directors. You are required to write a brief report to them as directors outlining the regulatory bodies that they will need to ensure compliance with.

## Question 1.10

Explain why directors of public companies and large proprietary companies must ensure that the company has an effective accounting system and list the general purpose financial reports required by AASB101.

# Comprehensive Assessment Activity

Gary and Anita Holt have approached your accounting firm, Get It Right (Suite 5, 20 Correct Ave, Kew, Victoria, 3195, ph. 03 1234 4321), to discuss the procedure to form a company.

The business details are as follows:

| | |
|---|---|
| **Business name and address:** (Registered Office and occupied by Holt Pty Ltd) | Holt Pty Ltd (this is not identical to any other business name). 45 Industrial Avenue Braeside, Victoria 3195 |
| **Type of company required:** | Private (limited by shares) |
| **Owners and directors:** | Gary Holt 12 The Esplanade Carrum, Victoria, 3197 Born 16 July 1966, Sydney — Anita Holt (nee Singh) 12 The Esplanade Carrum, Victoria, 3197 Born 21 May 1970, Delhi, India |
| **Company Secretary:** | Paula Banks 455 The Highway Berwick, Victoria, 3806 Born 1 September 1974, Melbourne |
| **Australian Business Number:** | 62 458 788 897 |
| **Size of business:** | *Gross Assets $15m* *Sales $120m* *65 employees* |
| **Share capital:** | Gary and Anita have determined that they will each hold 100 000 $1.00 ordinary shares in the company which must be paid for in cash immediately |
| **Constitution:** | Replaceable rules to apply |

The senior accountant of your accounting firm has requested you to undertake the following tasks which must be presented for appraisal:

a  obtain an Application for Registration of a Company from the ASIC website and complete it on behalf of the clients using today's date;

b  prepare journal entries to record the incorporation of the company using today's date and the costs of establishment which are to include your firm's fee of $3000 (plus GST) plus the lodging fee; and

c  write a brief report informing the company directors of their financial reporting responsibilities and the financial records they will need to maintain to ensure compliance with the Corporations Act.

# Assessment Checklist

Complete the following checklist to identify if you consider yourself capable of being assessed against each of the following outcomes.

| I can: | Chapter reference | Check ✓ |
| --- | --- | --- |
| differentiate between a reporting entity and a non-reporting entity | 1.2 | |
| explain the reporting obligations of a reporting entity | 1.2 | |
| define an incorporated entity | 1.3 | |
| differentiate between the public and private companies | 1.3 | |
| distinguish between small and large proprietary companies | 1.3 | |
| describe different types of shares | 1.4 | |
| explain the advantages of the company forms of business ownership | 1.5 | |
| describe the procedures required to register a company | 1.6 | |
| record the issue of shares to establish a company | 1.7 | |
| record the costs of establishment | 1.8 | |
| explain the role of ASIC | 1.9 | |
| explain the role of the ASX | 1.9 | |
| explain the role of the AASB | 1.9 | |
| explain why the Corporations Act requires financial records to be maintained | 1.10 | |

# CHAPTER 2

## COMPANY SHARE ISSUES

## WHAT YOU WILL LEARN IN THIS CHAPTER

Upon satisfactory completion of this chapter you should be able to:
- explain how a public company issues shares to the public;
- account for public company share issues; and
- define and account for share transaction costs.

**Are you already competent at these tasks?**
If you have already accomplished these tasks as a result of your recent workplace or training experiences you may wish to proceed to the Comprehensive Assessment Activity at the end of this chapter to assess your skills in these areas.

## 2.1    INTRODUCTION

Companies seeking finance to acquire assets, to expand the business or repay debt may issue shares. This chapter examines how companies issue shares and their associated accounting requirements.

## 2.2    COMPANY SHARE ISSUES

When a company requires finance it can choose to raise the funds by borrowing (debt finance) or it may issue shares (equity finance). Where equity finance is chosen the issue of shares will be governed by the Corporations Act which provides for different outcomes for private and public companies.

The Corporations Act precludes private companies from issuing shares to the public, thereby restricting the raising of equity finance to existing shareholders, directors and employees, whilst public companies are permitted to issue shares to the public.

When a public company issues shares to the public it must issue a prospectus in accordance with the requirements of the Corporations Act. The prospectus sets out information about the company and its directors, details of the share issue and includes an application form which must be completed and lodged with the company along with the payment stipulated in the prospectus. The directors will then decide to accept or reject the applicant's offer to purchase shares. Successful applicants then become shareholders and refunds are returned to unsuccessful applicants.

When a private company issues shares it is not required to issue a prospectus and it is not permitted to offer shares to the public at large. Instead it must restrict a share offering to existing employees, directors and its employees.

## 2.3    ISSUE PRICE OF SHARES

When a company issues shares the directors are free to place any terms and conditions they consider appropriate to the share issue. This includes placing a value on the shares and when they are to be paid. In setting the share price directors would need to give consideration to a range of factors, including:
- the maximisation of shareholder wealth as issuing shares will dilute the value of existing shareholder wealth;
- the effect on the market price of existing shares which would normally decrease the share price;
- the volume of shares to be offered to raise the capital required; and
- the expectation of future profits and dividends to service the new shares.

Consequently, over time as a company issues more shares they may not have the same issue price. For example, a company may have issued a prospectus offering shares to the public at $1.00 each in one year and in the following year issue another prospectus offering shares at $1.20 each or even $0.90 each.

## 2.4    REGISTER OF MEMBERS

When a company issues shares it is required by the Corporations Act to maintain a Register of Members that contains:
- each member's name and address;
- the date of entry of the member to the register;
- the date of the allotment of shares to the member;
- the number of shares allotted to the member and the total number of shares held;
- the class of shares, share numbers or share certificate numbers held by each member; and
- the amount that remains unpaid on the shares.

The Register of Members assists the company in identifying the name of the shareholder who is to receive dividends when declared. Companies can issue dividends 'ex-div' (where the buyer of a share obtains the share without a dividend which is paid to the seller of the share) or 'cum-div' (where the buyer of a share obtains the share with a dividend that has been declared but not yet paid).

## 2.5 ACCOUNTING FOR A PRIVATE COMPANY SHARE ISSUE

When a private company issues shares to its existing shareholders, directors or to its employees the directors must determine the specifics of the share issue including the type of shares to be issued, the issue price of the share, the people to whom the share will be allocated, the date of allocation and the date by which the shareholder must pay for the share.

Accounting entries are required when shares are allocated to shareholders and when payment is received for the shares.

### Illustration

Banks Pty Ltd was established on 1 July with 50 000 $1.00 ordinary shares issued to its founding members. The company's statement of financial position on this date was as follows:

**Banks Pty Ltd**
**Statement of financial position**
**at 1 July**

| Shareholders' equity | $ |
|---|---|
| Share capital | |
| Ordinary shares (50 000 @ $1.00 each) | 50 000 |
| Total shareholders' equity | 50 000 |
| Assets | |
| Bank | 50 000 |
| Total assets | 50 000 |

On 1 October the directors decided to raise $100 000 by issuing 100 000 $1.00 ordinary shares to the company's existing shareholders and its employees. The share issue required investors to accept or reject the share offer by 30 October. Allocation of the shares would take place on 15 November with payment to be made by 30 November.

All shares offered were accepted and payment was made by the due date.

The entries to record the share issue and the receipt of money would be as follows:

**1 Allotment of shares**

**General journal**

| Date | Details | Debit | Credit |
|---|---|---|---|
| | | $ | $ |
| 15 Nov | Accounts receivable (share allotment) | 100 000 | |
| | Share capital – ordinary shares | | 100 000 |
| | *Issued 100 000 ordinary shares at $1.00 per share* | | |

**2 Receipt of share moneys**

**General journal**

| Date | Details | Debit | Credit |
|---|---|---|---|
| | | $ | $ |
| 30 Nov | Bank | 100 000 | |
| | Accounts receivable (share allotment) | | 100 000 |
| | *Cash received for issue of 100 000 $1.00 ordinary shares* | | |

The general ledger arising from these entries would appear as follows:

### General ledger – Baronga Ltd

| Date | Particulars | Debit $ | Credit $ | Balance $ |
|---|---|---|---|---|
| **Share capital – ordinary shares** | | | | |
| 1 July | Balance | | | 50 000 Cr |
| 15 Nov | Accounts receivable (share allotment) | | 100 000 | 150 000 Cr |
| **Accounts receivable (share allotment)** | | | | |
| 15 Nov | Share capital – Ordinary shares | 100 000 | . | 100 000 Dr |
| 30 Nov | Bank | | 100 000 | Nil |
| **Bank** | | | | |
| 1 July | Balance | | | 50 000 Dr |
| 15 Nov | Accounts receivable (share allotment) | 100 000 | | 150 000 Dr |

The company's statement of financial position after the share issue would be as follows:

### Banks Pty Ltd
### Statement of financial position
### at 30 November

| Shareholders' equity | $ |
|---|---|
| Share capital | |
| Ordinary shares (150 000 @ $1.00 each) | 150 000 |
| Total shareholders' equity | 150 000 |
| Assets | |
| Bank | 150 000 |
| Total assets | 150 000 |

# Question 2.1

Using the following information for Smart Pty Ltd you are required to:

a   prepare journal entries to record the allocation and payment for shares issued; and

b   prepare a statement of financial position at 30 June.

Smart Pty Ltd's financial position at 1 July was as follows:

### Smart Pty Ltd
### Statement of financial position
### at 1 July

| Shareholders' equity | $ |
|---|---|
| Share capital | |
| Ordinary shares (100 000 @ $5.00 each) | 500 000 |
| Total shareholders' equity | **500 000** |
| Assets | |
| Bank | 50 000 |
| Plant and equipment | 450 000 |
| Total assets | 500 000 |

- On 1 January the directors decided to raise $250 000 by issuing 50 000 ordinary shares to existing shareholders at $5.00 each.
- On 31 January the shares were allotted to shareholders.
- On 28 February money was received for the shares issued.

## Question 2.2

On 1 March Grant and Blake registered Two Boys Brewery Pty Ltd taking 5000 $10.00 preference shares each in the company as founding members. They paid for the shares on 20 March.

On 1 May they offered their four parents 25 000 ordinary shares each at $1.00 and allocated the shares on 20 May. Payment for the shares was received on 20 June.

You are required to:

a prepare journal entries to record the shares issues; and

b prepare the shareholders' equity section of the statement of financial position as at 30 June.

## 2.6 PROCEDURE FOR ISSUING SHARES BY A PUBLIC COMPANY

A public company can raise capital by issuing shares to selected investors. This is referred to as a 'private placement'. This allows the company to negotiate large sums of money with chosen investors and avoids the complications associated with issuing shares to the public in general via a prospectus.

The Corporations Act requires a public company to prepare a prospectus when it is offering shares to the public. The prospectus contains information about the company which assists prospective shareholders in evaluating the company's prospects as an investment and the terms associated with the shares being issued. The prospectus must also contain an application form which allows the prospective shareholder to make an offer to purchase shares.

In contract law, a prospectus is not an offer by the company but an 'invitation to treat' meaning to 'invite an offer' from potential investors. Prospective shareholders must complete and lodge the application form together with the amount required to be paid with the company (or its solicitor). The application constitutes an offer by the applicant to the company.

If the company accepts the offer, the applicant is issued shares and becomes a shareholder in the company. Where an applicant's offer is unsuccessful the applicant is refunded their application money.

The terms and conditions of the prospectus should include:

- the class of share and the number of shares being issued;
- the share price;
- how and when payment for the share is required; and
- how and when shares will be allotted.

The accounting entries associated with issuing shares under a public company prospectus are directly associated with the legal requirements associated with the issue of shares under a prospectus. These requirements are as follows:

1 The company makes the approved prospectus, together with an application form attached, available to the prospective investors. The application form is completed by the prospective shareholder and forwarded together with money to the company (or its solicitor).

The Corporations Act requires application money received from prospective shareholders making an offer on a prospectus to be deposited into a 'trust account' with a financial institution until shares are allotted.

2 On the allotment date directors will:

- identify successful applicants and accept their offer to purchase shares. Successful applicants are issued with a share certificate as consideration for their offer and become shareholders with their names recorded in the Register of Members; and

- identify unsuccessful applicants. If an applicant's offer is rejected or the applicant is not allotted the full amount of shares applied for, the applicant's money is refunded from the trust account.

3 After allotment has been made and refunds given, the company can then transfer the application money from the trust account to its general purpose bank account.

### Illustration

On 1 August the directors of Baronga Ltd issued a prospectus inviting applications for 200 000 preference shares at $4.00 each payable in full on application by 30 September. By the closing date applications had been received for 230 000 shares. On 1 October the directors allotted 200 000 shares at $4.00 each to successful applicants, refunded unsuccessful applicants for 30 000 shares and transferred money from the trust account to the general bank account.

The critical dates, transactions and amounts from this prospectus are:

| | | | |
|---|---|---|---|
| Application money received | 30 September | (230 000 × $4.00) = | **$920 000** |
| Value of shares issued | 1 October | (200 000 × $4.00) = | **$800 000** |
| Amount refunded | 1 October | (30 000 × $4.00) = | **$120 000** |
| Amount transferred | 1 October | (200 000 × $4.00) = | **$800 000** |

## Question 2.3

Select the best answer to each of the following questions.

**1**  Which of the following types of companies are permitted to issue shares to the public?
   **a**  small proprietary companies;
   **b**  large proprietary companies; or
   **c**  public companies?

**2**  A prospectus from a legal perspective is:
   **a**  an offer;
   **b**  an acceptance; or
   **c**  an invitation to treat?

**3**  A completed application form on a prospectus constitutes:
   **a**  an offer
   **b**  an acceptance; or
   **c**  an offer to treat?

**4**  Application money received from an applicant to a prospectus must be:
   **a**  held in a safe;
   **b**  banked; or
   **c**  held in a trust account?

**5**  From the following information relating to a prospectus issued by Carreara Ltd, calculate the following:
   **a**  applications money received;
   **b**  value of shares allotted;
   **c**  amount refunded to unsuccessful applicants; and
   **d**  amount transferred from bank trust to bank general.

On 1 April the directors issued a prospectus inviting applications for 500 000 ordinary shares at $1.50 each, payable in full on application. When applications closed on 30 May, applications for 650 000 shares had been received. On 4 June the directors met and allotted shares to successful applicants and made refunds to unsuccessful applicants.

## 2.7   ACCOUNTING FOR PUBLIC COMPANY SHARE ISSUES

When shares are issued via a prospectus the terms of payment would be included in the prospectus and may include the following scenarios:
**a**   payment in full on application; or
**b**   payment by instalments.

Companies issuing a prospectus may also find that the number of shares applied for by the applicants may exceed the number of shares on offer. This is referred to as an 'oversubscription' and will require refunds to successful applicants.

## Shares issued fully paid on application

To account for the issue of shares on a prospectus, where applicants are required to pay in full on application where the prospectus has been oversubscribed, the following entries are required:

1  bank money received in a trust account;
2  allot shares to successful applicants and make refunds to unsuccessful applicants; and
3  transfer trust money to the general bank account.

 **Illustration**

Baronga Ltd was established on 1 June with 100 000 $1.00 ordinary shares issued to its founding members. The company's statement of financial position on this date was as follows:

**Baronga Ltd**
**Statement of financial position**
**at 1 June**

| Shareholders' equity | $ |
|---|---|
| Share capital | |
|    Ordinary shares (100 000 @ $1.00 each) | 100 000 |
| Total shareholders' equity | 100 000 |
| Assets | |
| Bank | 100 000 |
| Total assets | 100 000 |

On 1 August the directors issued a prospectus inviting applications for 200 000 preference shares at $4.00 each payable in full on application ($800 000) by 30 September.

By the closing date applications had been received for 230 000 shares ($920 000).

On 1 October the directors:

• allotted 200 000 shares at $4.00 each to successful applicants ($800 000); and
• refunded unsuccessful applicants for 30 000 shares at $4.00 each ($120 000).

The journal entries recording these transactions would be as follows:

**1  Receipt of application moneys**

**General journal**

| Date | Details | Debit | Credit |
|---|---|---|---|
| | | $ | $ |
| 30 Sept | Bank trust – preference shares | 920 000 | |
| |    Applications liability – preference shares | | 920 000 |
| | *Received applications for 230 000 shares @ $4.00 per share* | | |

**2  Allotment of shares to successful applicants and make refunds to unsuccessful applicants**

**General journal**

| Date | Details | Debit | Credit |
|---|---|---|---|
| | | $ | $ |
| 1 Oct | Applications liability – preference shares | 920 000 | |
| |    Share capital – preference shares | | 800 000 |
| |    Bank trust – preference shares | | 120 000 |
| | *Issued 200 000 shares at $4.00 per share and made refunds for 30 000 shares @ $4.00 each* | | |

### 3  Transfer money held in trust to general bank account

**General journal**

| Date | Details | Debit | Credit |
|------|---------|-------|--------|
|      |         | $     | $      |
| 1 Oct | Bank general | 800 000 | |
|       | Bank trust – preference shares | | 800 000 |
|       | *Transferred share money held in trust* | | |

The general ledger arising from these entries would appear as follows:

**General ledger – Baronga Ltd**

| Date | Particulars | Debit | Credit | Balance |
|------|-------------|-------|--------|---------|
|      |             | $     | $      | $       |
| **Bank trust – preference shares** | | | | |
| 30 Sept | Applications – preference shares | 920 000 | | 920 000 Dr |
| 1 Oct | Applications – preference shares | | 120 000 | 800 000 Dr |
|       | Bank general | | 800 000 | Nil |
| **Applications liability – preference shares** | | | | |
| 30 Sept | Bank trust – preference shares | | 920 000 | 920 000 Cr |
| 1 Oct | Share capital – preference shares | 800 000 | | 120 000 Cr |
|       | Bank trust – preference shares | 120 000 | | Nil |
| **Share capital – preference shares** | | | | |
| 1 Oct | Applications – preference shares | | 800 000 | 800 000 Cr |
| **Bank general** | | | | |
| 1 July | Balance | | | 100 000 Dr |
| 1 Oct | Bank trust – preference shares | 800 000 | | 900 000 Dr |

The company's statement of financial position after the share issue would be as follows:

**Baronga Ltd**
**Statement of financial position**
**at 1 October**

| Shareholders' equity | $ |
|----------------------|---|
| Share capital | |
|    Ordinary shares (100 000 @ $1.00 each) | 100 000 |
|    Preference shares (200 000 @ $4.00 each) | 800 000 |
| Total shareholders' equity | 900 000 |
| Assets | |
| Bank general | 900 000 |
| Total assets | 900 000 |

## Question 2.4

Carreara Ltd's shareholders' equity is shown in the following financial statement:

**Carreara Ltd**
**Statement of financial position (extract)**
**at 1 March**

| Shareholders' equity | $ |
|---|---|
| Share capital | |
| Deferred shares (20 000 @ $5.00 each) | 100 000 |

On 1 April the directors issued a prospectus inviting applications for 500 000 ordinary shares at $1.50 each payable in full on application.

When applications closed on 30 May, applications for 650 000 shares had been received.

On 4 June the directors met and allotted shares to successful applicants and made refunds to unsuccessful applicants.

You are required to prepare:

a   all journal entries (in general journal format); and

b   the shareholders' equity section of the statement of financial position as at 30 June.

## Question 2.5

Drummond Ltd was registered on 1 September with three members, each agreeing to take 50 000 ordinary shares at an issue price of $1.00 each.

The money owing by the subscribers was received on 30 September.

On 20 October the directors met and agreed to issue a prospectus inviting offers for 200 000 preference shares at an issue price of $3.00 each, payable in full by 28 November.

By the closing date applications had been received for 240 000 preference shares.

The directors met on 30 November and allotted shares to successful applicants and refunded unsuccessful applicants.

You are required to:

a   prepare journal entries for the period 1 September to 30 November; and

b   prepare the statement of financial position as at 30 November.

## Shares issued payable by instalments

A prospectus may require applicants to make payments with an initial amount on application followed by instalments.

The conditions for paying by instalment would be included in the prospectus to inform applicants that if they are successful in being allotted shares they must commit to paying additional instalments.

The company can request an instalment:

- **On allotment:** when shares are allotted to successful applicants, and/or
- **In a call:** request a payment in the future, commonly referred to as a 'call'.

When an instalment is made the company will issue an 'allotment letter' or a 'call notice' requesting payment by a specified date.

### Shares issued payable on allotment

A company may issue a prospectus requiring applicants to make an initial payment to be included with the application form and a final payment to be made after the shares are allotted.

The journal entries to record the share transactions under these terms of payment are the same as in the previous illustration; however, additional entries are required upon the allotment of the shares. These entries are to record the amount owing by the shareholders when the shares are allotted, and to record the receipt of money by the shareholders when the final instalment is made.

## Illustration

On 1 May Annandale Ltd's shareholders' equity was as follows:

**Annandale Ltd**
**Statement of financial position (extract)**
**at 1 May**

| Shareholders' equity | $ |
|---|---|
| Share capital | |
| Ordinary shares (50 000 @ $2.00 each) | 100 000 |

On 10 May a prospectus was issued inviting applications for 100 000 ordinary shares @ $3.00 each payable as follows:
- $2.00 on application (with 31 May being the closing date for applications); and
- $1.00 on allotment (payable by 20 June).
Applications were received for 120 000 shares @ $2.00 each ($240 000).
On 1 June the directors:
- allotted 100 000 shares @ $2.00 each ($200 000); and
- made refunds for 20 000 shares @ $2.00 each ($40 000).
The journal entries to record these transactions would be as follows:

**1   Receipt of application moneys**

**General journal**

| Date | Details | Debit | Credit |
|---|---|---|---|
| | | $ | $ |
| 31 May | Bank trust – ordinary shares | 240 000 | |
| | Applications liability – ordinary shares | | 240 000 |
| | *Received applications for 120 000 shares @ $2.00 per share* | | |

**2   Allotment of shares to successful applicants and make refunds to unsuccessful applicants**

**General journal**

| Date | Details | Debit | Credit |
|---|---|---|---|
| | | $ | $ |
| 1 June | Applications liability – ordinary shares | 240 000 | |
| | Share capital – ordinary shares | | 200 000 |
| | Bank trust – ordinary shares | | 40 000 |
| | *Issued 100 000 shares @ $2.00 per share and made refunds for 20 000 shares @ $2.00 each* | | |

**3 Transfer money held in trust to general bank account**

**General journal**

| Date | Details | Debit | Credit |
|---|---|---|---|
| | | $ | $ |
| 1 June | Bank general | 200 000 | |
| | Bank trust – ordinary shares | | 200 000 |
| | *Transferred share money held in trust* | | |

**4   Request allotment money**

On the day the shares are allotted on 1 June the shareholders who were allotted shares will also be forwarded the share allotment letter, informing them of the shares allotted and requesting the final instalment to be paid by 20 June. As 100 000 shares were allotted and the final instalment is $1.00 per share the amount owing is $100 000.

General journal

| Date | Details | Debit | Credit |
|---|---|---|---|
| | | $ | $ |
| 1 June | Allotment – ordinary shares | 100 000 | |
| | Share capital – ordinary shares | | 100 000 |
| | *Requested final instalment of $1.00 per share on 100 000* | | |
| | *shares issued on allotment* | | |

**5   The entry to record the receipt of the final instalment of $100 000 would be as follows:**

General journal

| Date | Details | Debit | Credit |
|---|---|---|---|
| | | $ | $ |
| 20 June | Bank general | 100 000 | |
| | Allotment – ordinary shares | | 100 000 |
| | *Received payment of final instalment of $1.00 per share on* | | |
| | *100 000 shares* | | |

Annandale's shareholder's equity after these transactions would be as follows:

**Annandale Ltd**
**Statement of financial position (extract)**
**at 20 June**

| Shareholders' equity | $ |
|---|---|
| Share capital | |
| Ordinary shares (50 000 @ $2.00 each) | 100 000 |
| Ordinary shares (100 000 @ $3.00 each) | 300 000 |
| Total shareholders' equity | 400 000 |

# Question 2.6

From the following information for Inverloch Ltd you are required to:

a   prepare the journal entries to record the above share transactions; and

b   prepare the shareholder's equity section of the statement of financial position on 30 April.

On 1 March Inverloch Ltd's financial position included the following share capital.

**Inverloch Ltd**
**Statement of financial position (extract)**
**at 1 March**

| Shareholders' equity | $ |
|---|---|
| Share capital | |
| Ordinary shares (100 000 @ $2.00 each) | 200 000 |

On 5 March a prospectus was issued inviting applications for 300 000 ordinary shares with an issue price of $2.50 payable in two instalments:

- $1.00 on application (payable by 31 March); and
- $1.50 on allotment (payable by 30 April).

Applications closed on 31 March for 350 000 shares.

On 1 April the directors allotted shares, made refunds and issued allotment letters.

All allotment money was received on 30 April.

## Question 2.7

Jackaroo Ltd has provided the following information from which you are required to:

a    prepare journal entries to record all share transactions; and

b    prepare a statement of financial position as at 30 March.

Jackaroo Ltd was registered as a public company on 15 January with 10 subscribers taking 500 ordinary shares each at an issue price of $1.00 each. The subscribers paid for their shares on 20 January.

A prospectus was issued on 18 February inviting the public to apply for 100 000 ordinary shares at an issue price of $1.20 each payable:

- $0.80 on application by 1 March; and
- $0.40 on allotment.

When applications closed on 1 March, 160 000 shares had been applied for. On 5 March the directors formally allotted the share to successful applicants and made refunds to unsuccessful applicants. Allotment letters were issued requesting payment of the second instalment by 30 March.

On 30 March all allotment money had been received.

### Shares issued payable on a call

When a company is raising capital via a share issue it may plan to collect some of the money in the future. This is referred to as a 'call'. The prospectus would indicate the amount that should be paid for on application to the prospectus, the amount payable on allotment (if any) and the amount(s) to be called in the future.

The journal entries required for a share issue involving a call are initially the same as described in previous illustrations. However, additional entries are required to make the call on the shares and to record the money received on the call.

## Illustration

On 1 March 2012 Anglesea Ltd issued a prospectus inviting applications for 50 000 ordinary shares at $6.00 each payable:

- $3.00 on application;
- $2.00 on allotment of shares; and
- $1.00 on a future call.

By 30 April shares had been allotted to successful applicants and payment had been received for the application and allotment of $5.00 per share ($250 000). The company's statement of financial position at this date included the following share capital:

**Anglesea Ltd**
**Statement of financial position (extract)**
**at 30 April**

| Shareholders' equity | $ |
|---|---|
| Share capital | |
| Ordinary shares (50 000 $6.00 shares paid to $5.00 each) | 250 000 |

On 1 August the directors issued a call notice requesting the final instalment of $1.00 per share on the 50 000 shares to be paid by 31 August.

The two entries required to record the call would be as follows:

**1   Record the issue of the call notice requesting payment for 50 000 shares @ $1.00 each**

**General journal**

| Date | Details | Debit | Credit |
|------|---------|-------|--------|
|      |         | $ | $ |
| 1 Aug | Call – ordinary shares | 50 000 | |
|      |     Share capital – ordinary shares | | 50 000 |
|      | *Requested final instalment of $1.00 per share on 50 000 shares.* | | |

**2   Record the receipt of the call money**

**General journal**

| Date | Details | Debit | Credit |
|------|---------|-------|--------|
|      |         | $ | $ |
| 31 Aug | Bank general | 50 000 | |
|      |     Call – ordinary shares | | 50 000 |
|      | *Received payment of final instalment of $1.00 per share on 50 000 shares* | | |

The company's financial position after the call would be as follows:

**Anglesea Ltd**
**Statement of financial position**
**at 31 August**

| Shareholders' equity | $ |
|----------------------|---|
| Share capital | |
|     Ordinary shares (50 000 @ $6.00 each) | 300 000 |
| Total shareholders' equity | 300 000 |
| Assets | |
| Bank | 300 000 |
| Total assets | 300 000 |

## Question 2.8

On 31 March OPQ Ltd issued a prospectus inviting applications for 150 000 $1.50 ordinary shares. The terms of payment were:

- $0.50 on application payable by 14 May, with allotment occurring on 21 May;
- $0.50 on allotment payable by 31 May; and
- $0.50 in one call to take effect on 31 July and payable by 31 August.

  From the information provided, you are required to prepare:
  a   journal entries to record the call transactions; and
  b   the shareholders' equity section of the statement of financial position as at 31 August.

## 2.8   CALLS IN ARREARS

When a call on shares is made, the company may not receive all call money owing by shareholders – that is, the call money is owing. Where the call account remains with a debit balance after the final date for payment of a call, the balance represents 'calls in arrears' or 'calls owing'.

The calls in arrears account should be classified as a shareholders' equity account and be disclosed as a reduction of share capital in the statement of financial position.

A company's constitution may include clauses specifying that shareholders who have not paid for calls on shares may forfeit the shares and that the shares can be reissued.

 **Illustration**

On 1 February Yamba Ltd issued a prospectus inviting applications for 300 000 ordinary shares at $2.00 each payable by instalments:
- $1.00 on application by 1 April with allotment on 1 March;
- $0.60 on allotment payable by 1 June; and
- $0.40 on a call.

On 1 December the directors issued a call notice on the 300 000 shares @ $0.40 each ($120 000) payable by 1 February.

The entries to record the call notice would be as follows:

**General journal**

| Date | Details | Debit | Credit |
|------|---------|-------|--------|
|      |         | $     | $      |
| 1 Dec | Call – ordinary shares | 120 000 | |
|       |     Share capital – ordinary shares | | 120 000 |
|       | *Requested final instalment of $0.40 per share on 300 000 shares* | | |

By 1 February calls had been received on 280 000 shares @ $0.40 each ($112 000). This would be recorded as follows:

**General journal**

| Date | Details | Debit | Credit |
|------|---------|-------|--------|
|      |         | $     | $      |
| 1 Feb | Bank – general account | 112 000 | |
|       |     Call – ordinary shares | | 112 000 |
|       | *Received final instalment of $0.40 per share on 280 000 shares* | | |

The ordinary shares account (after allotting shares and requesting the call) and call account (after receiving the call) would be as follows:

**General ledger – Yamba Ltd**

| Date | Particulars | Debit | Credit | Balance |
|------|-------------|-------|--------|---------|
|      |             | $     | $      | $       |
| Share capital – ordinary shares | | | | |
| 1 March | Applications (deposit $1.00 × 300 000) | | 300 000 | 300 000 Cr |
|         | Allotment (1st instalment $0.60 × 300 000) | | 180 000 | 480 000 Cr |
| 1 Dec | Call (2nd instalment $0.40 × 300 000) | | 120 000 | 600 000 Cr |
| Call | | | | |
| 1 Dec | Share capital – ordinary shares | 120 000 | | 120 000 Dr |
| 1 Feb | Bank | | 112 000 | 8 000 Dr |

These accounts would be disclosed in the statement of financial position as follows:

**Yamba Ltd**
**Statement of financial position (extract)**
**at 31 August**

| Shareholders' equity | $ |
| --- | --- |
| Share capital | |
| Ordinary shares (300 000 @ $2.00 each) | 600 000 |
| Less calls in arrears (20 000 @ $0.40 each) | 8 000 |
| Total shareholders' equity | 592 000 |

## Question 2.9

From the following information on Jindabyne Ltd you are required to prepare:
a   journal entries to account for all share transactions;
b   the shareholders' equity section of the statement of financial position as at 20 December.
   On 7 February the directors of Jindabyne Ltd issued a prospectus inviting applicants for 250 000 preference shares at $3.50 each payable as follows:
- $2.00 on application;
- $1.00 on allotment; and
- $0.50 in future calls.
   On 15 March applications were received for 300 000 shares with application money.
   On 30 March directors allotted shares, made refunds and issued allotment letters.
   On 31 July all allotment money was received.
   On 28 November directors issued a call notice for the final instalment.
   On 20 December call money on 240 000 shares was received.

## Question 2.10

On 1 June Korumburra Ltd was registered, with 10 members each agreeing to take 20 000 preference shares at an issue price of $10.00 each. Payment for these shares was made on 15 June.
   On 25 July the directors issued a prospectus inviting applications for 400 000 ordinary shares with an issue price of $5.00 payable as follows:
- $2.00 on application;
- $1.50 on allotment; and
- $1.50 in calls.
   Prospectus applications closed on 31 August with 450 000 shares applied for.
   On 10 September shares were allotted, refunds made and allotment letters were issued.
   Allotment money was received on 1 October.
   On 15 April a call of $1.50 was made.
   By 30 May call money had been received on 380 000 shares.

You are required to prepare:
a   general journal entries to record all share issues; and
b   the shareholders' equity section of the statement of financial position as at 31 May.

## 2.9   COSTS ASSOCIATED WITH A SHARE ISSUE

When a company prepares a prospectus and issues shares it will incur costs for preparing, issuing and registering the prospectus. These costs can be referred to as 'transaction costs'.

AASB132: Financial Instruments: Disclosure and Presentation requires transaction costs of an equity transaction to be accounted for as a deduction from equity. Hence, transaction costs should be transferred to the share capital account, thereby reducing share capital issued.

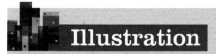

## Illustration

Clematis Ltd issued 100 000 $2.00 ordinary shares via a prospectus. Transaction costs associated with the share issue totalling $5500 (including GST) were paid on 15 December.

The journal entry to record this payment would be as follows:

### General journal

| Date | Details | Debit | Credit |
|------|---------|-------|--------|
|      |         | $     | $      |
| 15 Dec | Transaction costs – ordinary shares | 5 000 | |
|      | GST paid | 500 | |
|      | Bank | | 5 500 |
|      | *Paid transaction costs* | | |

In accordance with AASB132: Financial Instruments, these transaction costs must be deducted from equity. This can be achieved by allocating the costs against the number of shares issued. As transaction costs of $5000 were incurred on 100 000 shares issued, the cost per share is $0.05.

The entry to deduct transaction costs directly from the shares issued would be as follows:

### General journal

| Date | Details | Debit | Credit |
|------|---------|-------|--------|
|      |         | $     | $      |
| 15 Dec | Share capital – ordinary shares | 5 000 | |
|      | Transaction costs – ordinary shares | | 5 000 |
|      | *Allocated transaction costs against equity* | | |

The statement of financial position would disclose the ordinary shares as follows:

### Clematis Ltd
### Statement of financial position (extract)

| Shareholders' equity | $ |
|----------------------|---|
| Share capital | |
| Ordinary shares (100 000 @ $2.00 each) | 200 000 |
| Less transaction costs (100 000 @ $0.05 each) | 5 000 |
| Ordinary shares (100 000 @ $1.95 each) | 195 000 |

## Question 2.11

Using the following information provided by Noosa Ltd you are required to:

a   record all transactions in the general journal; and

b   prepare the shareholder's equity section of the statement of financial position at 20 September.

Noosa Ltd on 1 August issued a prospectus inviting applications for 500 000 preference shares @ $4.00 each payable in full on application.

By 31 August applications had been received for 520 000 ordinary shares.

The directors met on 15 September and allotted shares and issued refunds.

On 20 September the company paid $11 000 in transaction costs (GST inclusive) associated with the prospectus.

## Question 2.12

From the following information on Horsham Ltd you are required to:

a   record all transactions in the general journal; and

b   prepare an extract of the statement of financial position at 7 May showing shareholders' equity.

Horsham Ltd is a public company with an existing share capital of 200 000 deferred shares fully paid at $5.00 each.

On 20 June a prospectus was issued inviting applications for 600 000 ordinary shares at $7 per share payable:

- $3.00 on application;
- $1.50 on allotment; and
- $2.50 in calls.

By 5 August applications had been received for 640 000 ordinary shares.

On 7 August the directors allotted shares to successful applicants and refunded unsuccessful applicants and issued allotment letters.

On 14 September allotment money was received.

On 16 September transaction costs of $13 200 inclusive of GST were paid.

On 2 April the directors made a call of $2.50 on the ordinary shares.

On 7 May all required call money was received with the exception of calls on 5 000 shares.

## 2.10   PUBLIC COMPANY SHARE ISSUE TRANSACTIONS SUMMARY

1   Receipt of application money, allotment of shares, refunds and bank transfer:

### General journal

| Date | Details | Debit | Credit |
|------|---------|-------|--------|
|      |         | $     | $      |
|      | Bank trust | Dr |      |
|      |      Applications liability |   | Cr |
|      | *Receipt of application moneys* |   |   |
|      | Applications liability | Dr |   |
|      |      Share capital |   | Cr |
|      | *Allotment of shares to successful applicants* |   |   |
|      | Applications liability | Dr |   |
|      |      Bank trust |   | Cr |
|      | *Refunds to unsuccessful applicants* |   |   |
|      | Bank general | Dr |   |
|      |      Bank trust |   | Cr |
|      | *Transfer of money held in trust* |   |   |

2   Request for instalment on allotment and receipt of allotment money:

### General journal

| Date | Details | Debit | Credit |
|------|---------|-------|--------|
|      |         | $     | $      |
|      | Allotment | Dr |   |
|      |      Share capital |   | Cr |
|      | *Request for allotment instalment* |   |   |
|      | Bank general | Dr |   |
|      |      Allotment |   | Cr |
|      | *Receipt of allotment money* |   |   |

3    Request for instalment on call and receipt of call money:

**General journal**

| Date | Details | Debit | Credit |
|------|---------|-------|--------|
|  |  | $ | $ |
|  | Call | Dr |  |
|  |     Share capital |  | Cr |
|  | *Request for call instalment* |  |  |
|  | Bank general | Dr |  |
|  |     Call |  | Cr |
|  | *Receipt of call money* |  |  |

4    Payment of share issue costs and allocation to share capital:

**General journal**

| Date | Details | Debit | Credit |
|------|---------|-------|--------|
|  |  | $ | $ |
|  | Transaction costs | Dr |  |
|  | GST paid | Dr |  |
|  |     Share capital |  | Cr |
|  | *Payment of share issue costs* |  |  |
|  | Share capital | Dr |  |
|  |     Transaction costs |  | Cr |
|  | *Allocation of transaction costs* |  |  |

## Question 2.13

From the following information on Gumbone Ltd, you are required to:

**a**    record all transactions in general journal format; and

**b**    prepare a statement of financial position as at 30 October.

| Date | Transaction |
|------|-------------|
| 17 January | Gumbone Ltd was registered as a public company limited by shares with five subscribers being issued a total of 15 000 deferred shares at of $3.00 per share |
| 6 February | Subscriber money received |
| 1 March | Prospectuses were issued for 600 000 ordinary shares at a price of $6.00 per share payable: |
| | $2.50 on application; |
| | $2.00 on allotment; and |
| | one call of $1.50 payable when required by the directors |
| 2 April | Application money had been received for 620 000 ordinary shares |
| 3 April | Shares allotted, refunds made and allotment letters sent to successful applicants |
| 5 April | Paid for: |
| | costs of establishment of $11 000 (inclusive of GST); and |
| | share issue expenses of $0.05 per issued share (plus GST) |
| 6 May | Allotment money was received in full by the due date |
| 1 August | Call notice on ordinary shares issued |
| 30 October | Call money received on 590 000 shares |

# Question 2.14

Mannix Ltd's share capital on 1 February consisted of 10 000 $1.00 ordinary shares. The directors required capital for expansion purposes and decided to issue a prospectus inviting applications for 500 000 ordinary shares at $1.00 each, payable as follows:

- $0.25 on application;
- $0.25 on allotment; and
- $0.50 in two calls.

The following transactions were incurred as a result of this prospectus.

| Date | Transaction |
|---|---|
| 15 April | Applications received for 550 000 shares |
| 25 April | Directors allot shares, make refunds and issue allotment notices |
| 30 May | Allotment money received |
| 1 July | Paid transaction costs of $5500 including GST |
| 31 December | Call of $0.30 made on ordinary shares |
| 28 February | All call money received |
| 1 June | Final call of $0.20 made on ordinary shares |
| 30 June | Call money received on 495 000 shares |

You are required to prepare:

a   journal entries to account for all share transactions; and

b   the shareholders' equity section of the statement of financial position at 30 June.

# Comprehensive Assessment Activity

The following transactions have been provided by Warburton Ltd.

| Date | Transaction |
|---|---|
| 12 January | The company was registered as a public company limited by shares with five subscribers, each agreeing to purchase 3000 fully paid ordinary shares at a price of $5.00 per share |
| 14 January | Money received from subscribers |
| 16 February | Establishment costs totalling $6600 (GST inclusive) were paid |
| 20 March | Prospectus issued, inviting applications for: 150 000 preference shares at a price of $8.00 per share payable: *$4.00 on application; and* *$4.00 on allotment* |
| 25 March | Prospectus issued, inviting applications for: 800 000 ordinary shares at a price of $5.00 per share payable: *$1.75 on application;* *$1.50 on allotment; and* *the balance in calls when required* |
| 28 June | Closing date for both preference and ordinary share applications *200 000 preference shares applications* *1 000 000 ordinary shares applications* |
| 1 August | Shares allotted, refunds made and allotment letters issued |
| 10 August | Transaction costs amounting to $0.11 per share (GST inclusive) were paid |
| 15 September | All allotment money received |
| 15 November | Call notice issued on ordinary shares for $1.00 per share |
| 30 December | Call money received on 775 000 ordinary shares |

You are required to:
a  record all transactions in the general journal; and
b  prepare the shareholders' equity section of the statement of financial position as at 31 December.

# Assessment Checklist

Complete the following checklist to identify if you consider yourself capable of being assessed against each of the following outcomes.

| I can: | Chapter reference | Check ✓ |
|---|---|---|
| explain the law in relation to corporate entity share issues | 2.2 | |
| explain the purpose of a Register of Members | 2.4 | |
| account for a share issue by a private company | 2.5 | |
| explain the purpose of a share prospectus and its relationship to accounting entries | 2.6 | |
| account for the receipt of prospectus application money | 2.7 | |
| record the issue of shares to successful applicants | 2.7 | |
| record refunds to unsuccessful applicants | 2.7 | |
| explain the purpose of an allotment letter | 2.7 | |
| account for shares issued on allotment | 2.7 | |
| record the receipt of allotment money | 2.7 | |
| explain the purpose of a call notice | 2.7 | |
| account for shares issued on a call | 2.7 | |
| record the receipt of call money | 2.7 | |
| identify and account for calls in arrears | 2.8 | |
| account for transaction costs on a share issue | 2.9 | |

# CHAPTER 3

## ACCOUNTING FOR DEBENTURES

## WHAT YOU WILL LEARN IN THIS CHAPTER

Upon satisfactory completion of this chapter you should be able to:
- describe the characteristics of a debenture;
- define and differentiate between types of debentures;
- account for the issue of debentures;
- record debentures in the financial statements;
- account for interest payments on debentures; and
- account for the redemption of debentures.

**Are you already competent at these tasks?**
If you have already accomplished these tasks as a result of your recent workplace or training experiences you may wish to proceed to the Comprehensive Assessment Activity at the end of this chapter to assess your skills in these areas.

## 3.1  INTRODUCTION

Companies seeking finance may use debt funds (debt finance) rather than issue shares (equity finance). Debt finance may be considered more desirable as a source of funds as it does not impact on shareholders' wealth as a share issue does. Instead debt acquired is serviced through principal and interest repayments and paid out over an agreed period of time. A common source of debt finance for public companies is the issue of debentures.

This chapter examines the nature of debentures and their associated accounting requirements.

## 3.2  DEBENTURE FINANCE

A public company can issue debentures to the general public through the issue of a prospectus together with an application, or it can make a private placement of debentures to one or a few lenders for very large amounts. Private companies are generally precluded from raising finance by issuing a prospectus to the public for a debenture issue.

A debenture is a long-term loan normally acquired for asset purchases where the borrower (the company) enters into a loan contract with the lender (referred to as the debenture holder) and agrees to:
- make annual interest payments during the term of the loan; and
- repay the loan principal at the end of the loan period.

Debentures differ to term loans or hire purchase agreements where the amount borrowed is repaid over time with payments covering both principal and interest until the loan is paid out.

Debenture contracts between borrowers and debenture holders may be 'secured' or 'unsecured'. A secured debenture provides the debenture holder with security over a specific asset such as land or buildings of the borrower, or the debenture may have a floating charge over all assets, such as inventories, rather than on a specific asset. If the borrower defaults on repayment the debenture holder may acquire the borrower's asset(s) as compensation.

The Corporations Act requires that a debt can be only described as a 'debenture' if it is fully secured by a charge or security over the borrowing company's assets. Where a debenture is unsecured the borrower is required to identify the debt instrument as an 'unsecured note'.

When a company (the borrower) issues a debenture the debenture holder is issued with a debenture certificate which the debenture holder can retain or trade on the stock exchange, thereby transferring its ownership to another party, who then becomes the new debenture holder. The details of debenture holders must be recorded in a Register of Debenture Holders maintained by the borrower. This allows the lender to ensure that annual interest payments and the principal repayment at the end of the debenture period are paid to the correct debenture holder.

Debentures do not have a specified form but typically have an issue price or par value of $1000 each or $10 000 each and can be purchased in varying quantities; for example, 5000 debentures at $1000 each or 500 debentures at $10 000 each.

The Corporations Act requires the company issuing the debenture to appoint a trustee who monitors the borrower to safeguard the interests of the debenture holders, and the company must provide appropriate clear disclosure of all matters relating to the debentures as part of its financial reports.

### Question 3.1

Explain how repayments on a bank loan differ to repayments on a debenture loan.

## 3.3  ISSUING A DEBENTURE PROSPECTUS

The procedure for issuing debentures is similar to the procedure for issuing share capital via a prospectus. Where a debenture prospectus is issued to the public the procedure involves the following:
1  The company makes the approved prospectus, together with an application form attached, available to prospective investors. A prospective lender completes and lodges the application form together with the

application money with the company (or its agent) where it must be deposited into a 'trust account' with a financial institution until debenture certificates are allotted.

2 On the debenture allotment date directors identify successful debenture applicants and accept their offer to purchase debentures. Successful applicants are issued with debenture certificates as consideration for their offer and become debenture holders with their names recorded in the Register of Debenture Holders. If an applicant's offer is rejected or the applicant is not allotted the full amount of debentures applied for, the applicant's money is refunded from the trust account.

3 After debenture allotment has been made and refunds given, the company then transfers the application money from the trust account to its general purpose bank account.

## 3.4 ACCOUNTING FOR A DEBENTURE ISSUE

To account for the issue of debentures on a prospectus where applicants are required to pay in full on application, and where the prospectus has been oversubscribed, the following entries are required:

1 application money received and deposited in a trust account;
2 allot debentures to successful applicants and make refunds to unsuccessful applicants; and
3 transfer trust money to the general bank account.

 **Illustration**

On 1 May 2014 Grampians Ltd issued a prospectus inviting applications for 100 debentures at $10 000 each attracting an interest rate of 10% p.a. payable on 31 December and 30 June each year with the debenture maturing on 30 June 2020.

By the closing date of 1 June, applications were received for 110 debentures.

On 30 June 2014 the directors allotted the debentures, with the balance being refunded.

The journal entries and general ledger postings for this prospectus would be as follows:

1 **Receipt of application moneys**

### General journal

| Date | Details | Debit | Credit |
|------|---------|-------|--------|
| 2014 | | $ | $ |
| 1 June | Bank trust – debentures | 1 100 000 | |
| | Applications liability – debentures | | 1 100 000 |
| | *Received applications for 110 debentures @ $10 000 each* | | |

2 **Allotment debentures to successful applicants and make refunds to unsuccessful applicants**

### General journal

| Date | Details | Debit | Credit |
|------|---------|-------|--------|
| 2014 | | $ | $ |
| 30 June | Applications liability – debentures | 1 100 000 | |
| | Debentures liability | | 1 000 000 |
| | Bank trust – debentures | | 100 000 |
| | *Issued 100 debentures @ $10 000 each and made refunds for 10 debentures @ $10 000 each* | | |

3    Transfer money held in trust to general bank account

General journal

| Date | Details | Debit | Credit |
|---|---|---|---|
| 2014 | | $ | $ |
| 30 June | Bank general | 1 000 000 | |
| |     Bank trust – debentures | | 1 000 000 |
| | *Transferred debenture money held in trust* | | |

The general ledger arising from these entries would appear as follows:

**General ledger of Grampians Ltd**

| Date | Particulars | Debit | Credit | Balance |
|---|---|---|---|---|
| | | $ | $ | $ |
| **Bank trust – debentures** | | | | |
| 1 June 2014 | Applications – debentures | 1 100 000 | | 1 100 000   Dr |
| 30 June 2014 | Applications – debentures | | 1 000 000 | 100 000   Dr |
| | Bank general | | 100 000 | Nil |
| **Applications liability – debentures** | | | | |
| 1 June 2014 | Bank trust – debentures | | 1 100 000 | 1 100 000   Cr |
| 30 June 2014 | Debenture liability | 1 000 000 | | 100 000   Cr |
| | Bank trust – debentures | 100 000 | | Nil |
| **Debenture liability** | | | | |
| 30 June 2014 | Applications – debentures | | 1 000 000 | 1 000 000   Cr |
| **Bank general** | | | | |
| 30 June 2014 | Bank trust – debentures | 1 000 000 | | 1 000 000   Dr |

The debenture liability would be disclosed in the statement of financial position as follows:

**Grampians Ltd**
**Statement of financial position (extract)**
**at 30 June 2014**

| Non-current liabilities | $ |
|---|---|
|    Debentures | 1 000 000 |

# Question 3.2

On 1 May 2014 Robertson Ltd issued a prospectus inviting applications for 800 debentures at $1000 each payable in full on application. The terms of the debenture include 8% p.a. interest payable six-monthly, with a maturity date of 30 June 2020.

Applications for 825 debentures had been received by the closing date of 1 June 2014.

On 30 June 2014 the directors allotted 800 debentures, issued debenture certificates to successful applicants and refunded unsuccessful applicants.

You are required to prepare:

a   journal entries to record all transactions; and

b   show the debentures in the statement of financial position at 30 June 2014.

## Question 3.3

From the following information provided in respect of Taree Ltd's debenture transactions you are required to prepare:

a   journal entries to record all transactions; and

b   show the debentures in the statement of financial position to 31 December 2014.

Taree Ltd issued a prospectus on 1 November 2014 inviting applications for 500 debentures at $1000 each payable in full on application. Debenture terms were 10% p.a., interest paid quarterly maturing on 30 June 2024. By 10 December 2014, the closing date for applications, applications had been received for 600 debentures. On 31 December 2014 the directors allotted debentures to successful applicants and made appropriate refunds.

## 3.5   ACCOUNTING FOR DEBENTURE INTEREST PAYMENTS

Debentures are serviced each year through the payment of interest, with the rate and dates of payment being specified in the prospectus. This may include interest paid monthly, quarterly, biannually or annually. Interest paid on debentures is classified as a finance cost, is included in the calculation of annual profit and is an allowable tax deduction for the borrower.

### Illustration

In the previous illustration, Grampians Ltd on 1 July 2014 allotted 100 debentures of $10 000 each totalling $1 000 000 attracting an interest rate of 10% p.a. payable six-monthly on 31 December and 30 June each year until 30 June 2020.

The annual interest amount payable would be $1 000 000 @ 10% = $100 000. This would be paid in two instalments of $50 000, on 31 December and 30 June each year until the debenture matures on 30 June 2020.

The journal entries to record the interest payments for the year ended 30 June 2015 would be as follows:

**1   Payment of interest**

**General journal**

| Date | Details | Debit | Credit |
|---|---|---|---|
| | | $ | $ |
| 31 Dec 2014 | Debenture interest expense | 50 000 | |
| | Bank general | | 50 000 |
| | *Paid interest on debentures* | | |
| 30 June 2015 | Debenture interest expense | 50 000 | |
| | Bank general | | 50 000 |
| | *Paid interest on debentures* | | |

**2   Transfer of interest expense to the profit and loss account.**

**General journal**

| Date | Details | Debit | Credit |
|---|---|---|---|
| | | $ | $ |
| 30 June 2015 | Profit and loss | 100 000 | |
| | Debenture interest expense | | 100 000 |
| | *Transferred expense account to profit and loss* | | |

The general ledger arising from these entries would appear as follows:

**General ledger of Grampians Ltd**

| Date | Particulars | Debit $ | Credit $ | Balance $ |
|---|---|---|---|---|
| **Debenture interest expense** | | | | |
| 31 Dec 2014 | Bank general | 50 000 | | 50 000 Dr |
| 30 June 2015 | Bank general | 50 000 | | 100 000 Dr |
| | Profit and loss | | 100 000 | Nil |
| **Bank general** | | | | |
| 31 Dec 2014 | Debenture interest expense | | 50 000 | ˙50 000 Cr |
| 30 June 2015 | Debenture interest expense | | 50 000 | 100 000 Cr |
| **Profit and loss** | | | | |
| 30 June 2015 | Debenture interest expense | 100 000 | | 100 000 Dr |

## Question 3.4

Robertson Ltd issued 800 debentures at $1000 on 30 June 2014, attracting 8% p.a. interest payable six-monthly with a maturity date of 30 June 2020.

>You are required to prepare the journal entries to record the interest transactions for the year ended 30 June 2015.

## Question 3.5

Taree Ltd issued 500 $1000 debentures on 21 December 2014 which attracted interest at 10% p.a. paid quarterly and maturing on 30 June 2024.

>You are required to prepare the journal entries to record the interest transactions for the year ended 30 June 2015.

## Question 3.6

On 1 May 2014 Borrow Ltd issued a prospectus inviting applicants for 600 debentures of $1000 each, attracting an interest rate of 12% p.a. payable monthly with the debenture maturing on 30 June 2020.

>By the closing date of 25 May, applications were received for 650 debentures.

>On 1 June 2014 the directors allotted the debentures and made refunds.

You are required to:

a prepare the journal entries to record:
   the transactions relating to the prospectus;
   the interest transactions for the year ended 30 June 2014; and
b show the liabilities section of the statement of financial position at 30 June 2014.

## 3.6 DEBENTURE REDEMPTION

When a debenture matures, the borrower is required to pay the debenture holder the amount borrowed. This is called 'debenture redemption'.

Most redemptions occur when the debenture matures; that is, the date specified in the prospectus. However, debentures can be redeemed before the maturity date, usually at a premium (an amount above the debenture's issue price), or at a discount (an amount below the issue price).

## Redemption at maturity

Redemption at the date of maturity requires the lender to repay the debenture holder the debenture's issue price in full at the end of the loan period.

### Illustration

In the continuing illustration, Grampians Ltd owed debenture holders $1 000 000 in respect of 100 debentures of $10 000 each, payable on maturity at 30 June 2020.

The journal entry to redeem the debenture would be as follows:

**General journal**

| Date | Details | Debit | Credit |
|------|---------|-------|--------|
| 2020 | | $ | $ |
| 30 June | Debenture liability | 1 000 000 | |
| |     Bank general | | 1 000 000 |
| | *Payment to redeem 100 debentures @ $10 000 each* | | |

The debenture liability account would appear as follows:

**General ledger of Grampians Ltd**
**Debenture liability**

| Date | Particulars | Debit | Credit | Balance |
|------|-------------|-------|--------|---------|
| | | $ | $ | $ |
| 30 June 2014 | Applications – debentures | | 1 000 000 | 1 000 000  Cr |
| 30 June 2020 | Bank general | 1 000 000 | | Nil |

## Question 3.7

Robertson Ltd issued 800 debentures at $1000 on 30 June 2014, attracting 8% p.a. interest payable six-monthly with a maturity date of 30 June 2020.

You are required to prepare the journal entry to record the redemption of the debentures on 30 June 2020.

## Question 3.8

Taree Ltd issued 500 $1000 debentures on 21 December 2014 which attracted interest at 10% p.a. paid quarterly and maturing on 30 June 2024.

You are required to prepare the journal entry to record the debenture redemption at 30 June 2024.

## Redemption prior to maturity at a premium

When a debenture is redeemed prior to maturity and the amount paid by the lender to the debenture holder is greater than its issue price, the debenture is redeemed at a premium in the hands of the lender.

This can occur where the lender wishes to pay out the debenture liability prior to its maturity and entices the debenture holder by offering more than the debenture is worth to compensate the debenture holder for loss of future interest. The lender, by paying more than the debenture's issue price, will incur an expense referred to as a 'premium or (loss) on debenture redemption'.

A 'premium on debenture redemption' can also arise where the debenture holder has placed the debenture on the stock exchange for sale and the debenture lender (the company that issued the debenture) purchases the debenture, paying a price above the debenture's original issue price.

## Illustration

Barton Ltd issued 500 debentures at $1000 each on 1 January 2015, redeemable on 31 December 2020. On 15 May 2018 Barton Ltd redeemed 100 debentures at $1050 each.

This redemption can be analysed as follows:

| | | |
|---|---|---|
| Amount paid to redeem debentures | 100 × $1 050 = | $105 000 |
| Issue price of debentures | 100 × $1 000 = | $100 000 |
| Premium (loss) on debenture redemption | 100 × $50 = | $5 000 |

The journal entries to redeem the debenture at a premium would be as follows:

**General journal**

| Date | Details | Debit | Credit |
|---|---|---|---|
| 2018 | | $ | $ |
| 15 May | Debenture liability | 100 000 | |
| | Loss (premium) on debenture redemption | 5 000 | |
| |    Bank general | | 105 000 |
| | *Payment to redeem 100 $1 000 debentures at a premium of $50 each* | | |
| | Profit and loss | 5 000 | |
| |    Loss (premium) on debenture redemption | | 5 000 |
| | *Transferred expense account to profit and loss* | | |

The debenture liability account would appear as follows:

**General ledger – Barton Ltd**

| Debenture liability | | | | |
|---|---|---|---|---|
| Date | Particulars | Debit | Credit | Balance |
| | | $ | $ | $ |
| 1 Jan 2015 | Applications – debentures | | 500 000 | 500 000  Cr |
| 15 May 2018 | Bank general | 100 000 | | 400 000  Cr |

## Question 3.9

In March 2015 Upper Ltd issued 1000 debentures at $1000 each with a maturity date of 1 April 2020. On 1 May 2019 Upper Ltd accepted an offer from a debenture holder to redeem 100 debentures at $1050 each.

You are required to record the journal entries associated with the redemption.

## Question 3.10

On 1 August 2015 Limit Ltd allotted 5000 debentures at $1000 each with a maturity date of 1 August 2020.

On 1 January 2019 Limit Ltd paid $1030 through the ASX to redeem 3000 debentures at a premium of $30 per debenture.

On 1 August 2020 the remaining debentures were redeemed at their face value.

You are required to:

a    record the journal entries for each redemption; and

b    show the debenture account in the general ledger.

## Redemption prior to maturity at a discount

When a debenture is redeemed prior to maturity and the amount paid by the lender to the debenture holder is less than its issue price, the debenture is redeemed at a discount in the hands of the lender.

This may occur where the debenture holder needs cash and is keen to redeem the debenture before the maturity date and offers the lender the opportunity to pay out the debenture by paying a price below the debenture's issue price (at a discount). It can also arise where the debenture holder is offering the debenture for sale on the stock exchange and the lender purchases the debenture by paying a price below the debenture's original issue price.

## Illustration

Hart Ltd issued 800 debentures at $1000 each on 1 May 2015, redeemable on 30 April 2020. On 1 June 2018 the company accepted an offer by a debenture holder to redeem 100 debentures at $980 each.

This redemption can be analysed as follows:

| Amount paid to redeem debentures | 100 × $980 = | $98 000 |
|---|---|---|
| Issue price of debentures | 100 × $1 000 = | $100 000 |
| Discount (gain) on debenture redemption | 100 × $20 = | $2 000 |

The journal entries to redeem the debenture at a discount would be as follows:

### General journal

| Date | Details | Debit | Credit |
|---|---|---|---|
| 2018 | | $ | $ |
| 1 June | Debenture liability | 100 000 | |
| |     Gain (discount) on debenture redemption | | 2 000 |
| |     Bank general | | 98 000 |
| | *Payment to redeem 100 $1 000 debentures at a discount of $20 each* | | |
| | Gain (discount) on debenture redemption | 2 000 | |
| |     Profit and loss | | 2 000 |
| | *Transferred income account to profit and loss* | | |

The debenture liability account would appear as follows:

### General ledger – Hart Ltd

| Debenture liability | | | | |
|---|---|---|---|---|
| Date | Particulars | Debit | Credit | Balance |
| | | $ | $ | $ |
| 1 May 2015 | Applications – debentures | | 800 000 | 800 000 Cr |
| 1 June 2018 | Bank general | 100 000 | | 700 000 Cr |

## Question 3.11

On 1 January 2015 Gibson Ltd allotted 4000 debentures at $1000 with a maturity date of 31 December 2020.

On 29 January 2017, 2000 debentures were redeemed at $960 each.

On 24 May 2018, 1500 debentures were redeemed at a discount of $50 per debenture.

You are required to:

**a** record the journal entries associated with each redemption; and

**b** show the debentures liability account in the general ledger.

## Question 3.12

Balmoral Ltd on 1 May 2015 issued 10 000 debentures at par value $1000 each with a maturity date of 1 June 2020.

On 3 June 2018 the directors redeemed 5000 debentures at $950 each.

On 1 June 2020 the remaining debentures were redeemed at par value.

You are required to:

**a** record the journal entries for each redemption; and

**b** show the debenture liability account in the general ledger.

# 3.7 PUBLIC COMPANY DEBENTURE TRANSACTIONS SUMMARY

1 Receipt of application money, allotment of debentures, refunds and bank transfer

| Details | Debit | Credit |
|---|---|---|
| | $ | $ |
| Bank trust – debentures | Dr | |
|     Applications liability – debentures | | Cr |
| *Receipt of application moneys* | | |
| Applications liability – debentures | Dr | |
|     Debenture liability | | Cr |
| *Allotment of debentures to successful applicants* | | |
| Applications liability – debentures | Dr | |
|     Bank trust | | Cr |
| *Refunds to unsuccessful applicants* | | |
| Bank general | Dr | |
|     Bank trust – debentures | | Cr |
| *Transfer of money held in trust* | | |

2 Annual payment of interest

| Details | Debit | Credit |
|---|---|---|
| | $ | $ |
| Debenture interest | Dr | |
|     Bank general | | Cr |
| *Payment of debenture interest* | | |

3 Redemption of debentures at maturity at issue price

| Details | Debit | Credit |
|---|---|---|
| | $ | $ |
| Debenture liability | Dr | |
|     Bank general | | Cr |
| *Payment to redeem debentures at issue price* | | |

4 Redemption of debentures above issue price

| Details | Debit | Credit |
|---|---|---|
| | $ | $ |
| Debenture liability | Dr | |
| Loss (premium) on debenture redemption | Dr | |
|     Bank general | | Cr |
| *Payment to redeem debentures above issue price* | | |

5 Redemption of debentures below issue price

| Details | Debit | Credit |
|---|---|---|
| | $ | $ |
| Debenture liability | Dr | |
|     Gain (discount) on debenture redemption | | Cr |
|     Bank general | | Cr |
| *Payment to redeem debentures below issue price* | | |

## Question 3.13

Cobargo Ltd, on 1 April 2015, issued a prospectus inviting applications for 900 debentures at $1000 each payable in full on application. The debenture terms included:

- full payment on application by 1 June 2015;
- interest paid annually at 10% p.a. on 30 June; and
- maturation on 30 June 2017.

By 1 June 2015 applications had been received for 950 debentures.

On 30 June 2015 the directors allotted debentures and issued refunds.

You are required to prepare general journal entries to record:

a the application and allotment of the debentures;

b the annual interest payments; and

c debenture redemption.

## Question 3.14

On 10 December 2015 Daylesford Ltd issued a prospectus inviting applications for 750 debentures at par value of $1000 each payable in full on application. Terms of issue were 6% p.a. interest payable quarterly with a maturity date of 31 July 2020.

On 29 January 2015 applications closed for the mortgage debentures. Applications were received for 800 debentures.

On 1 February 2015 the directors allotted debentures.

On 21 August 2017 directors redeemed 250 debentures at $1040 each.

On 19 February 2018 directors redeemed another 350 debentures at a discount of $100 per debenture.

On 31 July 2020 the remaining debentures were redeemed at their issue price.

You are required to prepare journal entries to record:

a the application and allotment of debentures;

b the various redemptions; and

c show the debenture liability account.

# Comprehensive Assessment Activity

The following transactions have been provided by Transit Ltd.

| Date | Transaction |
| --- | --- |
| **2015** | |
| 1 January | The company was registered as a public company limited by shares with four subscribers, each agreeing to purchase 10 000 fully paid ordinary shares at a price of $5.00 per share |
| 10 January | Money received from subscribers |
| 20 January | Establishment costs totalling $5500 (GST inclusive) were paid |
| 1 May | Share prospectus issued inviting applications for: |
| | 100 000 preference shares at a price of $10.00 per share payable: |
| | *$5.00 on application;* |
| | *$3.00 on allotment; and* |
| | *$2.00 on a single call* |
| 2 May | Debenture prospectus issued inviting applications for 500 debentures at $1000 each. Debenture terms included interest of 10% p.a. payable on 30 June with redemption in five years |
| 28 June | Closing date for both share and debenture applications |
| | *120 000 share applications* |
| | *650 debenture applications* |
| 1 July | Shares and debentures allotted, refunds made and share allotment letters issued |
| 10 August | Transaction costs of $0.11 per share (GST inclusive) were paid |
| 15 September | All allotment money received in full |
| **2016** | |
| 1 May | Call money made on shares |
| 30 June | Calls received on 99 000 shares |
| | Interest paid on debentures |
| | Debenture holders redeem 100 debentures at a discount of $100 each |

You are required to:

**a**  record all transactions in the general journal; and

**b**  prepare an extract of the statement of financial position at 30 June 2016 showing only liabilities and shareholders' equity.

# Assessment Checklist

Complete the following checklist to identify if you consider yourself capable of being assessed against each of the following outcomes.

| I can: | Chapter reference | Check ✓ |
|---|---|---|
| explain the financial characteristics of a debenture | 3.2 | |
| explain the purpose of a debenture prospectus | 3.2 | |
| explain the meaning of a secured debenture | 3.2 | |
| explain the meaning of an unsecured note | 3.2 | |
| explain the purpose of a register of debenture holders | 3.2 | |
| explain why debenture application money must be held in trust | 3.3 | |
| account for the receipt of debenture application money | 3.3 | |
| record the issue of debentures to successful applicants | 3.3 | |
| record refunds of debenture applications to unsuccessful applicants | 3.3 | |
| record debentures in a statement of financial position | 3.4 | |
| account for annual debenture interest payments | 3.4 | |
| account for redemption of debentures at a premium | 3.5 | |
| account for redemption of debentures at a discount | 3.5 | |
| account for redemption at maturity | 3.5 | |

# CHAPTER 4

## CONVERTING A
## NON-CORPORATE ENTITY
## TO A COMPANY

## WHAT YOU WILL LEARN IN THIS CHAPTER

Upon satisfactory completion of this chapter you should be able to:
- apply Accounting Standard AASB3: Business Combinations;
- account for the acquisition of a non-corporate business by company;
- apply Accounting Standard AASB13: Fair Value Measurement;
- apply Accounting Standard AASB116: Property Plant and Equipment; and
- prepare a statement of financial position after a business combination has occurred.

**Are you already competent at these tasks?**
If you have already accomplished these tasks as a result of your recent workplace or training experiences you may wish to proceed to the Comprehensive Assessment Activity at the end of this chapter to assess your skills in these areas.

## 4.1   INTRODUCTION

Non-corporate entities such as sole trader and partnership forms of business ownership may convert their existing business into a company. When a sole trader or partnership converts to a company the appropriate accounting standards must be followed. This chapter studies the accounting principles and standards required when converting a non-corporate entity to a company.

## 4.2   CONVERTING TO A COMPANY

Non-corporate entities may consider a change of business structure and incorporate as a company under the Corporations Act. Conversion to a corporate entity may be desirable in the following circumstances:

1   **To avoid unlimited liability:** The principle of unlimited liability affects sole trader and partnership forms of business which require their owners to take personal responsibility for the business debts when the business is unable to meet those debts.

   When a company is formed shareholders liability is limited to the issue price of the shares acquired, thereby giving them limited liability in relation to the debts of the business.

2   **To obtain increased capital:** Conversion to a company, particularly a public company, will allow the business to issue shares to the public and thereby increase capital contributions.

### Registering the company

Before a non-corporate entity can be converted to a corporate entity, a company must first be registered. The steps to register a company were covered in Chapter 1 and include:

**Step 1**   Register the business by obtaining an ABN and consider registering for GST.

**Step 2**   Adopt the Replaceable Rules or prepare a constitution.

**Step 3**   Allot shares to founding members.

**Step 4**   Appoint director(s) and a company secretary.

**Step 5**   Complete and lodge the application form.

 **Illustration**

Colin and Jane Wood own a partnership business called Wood Electrics. On 1 February they formed a proprietary company with their son Mark, called Woody's Pty Ltd, taking one ordinary share each at $1.00 per share as founding members. The accounting entries on incorporation of Woody's Pty Ltd and its financial position would be as follows:

**General journal – Woody's Pty Ltd**

| Date | Details | Debit | Credit |
|------|---------|-------|--------|
|      |         | $     | $      |
| 1 Feb | Subscribers | 3 | |
|      | Share capital – ordinary shares | | 3 |
|      | *Issued shares to subscribers on registration* | | |
|      | Bank | 3 | |
|      | Subscribers | | 3 |
|      | *Receipted money paid by subscribers* | | |

**Woody's Pty Ltd**
**Statement of financial position**
**at 1 February**

| Shareholders' equity | $ | |
|---|---|---|
| Share capital | | |
| Ordinary shares (3 @ $1.00 each) | | 3 |
| Total shareholders' equity | | 3 |
| Assets | | |
| Bank | | 3 |
| Total assets | | 3 |

## Acquiring net assets

Once the company has been established it can then purchase the net assets of the sole trader or partnership. This will require the company (the purchaser) and the sole trader or partnership (the vendor) to agree on the assets and liabilities and their values that will be acquired by the company.

# 4.3   APPROVED ACCOUNTING STANDARDS

When a company acquires the net assets of a non-corporate entity two entities are combining as one. The Accounting Standard AASB3: Business Combinations defines a business combination as:

> A transaction or other event in which an acquirer obtains control of one or more businesses.
>
> Source: http://www.aasb.gov.au

When a business is acquired the purchaser will buy the net assets of the vendor's business. The values of the assets and liabilities reported on the vendor's statement of financial position are reported at their carrying amounts. Accounting Standard AASB116: Property, Plant and Equipment defines carrying amount as *the amount at which an asset is recognised after deducting any accumulated depreciation and accumulated impairment losses.*

> AASB3: Business Combinations requires the net assets acquired in a business combination to be measured at their fair value with AASB13: Fair Value Measurement defining fair value as the price that would be received to sell an asset or paid to transfer a liability in an orderly transaction between market participants at the measurement date.
>
> Source: http://www.aasb.gov.au

Hence the carrying cost of assets of a non-corporate entity will be recorded in the company's accounts at their fair values.

When a company purchases the assets of another entity the purchaser must ensure that their fair values are brought to account in accordance with AASB3 and AASB116. Consequently the purchaser when recording the purchase of assets from another entity MUST:

- **Never** record accumulated depreciation on non-current assets. Always introduce the asset at its fair value. The fair value then becomes the cost price in the purchaser's accounts.
- **Always** recognise the full value of debtors as invoices have been issued and have the potential to be collected in full. To adjust the invoiced value to the fair value use the allowance for doubtful debts account to adjust the debtor's value.

## Illustration

Colin and Jane Wood have formed Woody's Pty Ltd to acquire the net assets of their partnership Wood Electrics. The assets and liabilities of Wood Electrics are reported on its financial statement at the following carrying costs:

| Assets | $ | $ | Liabilities | $ |
|---|---|---|---|---|
| Bank | | 20 000 | Creditors | 30 000 |
| Debtors | 32 000 | | Bank overdraft | 20 000 |
| Less allowance for doubtful debts | 2 000 | 30 000 | | |
| Stock | | 60 000 | | |
| Vehicle | 38 000 | | | |
| Less accumulated depreciation | 18 000 | 20 000 | | |
| | | 130 000 | | 50 000 |

Woody's Pty Ltd has agreed to take over Wood Electrics' creditors but not its bank overdraft and to purchase all of its assets at the following fair values:

| | $ |
|---|---|
| Bank | 20 000 |
| Debtors | 29 000 |
| Stock | 55 000 |
| Vehicle | 16 000 |

The fair values of the net assets that Woody's Pty Ltd would bring to account as a result of the conversion would be as follows:

| Assets | $ | $ | Liabilities | $ |
|---|---|---|---|---|
| Bank | | 20 000 | Creditors | 30 000 |
| Debtors | 32 000 | | | |
| Allowance for doubtful debts | 3 000 | 29 000 | | |
| Stock | | 55 000 | | |
| Vehicle | | 16 000 | | |
| | | 120 000 | | 30 000 |

Hence the net assets acquired equals:

| Net assets = | Assets | Less | Liabilities |
|---|---|---|---|
| = | $120 000 | – | $30 000 |
| = | | | $90 000 |

## Question 4.1

Bart is converting his sole trader business to a private company. The following table shows the current carrying amounts and fair values of the business assets. Using this information, identify the accounts and their balances that would be brought to account by the newly-formed company and calculate the value of assets purchased.

| | Sole Trader Carrying amounts | | Fair values |
|---|---|---|---|
| | $ | $ | $ |
| Cash at bank | | 10 000 | 10 000 |
| Debtors | | 50 000 | 45 000 |
| Vehicles | 42 000 | | |
| *Less* accumulated depreciation | 22 000 | 20 000 | 18 000 |
| Land and buildings | | 120 000 | 180 000 |

## Question 4.2

Fisk Pty Ltd has been set up by the owners of Fisk Partners to take over the assets of the partnership. The following table shows the asset values. Using this information identify the accounts and their balances that would be brought to account by Fisk Pty Ltd and calculate the value of the net assets acquired.

| | Fisk Partners Carrying amounts | | Fair values |
|---|---|---|---|
| | $ | $ | $ |
| Debtors | 150 000 | | |
| *Less* allowance for doubtful debts | 15 000 | 135 000 | 140 000 |
| Equipment | 80 000 | | |
| *Less* accumulated depreciation | 60 000 | 20 000 | 25 000 |
| Machinery | | 100 000 | 90 000 |
| Creditors | | 30 000 | 30 000 |

## 4.4   PURCHASE CONSIDERATION PAID TO THE VENDOR

Where the owner(s) of a non-corporate entity convert their businesses into a company, the purchaser and vendor (the seller) are physically the same person(s). However, from a business entity point of view, the purchaser and the vendor are separate entities. Hence the two entities must reach an agreement on the amount that the purchaser will pay the vendor in consideration for the assets and liabilities being acquired.

The purchase amount agreed is called the purchase price and may be in the form of cash, shares in the newly formed company, or a combination of both.

The purchase price paid may be equal to the value of the net assets acquired, above their value or below their fair value.

### Purchase consideration above the fair value of net assets

When a company acquires another entity it may pay a price in excess of the value of the net assets being acquired. This may occur where the purchaser believes that the business being purchased has a profitable future and a higher price is more reflective of its future earnings potential.

Where the purchase price exceeds the fair values of the net assets being acquired, the purchaser is required to bring to account goodwill in accordance with AASB3, which refers to goodwill as being the excess of the consideration (given by the purchaser) over the net assets acquired (from the vendor).

## Illustration

In the previous illustration Woody's Pty Ltd acquired the net assets of Wood Electrics at the following fair values:

| Assets | $ | $ | Liabilities | $ |
|---|---|---|---|---|
| Bank | | 20 000 | Creditors | 30 000 |
| Debtors | 32 000 | | | |
| Less allowance for doubtful debts | 3 000 | 29 000 | | |
| Stock | | 55 000 | | |
| Vehicle | | 16 000 | | |
| | | 120 000 | | 30 000 |

Net assets = Assets     Less     Liabilities

     =   $120 000     –     $30 000

     =               $90 000

If the consideration paid by Woody's Pty Ltd (the purchaser) to Wood Electrics (the vendor) totalled $100 000 the goodwill amount would be $10 000, calculated as follows:

Goodwill = Assets     Less     Net assets

     =   $100 000     –     $90 000

     =               $10 000

## Question 4.3

Drayon Ltd purchased the business belonging to Lance Holt on 1 July for $650 000. On this date the carrying amounts and the agreed fair values of Lance's assets were as follows.

| | Carrying amounts | | Fair values |
|---|---|---|---|
| | $ | $ | $ |
| Inventory | | 100 000 | 110 000 |
| Debtors | 40 000 | | |
| Less allowance for doubtful debts | 5 000 | 35 000 | 32 000 |
| Plant and equipment | | 500 000 | 450 000 |
| Vehicles | 80 000 | | |
| Less accumulated depreciation | 60 000 | 20 000 | 25 000 |

Assuming Lance had no liabilities, you are required to calculate the amount of goodwill that Drayon Ltd should bring to account in respect of the above purchase.

## Question 4.4

The assets and liabilities of Martha's Fashions included the following:

| Assets | $ | $ | Liabilities | $ |
|---|---|---|---|---|
| Debtors | 50 000 | | Creditors | 20 000 |
| Less allowance for doubtful debts | 2 000 | 48 000 | Bank overdraft | 30 000 |
| Stock | | 30 000 | | |
| Equipment | 60 000 | | | |
| Less accumulated depreciation | 40 000 | 20 000 | | |

Martha's Pty Ltd has agreed to acquire Martha's Fashions for $100 000 by:
- taking over its creditors but not its bank overdraft; and
- purchasing all of the assets at the following fair values:

| | |
|---|---|
| Debtors | $45 000 |
| Stock | $32 000 |
| Equipment | $25 000 |

You are required to itemise the accounts and their balances (including goodwill) that would be recorded in the books of Martha's Pty Ltd.

## Purchase consideration below the fair value of net assets

It may also be possible for a company to pay consideration less than the fair value of the net assets being acquired. Where the purchaser pays less than the fair values of the net assets acquired, AASB3: Business Combinations requires the difference to be included in the calculation of profit and loss for the year.

For example, ABC Ltd purchased a business paying consideration of $80 000. The fair value of the business assets was $100 000. Consequently, a discount on acquisition of $20 000 would be recognised by ABC Ltd in its income statement.

## Question 4.5

Smart Ltd acquired the net assets of West Trading, paying $200 000 for the business. The fair value of the net assets acquired was:

| | $ | $ |
|---|---|---|
| Debtors | 12 000 | |
| Less allowance for doubtful debts | 2 000 | 10 000 |
| Stock on hand | | 40 000 |
| Land and buildings | | 150 000 |
| Equipment | 100 000 | |
| Less accumulated depreciation | 90 000 | 10 000 |

You are required to state the values that would be recorded in the accounts of Smart Ltd on the date of acquisition.

## 4.5 ACCOUNTING ENTRIES TO PURCHASE ANOTHER ENTITY

When a company acquires the assets of a sole trader or a partnership, the company becomes the 'purchaser' and the sole trader or partnership becomes the vendor.

The vendor who is selling the net assets to the company will require payment for the assets. This may take the form of cash, the issue of shares in the company, or both.

The steps involved in the accounts of the purchasing company are as follows:

**Step 1** Identify the assets to be acquired and their fair values.
**Step 2** Identify the liabilities to be acquired.
**Step 3** Calculate the amount to be paid to the vendor for the net assets acquired.
**Step 4** Calculate the amount of goodwill (or discount on acquisition).
**Step 5** Record the net assets acquired and the payment to the vendor.

### Purchase consideration above the fair value of net assets

Where the purchase price exceeds the fair values of the net assets acquired, the purchaser is required to bring to account goodwill in accordance with AASB3.

### Illustration

In the previous illustrations Woody's Pty Ltd which has a share capital of $3.00 paid $100 000 to acquire $90 000 in net assets of Wood Electrics and recognised $10 000 in goodwill on the acquisition.

Woody's Pty Ltd would undertake the following procedures to record the acquisition:

**Step 1** Purchase all of the assets of Wood Electrics at the following fair values:

| | |
|---|---|
| Bank | $20 000 |
| Debtors | $29 000 |
| Stock | $55 000 |
| Vehicle | $16 000 |
| Total | $120 000 |

**Step 2** Take over Wood Electric's creditors totalling $30 000, but not the bank overdraft.
**Step 3** Pay the partnership $100 000. Each partner is to receive: $45 000 in fully paid ordinary shares at $1.00 each in Woody's Pty Ltd, plus $5000 cash to be paid on 30 April.
**Step 4** Calculation of goodwill on acquisition.

| Net assets = | Assets | Less | Liabilities |
|---|---|---|---|
| = | $120 000 | – | $30 000 |
| = | $90 000 | | |

| Goodwill = | Consideration | Less | Net assets |
|---|---|---|---|
| = | $100 000 | – | $90 000 |
| = | $10 000 | | |

**Step 5**  Record the net assets acquired, any goodwill and the vendor(s) consideration. The journal entry required would be as follows:

**Woody's Pty Ltd**
**General journal**

| Date | Particulars | Debit | Credit |
|------|-------------|-------|--------|
| | | $ | $ |
| 1 Feb | Bank | 20 000 | |
| | Debtors | 32 000 | |
| | Stock | 55 000 | |
| | Vehicle | 16 000 | |
| | Goodwill | 10 000 | |
| | Allowance for doubtful debts | | 3 000 |
| | Creditors | | 30 000 |
| | Vendor liability – C. Wood (due 30 April) | | 5 000 |
| | Vendor liability – J. Wood (due 30 April) | | 5 000 |
| | Share capital – ordinary shares | | 90 000 |
| | *To record the takeover of Woody's Electrics.* | | |

The financial position after the acquisition of the net assets of Wood Electrics would be as follows:

**Woody's Pty Ltd**
**Statement of financial position**
**at 1 February**

| Shareholders' equity | $ | $ |
|----------------------|---|---|
| Share capital | | |
| Ordinary shares (90 003 @ $1.00 each) | | 90 003 |
| Total shareholders' equity | | 90 003 |
| Assets | | |
| Bank | | 20 003 |
| Debtors | 32 000 | |
| *Less* allowance for doubtful debts | 3 000 | 29 000 |
| Stock | | 55 000 |
| Vehicle | | 16 000 |
| Goodwill | | 10 000 |
| Total assets | | 130 003 |
| Less liabilities | | |
| Creditors | 30 000 | |
| Vendor liability – C. Wood (due 30 April) | 5 000 | |
| Vendor liability – J. Wood (due 30 April) | 5 000 | 40 000 |
| Net assets | | 90 003 |

## Question 4.6

Peta Powers owns a sole trader business called Powers Plants. On 1 May she formed a proprietary company with her mother Mary, called Powers Pty Ltd. Peta and Mary took 1000 ordinary shares each at $1.00 per share as founding members.

The company statement of financial position after its incorporation was as follows:

**Powers Pty Ltd**
**Statement of financial position**
**at 1 May**

| Shareholders' equity | $ |
|---|---|
| Share capital | |
| Ordinary shares (2 000 @ $1.00 each) | 2 000 |
| Total shareholders' equity | 2 000 |
| Assets | |
| Bank | 2 000 |
| Total assets | 2 000 |

The asset and liabilities of Peta's sole trader business Power Plants included the following:

| Assets | $ | $ | Liabilities | $ |
|---|---|---|---|---|
| Debtors | 12 000 | | Creditors | 10 000 |
| Less allowance for doubtful debts | 2 000 | 10 000 | Bank overdraft | 40 000 |
| Stock | | 20 000 | | |
| Vehicle | 52 000 | | | |
| Less accumulated depreciation | 22 000 | 30 000 | | |

Peta and Mary as company directors agreed that Powers Pty Ltd would:

- Purchase all of the assets of Powers Plants at the following fair values:

  Debtors          $11 000

  Stock            $22 000

  Vehicle          $29 000

- Take over Powers Plants creditors but not the bank overdraft.
- Pay Peta the immediate allocation 40 000 fully paid ordinary shares at $1.00 each, plus $20 000 cash in 12 months.

You are required to:

**a**   record the general journal entry in the books of Power's Pty Ltd to take over Powers Plants; and

**b**   prepare Powers Pty Ltd's statement of financial position after the conversion.

## Question 4.7

On 1 July W. and J. Arden registered Arden's Pty Ltd, taking 50 000 $2.00 ordinary shares each with the intention of acquiring the net assets of their partnership, Arden Plumbing Supplies.

The account balances of the partnership Arden Plumbing Supplies included the following carrying amounts:

| Assets | $ | $ | Liabilities | $ |
|---|---|---|---|---|
| Cash at bank | | 4 000 | Creditors | 32 000 |
| Debtors | | 40 000 | | |
| Plumbing supplies | | 72 000 | | |
| Equipment | 36 000 | | | |
| Less accumulated depreciation | 12 000 | 24 000 | | |

### Additional information

- The directors of the company agreed to take over all the assets and liabilities of Arden Plumbing Supplies at the following fair values:

| | |
|---|---|
| Cash at bank | $4 000 |
| Debtors | $38 000 |
| Plumbing supplies | $70 000 |
| Equipment | $20 000 |
| Creditors | $32 000 |

- Purchase consideration consisted of each partner accepting 25 000, $2.00 ordinary shares immediately in the capital of Arden Plumbing Supplies Pty Ltd plus $50 000 cash payable on 31 July.

You are required to prepare Arden Pty Ltd's:

a  general journal entry recording the acquisition of Arden Plumbing Supplies; and

b  statement of financial position after the takeover.

## Question 4.8

Brad and Julie operate independent sole trader businesses in the same industry. Their respective account balances consisted of:

| Brad | | Julie | |
|---|---|---|---|
| | $ | | $ |
| Bank overdraft | (10 000) | Bank | 10 000 |
| Debtors | 50 000 | Vehicle | 75 000 |
| Allowance for doubtful debts | (2 000) | Accumulated depreciation | (15 000) |

They decided to combine their businesses and form a private company called Bradulie Pty Ltd and acquire the net assets of each sole trader business.

The transactions to form the company and acquire the sole trader businesses were as follows:

| Date | Transaction |
|---|---|
| 1 April | Bradulie Ltd was incorporated with Brad and Julie each taking 20 000 $2.00 ordinary shares as subscribers |
| 10 April | Brad and Julie pay for their shares |
| 15 April | Brad's sole trader business assets are acquired by Bradulie Ltd for $50 000 with debtors' fair value being $49 000. Brad was issued with 20 000 $2.00 ordinary shares in Bradulie Pty Ltd and the balance in cash in 12 months |
| 20 April | Julie's sole trader business assets are acquired with the fair value of the vehicle being $50 000. Julie was issued with $2.00 ordinary shares in Bradulie Pty Ltd as full payment |

You are required to prepare:

a  the general journal entries recording the above transactions; and

b  Bradulie's statement of financial position after the conversion.

## Purchase consideration below the fair value of net assets

Where the purchaser pays less than the fair values of the net assets acquired, AASB3: Business Combinations requires the difference to be included in the calculation of profit and loss for the year.

### Illustration

M. Wilson operates a sole trader business trading as Frankston Wholesalers. On 1 March Wilson established a private company called Wilson's Pty Ltd by taking $10 000 in ordinary shares and placing the cash in the bank.

Wilson's Pty Ltd then acquired the net assets of Frankston Wholesalers for $60 000 cash. The net assets of Frankston Wholesalers at their fair values consisted of:

| Assets | $ | $ | Liabilities | $ |
|---|---|---|---|---|
| Debtors control | 25 000 | | Creditors' control | 15 000 |
| Less allowance for doubtful debts | 5 000 | 20 000 | Bank loan | 25 000 |
| Stock | | 40 000 | | |
| Vehicle | | 60 000 | | |
| | | 120 000 | | 40 000 |

Net assets = Assets    Less    Liabilities
      = $120 000    −    $40 000
      = $80 000
Goodwill = Consideration    Less    Net assets
      = $60 000    −    $80 000
      = $20 000

The acquisition of the net assets, recognition of discount on acquisition and payment to the vendor could be recorded as follows:

**General journal – Wilson's Pty Ltd**

| Date | Particulars | Debit | Credit |
|---|---|---|---|
| | | $ | $ |
| 1 March | Debtors' control | 25 000 | |
| | Stock | 40 000 | |
| | Vehicle | 60 000 | |
| |      Allowance for doubtful debts | | 5 000 |
| |      Creditors control | | 15 000 |
| |      Bank loan | | 25 000 |
| |      Bank | | 60 000 |
| |      Discount on acquisition | | 20 000 |
| | *Acquired net assets of Frankston Wholesalers.* | | |
| | Discount on acquisition | 20 000 | |
| |      Profit and loss | | 20 000 |
| | *Transferred income to profit and loss* | | |

# Question 4.9

M. Cash is converting his existing business, Future Furniture, into a proprietary company called Style Pty Ltd with his brother, on 1 January.

You are required to prepare Style Pty Ltd's journal entry to record the acquisition of Future Furniture.

M. Cash has provided the following information:

**Future Furniture**
**Account balances at 1 January**

| Assets | $ | $ | Liabilities | $ |
|---|---|---|---|---|
| Debtors | | 40 000 | Creditors | 53 000 |
| Stock | | 80 000 | Bank overdraft | 10 000 |
| Shop furniture | 12 000 | | | |
| Less accumulated depreciation | 6 000 | 6 000 | | |

- All the assets were purchased at the following fair values:

  Debtors                $36 000
  Stock                  $75 000
  Shop furniture         $4 000

- Style Pty Ltd. took over the creditors but not the bank overdraft.
- Purchase consideration was the immediate allotment of 50 000 ordinary shares at $1.00 per share in Style Pty Ltd and a cash payment of $10 000 to be paid on 31 January.

# Question 4.10

Harford Pty Ltd was incorporated on 1 July to acquire the business of Donvale Retailers.

From the following information you are required to prepare the statement of financial position of Harford Pty Ltd at 1 July after the acquisition of Donvale Retailers.

- On 1 July Jani Harford as the sole shareholder paid for 10 000 $1.00 ordinary shares when she established Harford Pty Ltd.
- Donvale Traders account balances on July 1 were as follows:

| Assets | $ | $ | Liabilities | $ |
|---|---|---|---|---|
| Cash on hand | | 1 000 | Accounts payable | 39 000 |
| Accounts receivable | | 25 000 | Bank overdraft | 18 000 |
| Stock | | 40 000 | Bank loan | 14 000 |
| Shop premises | | 50 000 | | |
| Shop furniture | 8 000 | | | |
| Less Accumulated depreciation | 6 000 | 2 000 | | |
| Motor vehicles | 10 000 | | | |
| Less Accumulated depreciation | 6 000 | 4 000 | | |

- All assets were acquired with the following assets being revalued:

  Accounts receivable    $22 000
  Stock                  $38 000
  Shop premises          $7 000
  Motor vehicles         $3 000

- The only liability acquired was accounts payable.
- The sale agreement allowed provided the vendor with the immediate allotment of 80 000 ordinary shares at $1.00 each in Harford Pty Ltd.

# Comprehensive Assessment Activity

Leyton and Bec, who operate independent sole trader businesses in the same industry, have decided to combine their businesses and form a public company called Leybec Ltd. Their respective account balances were as follows:

| Leyton | | Bec | |
|---|---|---|---|
| | $ | | $ |
| Bank | 15 000 | Bank overdraft | (5 000) |
| Debtors | 30 000 | Motor vehicle | 65 000 |
| Allowance for doubtful debts | (5 000) | Accumulated depreciation | (15 000) |

You are required to:
**a**  prepare general journal entries for the following transactions; and
**b**  prepare a statement of financial position at June 30.

| Date | Transaction |
|---|---|
| 1 March | Leybec Ltd was incorporated, with Leyton and Bec as subscribers with each taking 50 000 $2.00 ordinary shares. |
| 5 March | Leyton and Bec pay for their shares |
| 1 April | Leyton's sole trader business net assets are acquired by Leybec Ltd for $63 000 with debtors' fair value being $28 000. Leyton will be issued with 25 000 $2.00 ordinary shares and the balance in cash in 12 months |
| | Bec's sole trader business net assets are acquired by Leybec Ltd for $50 000 with the fair value of the vehicle being $40 000. Bec will be issued with $2.00 ordinary shares as full payment |
| 1 May | A prospectus is issued offering 100 000 $5 preference shares payable $3.00 on application, $1.00 on allotment and $1.00 on a call when required. |
| | A prospectus is issued offering 2000 $100 debentures |
| 10 May | Closing date for share applications |
| | Applications received for 120 000 preference shares |
| | Applications received for 2050 debentures |
| 20 May | Shares and debentures are allotted to successful applicants and refunds made |
| 31 May | All allotment moneys received |
| 1 June | Establishment costs $5500 (inclusive of GST) paid |
| | Share issue costs $11 000 (inclusive of GST) paid |
| | Call made on preference shares |
| 30 June | Calls received on 90 000 preference shares |

# Assessment Checklist

Complete the following checklist to identify if you consider yourself capable of being assessed against each of the following outcomes.

| I can: | Chapter reference | Check ✓ |
| --- | --- | --- |
| explain why a non-corporate entity may seek incorporation | 4.2 | |
| define a business combination in accordance with AASB3 | 4.3 | |
| define the carrying cost and fair value of an asset in accordance with AASB13 and AASB116 | 4.3 | |
| explain how to treat doubtful debts on a business combination | 4.3 | |
| explain how to treat accumulated depreciation on a business combination | 4.3 | |
| recognise and calculate goodwill in accordance with AASB3 | 4.4 | |
| recognise and calculate discount on acquisition on a business combination | 4.4 | |
| account for the acquisition of net assets on a business combination | 4.4 | |

# CHAPTER 5

## PREPARING THE PROFIT AND LOSS ACCOUNT

## WHAT YOU WILL LEARN IN THIS CHAPTER

Upon satisfactory completion of this chapter you should be able to:
- account for the impairment of goodwill;
- account for the revaluation of investment assets;
- account for income tax under the Pay As You Go system;
- adjust income tax expense and income tax payable; and
- prepare the profit and loss account.

**Are you already competent at these tasks?**
If you have already accomplished these tasks as a result of your recent workplace or training experiences you may wish to proceed to the Comprehensive Assessment Activity at the end of this chapter to assess your skills in these areas.

## 5.1    INTRODUCTION

On 30 June each year companies need to make end-of-year adjustments in the accounts and calculate the profit for the financial year.

This chapter examines how profit can be determined from the general ledger accounts including entries to impair assets and account for income tax.

## 5.2    DETERMINING PROFIT FROM THE ACCOUNTS

A company's profit can be determined by transferring all revenue (income) and expense accounts to the profit and loss account.

### Illustration

The following illustration shows the revenue and expense account of Bart Ltd closed to the profit and loss account to reveal a profit of $235 000 for the year ended 30 June.

### General ledger – Bart Ltd

| Date | Details | Debit $ | Credit $ | Balance $ | |
|------|---------|---------|----------|-----------|---|
| **Sales** | | | | | |
| 30 June | Balance | | | 500 000 | Cr |
| | Profit and loss | 500 000 | | Nil | |
| **Cost of goods sold** | | | | | |
| 30 June | Balance | | | 120 000 | Dr |
| | Profit and loss | | 120 000 | Nil | |
| **Wages** | | | | | |
| 30 June | Balance | | | 50 000 | Dr |
| | Profit and loss | | 50 000 | Nil | |
| **Depreciation** | | | | | |
| 30 June | Balance | | | 20 000 | Dr |
| | Profit and loss | | 20 000 | Nil | |
| **Directors' fees** | | | | | |
| 30 June | Balance | | | 15 000 | Dr |
| | Profit and loss | | 15 000 | Nil | |
| **Operating expenses** | | | | | |
| 30 June | Balance | | | 60 000 | Dr |
| | Profit and loss | | 60 000 | Nil | |
| **Dividends received** | | | | | |
| 30 June | Balance | | | 15 000 | Cr |
| | Profit and loss | 15 000 | | Nil | |
| **Profit and loss** | | | | | |
| 30 June | Sales | | 500 000 | 500 000 | Cr |
| | Cost of goods sold | 120 000 | | 380 000 | Cr |
| | Wages | 50 000 | | 330 000 | Cr |
| | Depreciation | 20 000 | | 310 000 | Cr |
| | Directors' fees | 15 000 | | 295 000 | Cr |
| | Operating expenses | 60 000 | | 235 000 | Cr |
| | Dividends received | | 15 000 | 250 000 | Cr |

## Question 5.1

Hartford Ltd has provided you with the following account balances at 30 June. You are required to prepare the company's profit and loss account to determine its annual profit.

| Account Name | Debit | Credit |
|---|---|---|
| | $ | $ |
| Advertising | 36 000 | |
| Bad and doubtful debts | 15 000 | |
| Cost of goods sold | 400 000 | |
| Directors' fees | 50 000 | |
| Discount revenue | | 6 000 |
| Depreciation expenses | 15 000 | |
| Establishment costs | 16 000 | |
| Interest on loans | 14 000 | |
| Operating expenses | 85 000 | |
| Profit on sale of equipment | | 35 000 |
| Sales | | 1 000 000 |
| Wages | 90 000 | |

## 5.3 IMPAIRMENT OF ASSETS

In addition to transferring revenue and expense accounts to the profit and loss account, companies may need to impair assets in accordance with Australian Accounting Standard AASB136: Impairment of Assets.

Entities normally report assets at their carrying costs, which is the cost price of the asset less any adjustments. This valuation may, however, be greater than the assets recoverable amount, which is defined as the amount that could be received from its sale or from its use.

A vehicle, for example, may have a cost price of $50 000 and have been depreciated by $20 000 resulting in a carrying cost of $30 000, but it may only attract $25 000 if sold. Hence the vehicle is being carried at a higher valuation than its recoverable amount.

AASB136: Impairment of Assets requires assets to be reported at no more than their recoverable amount. Hence where an asset's carrying amount is greater than its recoverable amount it has been impaired in value and an impairment loss must be brought to account.

### Impairment of goodwill

A company will bring goodwill to account when it purchases another entity and pays a purchase price that exceeds the fair values of the net assets acquired in accordance with AASB3: Business Combinations.

When a company acquires another entity and pays a purchase price above the fair value of the net assets acquired, goodwill is brought to account. Goodwill is then reported as asset in the purchasing company's financial statements. (The topic accounting for goodwill was covered in Chapter 4.)

As goodwill represents the excess value paid for the net assets acquired from another entity, AASB136 requires the company at the end of the financial year in which it acquired the net assets, to calculate the fair value of the purchased entity and the replaceable value of the assets acquired to determine if their values have fallen.

If the recoverable amounts of the assets or the entity acquired are less than their carrying amounts they are overvalued and an impairment loss must be brought to account.

Note: AASB136 does not allow the carrying cost of goodwill to be increased if the fair value of the acquired entity increases after the date of acquisition, nor does it allow for impairment losses of goodwill to be reversed in a later period.

## Illustration

On 1 January Bart Ltd purchased the net assets of another entity consisting solely of shop fittings with a fair value at $800 000 for $1 000 000 and brought to account goodwill of $200 000.

On 30 June Bart Ltd estimated the fair value of the purchased entity to be $950 000 with the recoverable value of shop fittings acquired falling from $800 000 to $780 000.

The following table shows the comparison of values from the acquisition date to the date of reporting.

| 1 January | | 30 June | |
|---|---|---|---|
| Amount paid for investment | $1 000 000 | Fair value of investment | $950 000 |
| Less fair value of shop fittings | $800 000 | Less recoverable value of shop fittings | $780 000 |
| Equals goodwill valuation | $200 000 | Equals goodwill valuation | $170 000 |

These comparisons indicate:
- that the fair value of the investment has fallen by $50 000 from $1 000 000 to $950 000;
- a reduction in value of the shop fittings purchased by $20 000 falling from $800 000 to $780 000; and
- a fall of $30 000 in the value of goodwill from $200 000 to $170 000.

Hence the value of the carrying cost of the assets and goodwill have been impaired. The entry to record these impairments would be as follows:

**General journal – Bart Ltd**

| Date | Details | Debit | Credit |
|---|---|---|---|
| | | $ | $ |
| 30 June | Impairment loss – shop fittings | 20 000 | |
| | Shop fittings | | 20 000 |
| | *To reduce carrying cost of asset to replaceable value* | | |
| | Impairment loss – goodwill | 30 000 | |
| | Goodwill | | 30 000 |
| | *To record impairment loss of goodwill* | | |

The entry to transfer the impairment losses to the profit and loss account would be as follows:

**General journal – Bart Ltd**

| Date | Details | Debit | Credit |
|---|---|---|---|
| | | $ | $ |
| 30 June | Profit and loss | 50 000 | |
| | Impairment loss – shop fittings | | 20 000 |
| | Impairment loss – goodwill | | 30 000 |
| | Transfer of expenses to profit and loss | | |

The profit and loss account for Bart Ltd from the previous illustration would show these impairment losses as follows:

### General Ledger – Bart Ltd

| Date | Details | Debit | Credit | Balance |
|------|---------|-------|--------|---------|
|      |         | $ | $ | $ |
| **Profit and Loss** | | | | |
| 30 June | Sales | | 500 000 | 500 000  Cr |
|         | Cost of goods sold | 120 000 | | 380 000  Cr |
|         | Wages | 50 000 | | 330 000  Cr |
|         | Depreciation | 20 000 | | 310 000  Cr |
|         | Directors fees | 15 000 | | 295 000  Cr |
|         | Operating expenses | 60 000 | | 235 000  Cr |
|         | Dividends received | | 15 000 | 250 000  Cr |
|         | Impairment loss – Shop fittings | 20 000 | | 230 000  Cr |
|         | Impairment loss – Goodwill | 30 000 | | 200 000  Cr |

## Question 5.2

On 1 September Hartford Ltd acquired another entity for $600 000, purchasing equipment with a fair value of $400 000 and machinery valued at $100 000. On 30 June the acquired entity was valued at $550 000 with equipment having a recoverable value of $375 000 and machinery $90 000.

You are required to determine if the acquired entity and its associated assets have been impaired, and if so prepare the journal entries and transfer impairment losses to the profit and loss account.

### Impairment of investment assets

When a company purchases shares in another company as an investment it will find that the market value of the shares will rise and fall.

When the share market falls in value the carrying cost of the investment will be less than its market value, hence it will be overvalued. As its value has been impaired an impairment loss should be brought to account in accordance with AASB136.

When the share market recovers and the investment increases in value, the investment can be revalued upwards. However, AASB136 restricts any revaluation above the investment's original cost price.

## Illustration

Bart Ltd purchased shares in Crash Ltd at a cost price of $500 000. During the year the market value of the investment fell to $450 000 as a result of poor trading performance.

The journal entry to record the $50 000 impairment in the value of the investment to its recoverable amount would be as follows:

#### General journal – Bart Ltd

| Date | Particulars | Debit | Credit |
|------|-------------|-------|--------|
| | | $ | $ |
| 30 June | Impairment loss – investment in Crash Ltd | 50 000 | |
| | Accumulated writedown in investments | | 50 000 |
| | *Writedown of investments to market value* | | |
| | Profit and loss | 50 000 | |
| | Impairment loss – Investment in Crash Ltd | | 50 000 |
| | *Transfer expense to profit & loss* | | |

The updated profit and loss account showing the impairment loss on investments would be as follows:

#### General Ledger – Bart Ltd

| Date | Details | Debit | Credit | Balance |
|------|---------|-------|--------|---------|
| | | $ | $ | $ |
| **Profit and Loss** | | | | |
| 30 June | Sales | | 500 000 | 500 000 Cr |
| | Cost of goods sold | 120 000 | | 380 000 Cr |
| | Wages | 50 000 | | 330 000 Cr |
| | Depreciation | 20 000 | | 310 000 Cr |
| | Directors' fees | 15 000 | | 295 000 Cr |
| | Operating expenses | 60 000 | | 235 000 Cr |
| | Dividends received | | 15 000 | 250 000 Cr |
| | Impairment loss – shop fittings | 20 000 | | 230 000 Cr |
| | Impairment loss – goodwill | 30 000 | | 200 000 Cr |
| | Impairment loss – investment | 50 000 | | 150 000 Cr |

As a result of this adjustment the statement of financial position would show the following values for the investment:

#### Bart Ltd
#### Statement of financial position
#### as at 30 June (extract)

| Assets | $ | $ |
|--------|---|---|
| Shares in Crash Ltd | 500 000 | |
| *less* accumulated writedown in investments | 50 000 | 450 000 |

# Question 5.3

You are required to:

a  prepare the general journal entries for Hardy Ltd to record the following adjustments;

b  transfer expenses to profit and loss at the end of the financial year; and

c  show how the assets would be recorded in the statement of financial position.

The investment in TNT Ltd is to be revalued from its cost of $600 000 to its recoverable amount of $320 000.

During the year, goodwill of $100 000 was brought to account as a result of a business combination in which equipment was valued at $200 000. At 30 June the equipment has a recoverable amount of $190 000 and goodwill has been impaired by $15 000.

## Question 5.4

From the following extract of the general ledger and additional information of Stinger Ltd you are required to:

a   prepare the profit and loss account at 30 June; and

b   prepare the assets section of the statement of financial position at 30 June.

### Stinger Ltd
### Trial balance at 30 June (extract)

|  | Debit | Credit |
|---|---|---|
|  | $ | $ |
| Sales |  | 750 000 |
| Cost of goods sold | 320 000 |  |
| Wages | 130 000 |  |
| Costs of establishment | 22 000 |  |
| Advertising | 25 000 |  |
| Entertainment costs | 14 500 |  |
| Bad and doubtful debts | 8 000 |  |
| Profit on sale of equipment |  | 32 000 |
| Discount revenue |  | 2 500 |
| Vehicles | 100 000 |  |
| Goodwill | 50 000 |  |
| GST clearing |  | 16 000 |
| Investment in Ansett Ltd | 850 000 |  |
| Accumulated writedown of investment in Ansett Ltd |  | 150 000 |

#### Additional information

1.  Goodwill was established from a business combination in which vehicles were the only asset acquired. On 30 June the recoverable amount of vehicles acquired is $80 000 whilst the entity has been valued at $100 000.

2.  Investment in Ansett Ltd is to be revalued from its carrying cost at its recoverable amount of $600 000.

# 5.4   ACCOUNTING FOR INCOME TAX

When accounting for income tax companies must comply with the following requirements:
* the PAYG income tax system;
* the *Income Tax Assessment Act*; and
* Accounting Standard AASB112: Income Taxes.

## PAYG income tax system

Under the PAYG taxation system, companies are required to pay income tax to the Australian Taxation Office (ATO) quarterly, calculated as a percentage of each quarter's sales.

The ATO advises companies annually of the required percentage of sales that must be remitted as PAYG income tax. The percentage is determined from the information supplied on the previous year's taxation return and is calculated by dividing the income tax payable for the year by the assessable income earned in the same year. For example, if a company derived assessable income of $250 000 and had paid $25 000 income tax on that income, the percentage would be equal to 10% ($25 000 / $250 000).

The PAYG system requires companies to calculate the amount of tax payable at the end of each quarter. The following table shows the payment dates for each quarter's income tax liability.

| Quarter ending | Payment date |
| --- | --- |
| 30 September | 28 October |
| 31 December | 28 February |
| 31 March | 28 April |
| 30 June | 28 July |

At the end of the financial year income tax expensed is transferred to the profit and loss account and the final unpaid amount for the quarter ended 30 June is included in the Statement of Financial Position as a current liability.

## Illustration

Bart Ltd has been advised by the ATO that it has a PAYG income tax instalment rate of 10% of sales revenue.

For the quarter ended 30 September the company recorded sales income of $100 000, requiring the company to pay $10 000 in income tax by 28 October.

The journal entries to record the income tax expensed, the income tax liability and the payment of that liability would be as follows:

### General journal – Bart Ltd

| Date | Particulars | Debit | Credit |
| --- | --- | --- | --- |
| | | $ | $ |
| 30 Sept | Income tax expense | 10 000 | |
| | Income tax payable | | 10 000 |
| | To record income tax payable | | |
| 28 Oct | Income tax payable | 10 000 | |
| | Bank | | 10 000 |
| | To record income tax payable paid | | |

The resulting ledger accounts would be as follows:

### General ledger – Bart Ltd

| Date | Details | Debit | Credit | Balance |
| --- | --- | --- | --- | --- |
| | | $ | $ | $ |
| Income tax expense | | | | |
| 30 Sept | Income tax payable | 10 000 | | 10 000  Dr |
| Income tax payable | | | | |
| 30 Sept | Income tax expense | | 10 000 | 10 000  Cr |
| 28 Oct | Bank | 10 000 | | Nil |

If Bart Ltd recorded sales income of $120 000, $150 000 and $130 000 for the next three quarters with a PAYG income tax rate of 10% on sales, the company would have recorded income tax of $12 000, $15 000 and $13 000 respectively.

At the end of the financial year the income tax accounts would appear as follows:

### General ledger – Bart Ltd

| Date | Details | Debit $ | Credit $ | Balance $ |
|---|---|---|---|---|
| **Income tax expense** | | | | |
| 30 Sept | Income tax payable | 10 000 | | 10 000 Dr |
| 31 Dec | Income tax payable | 12 000 | | 22 000 Dr |
| 31 Mar | Income tax payable | 15 000 | | 37 000 Dr |
| 30 June | Income tax payable | 13 000 | | 50 000 Dr |
| **Income tax payable** | | | | |
| 30 Sept | Income tax expense | | 10 000 | 10 000 Cr |
| 28 Oct | Bank | 10 000 | | Nil Cr |
| 31 Dec | Income tax expense | | 12 000 | 12 000 Cr |
| 28 Feb | Bank | 12 000 | | Nil Cr |
| 31 Mar | Income tax expense | | 15 000 | 15 000 Cr |
| 28 Apr | Bank | 15 000 | | Nil Cr |
| 30 June | Income tax expense | | 13 000 | 13 000 Cr |

## Question 5.5

Drever Ltd has a PAYG instalment of 20% of sales. Quarterly sales for the year ended 30 June were as follows:

| 30 September | $700 000 |
|---|---|
| 31 December | $600 000 |
| 31 March | $750 000 |
| 30 June | $800 000 |

For the year ended 30 June you are required to prepare the income tax expense and income tax payable accounts.

## Question 5.6

From the following information of Conmar Ltd you are required to prepare:

a    journal entries recording the company's quarterly income tax transactions; and

b    the income tax accounts in the general ledger.

On 1 July the company owed $25 000 in income tax. This was paid on 28 July. The company's PAYG instalment amount is 15%.

Quarterly sales for the year ended 30 June were:

| | |
|---|---|
| 30 September | $150 000 |
| 31 December | $220 000 |
| 31 March | $180 000 |
| 30 June | $190 000 |

## The *Income Tax Assessment Act 1997*

Australian companies are required to lodge an annual income tax assessment with the ATO that complies with the *Income Tax Assessment Act*. The annual assessment includes the company's assessable income less allowable deductions to derive taxable income.

The company income tax rate (currently at 30%) is then applied to the taxable income to determine the amount of income tax that the company should have incurred during the financial year.

The income tax payable, calculated on taxable income at the end of the year, is then compared to the income tax expense calculated on the PAYG system during the year. Where the amounts differ an adjustment must be made.

If the company has not paid sufficient PAYG taxation instalments, it will owe tax to the ATO. If the company has paid too much tax, the ATO will issue a refund.

Under Australian income tax law:

1 certain items of revenue will never be included as income for taxation purposes; that is, non-assessable income; and

2 certain expense items will never be allowed as deductions for taxation purposes; that is, non-deductible expenses.

These non-assessable or non-deductible items, sometimes referred to as permanent differences, include:

3 **Exempt income:** In some cases, the Act will not treat specific items of revenue as assessable income for taxation purposes.

4 **Entertainment expenses:** Expenses associated with entertainment, which are subsequently written off against annual profits, may not be claimed as allowable deductions for taxation purposes unless they meet specific criteria.

5 **Establishment costs:** The costs of setting up a company written off against company profits are not allowable as taxation deductions.

6 **Impairment of assets:** The impairment of goodwill and the impairment of investments reduce a company's profit; however, these specific expenses cannot be claimed as allowable deductions for taxation purposes.

7 **Depreciation on buildings:** The annual depreciation of buildings by companies reduces the profit. However, for taxation purposes the depreciation on buildings may not be an allowable deduction from assessable income unless the expenditure meets specific criteria.

These non-assessable or non-deductible items of revenue and expense are referred to as permanent differences in that they will never be included in the calculation of taxable income; that is, permanently different. Hence they will need to be excluded in the calculation of taxable income.

## The accounting standard

Accounting Standard AASB112: Income Taxes requires a company's income tax expense to be equal to its current tax liability (based on its taxable income) plus adjustments for deferred taxes. This amount may differ to the income tax expense amount recorded during the year under the PAYG system which is calculated on a percentage of sales income.

Thus, at the end of the financial year, a company will need to calculate its income tax expense based on its taxable income, compare it to the income tax amount expensed during the year under the PAYG system and where a difference results, make an adjustment.

If the PAYG income tax expense is lower than the tax expense based on taxable income the amount will need to be increased. If it is lower, the income tax expense amount will need to be reduced.

# 5.5    THE EFFECT OF PERMANENT DIFFERENCES ON THE CALCULATION OF INCOME TAX

Permanent differences have an impact on the calculation of both income tax payable and income tax expense.

As permanent differences are non-assessable income or non-deductible expenses for taxation purposes they are excluded from the calculation of taxable income which is used to calculate income tax payable and income tax expense as shown in the following diagram.

**Figure 5.1**  Calculation of a company's income tax liability

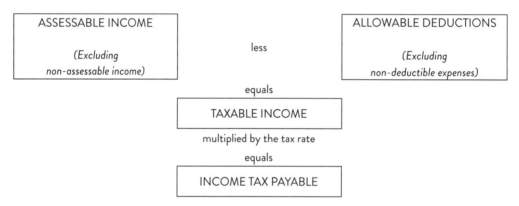

To ensure that income tax expense is calculated on a similar basis to taxable income, permanent differences also need to be excluded in the calculation of profit in accordance with AASB112. This is shown in the following diagram.

**Figure 5.2**  Income tax expense calculated on adjusted profit

Once income tax expense and income tax payable have been determined, adjustments can be made to their respective amounts which were recorded under the PAYG system throughout the year.

## Adjusting company income tax

When calculating a company's income tax payable at the end of the financial year the revenue and expenses included in the calculation of profit and loss may be classified as assessable income or allowable deductions and included in the calculation of taxable income.

Once taxable income has been determined the company's true taxation liability and taxation expense can be calculated.

If the amount of income tax recorded under the PAYG system is not equal to the amount based on the company's taxable income, an adjustment must be made as taxation will be understated or overstated.

### Understated income tax

When income tax expensed during the year under the PAYG system is lower than the tax liability calculated on taxable income at the end of the year, income tax has been understated, requiring an adjustment to increase both income tax expense and income tax liability.

### Illustration

Bart Ltd's profit and loss account, showing a profit before income tax of $150 000 and income tax account balances from previous illustrations, are as follows:

**General ledger – Bart Ltd**

| Date | Details | Debit $ | Credit $ | Balance $ |
|------|---------|---------|----------|-----------|
| **Profit and Loss** | | | | |
| 30 June | Sales | | 500 000 | 500 000 Cr |
| | Cost of goods sold | 120 000 | | 380 000 Cr |
| | Wages | 50 000 | | 330 000 Cr |
| | Depreciation | 20 000 | | 310 000 Cr |
| | Directors' fees | 15 000 | | 295 000 Cr |
| | Operating expenses | 60 000 | | 235 000 Cr |
| | Dividends received | | 15 000 | 250 000 Cr |
| | Impairment loss – shop fittings | 20 000 | | 230 000 Cr |
| | Impairment loss – goodwill | 30 000 | | 200 000 Cr |
| | Impairment loss – investment | 50 000 | | 150 000 Cr |
| **Income tax expense** | | | | |
| 30 June | Balance | | | 50 000 Dr |
| **Income tax payable** | | | | |
| 30 June | Balance | | | 13 000 Cr |

Bart Ltd's tax accountant has determined that the following revenues and expenses cannot be included as assessable income or allowable deductions for taxation purposes:

| | |
|---|---|
| Dividend income | $15 000  (not assessable) |
| Impairment loss – goodwill | $30 000  (not deductible) |
| Impairment loss – investments | $50 000  (not deductible) |

Using a **taxation calculation worksheet** the correct amounts of income tax expense and income tax payable can be determined, compared to PAYG taxation and the adjustment calculated as follows:

**Taxation calculation worksheet**

| | $ | $ |
|---|---|---|
| Profit (before tax) | 150 000 | |
| **Adjusted for permanent differences** | | |
| Subtract non-assessable income | | |
| Dividends income | 15 000 | 135 000 |
| Add back non-deductible expenses | | |
| Impairment loss – goodwill | 30 000 | |
| Impairment loss – investments | 50 000 | 80 000 |
| **Adjusted profit and taxable income** | | 215 000 |
| Multiplied by the tax rate | | × 30% |
| Income tax expense and income tax payable | | 64 500 |
| Less income tax expensed as PAYG | | 50 000 |
| Income tax adjustment | | 14 500 |

The worksheet reveals that income tax calculated on accounting profit and taxable income should be $64 500 for the year, whilst $50 000 has been accounted for under the PAYG system. Income tax has been underprovided by $14 500 and an adjusting entry is required.

The adjusting entry, the entry to transfer income tax expense to profit and loss and the account showing the adjustments, would be as follows:

**General journal – Bart Ltd**

| Date | Particulars | Debit | Credit |
|---|---|---|---|
| | | $ | $ |
| 30 June | Income tax expense | 14 500 | |
| | Income tax payable | | 14 500 |
| | *Adjustment for understated PAYG income tax* | | |
| | Profit and loss | 64 500 | |
| | Income tax expense | | 64 500 |
| | *Transferred account balance* | | |

General ledger – Bart Ltd

| Date | Details | Debit $ | Credit $ | Balance $ |
|---|---|---|---|---|
| **Income tax expense** | | | | |
| 30 June | Balance | | | 50 000 Dr |
| | Income tax payable (adjustment) | 14 500 | | 64 500 Dr |
| | Profit and loss | | 64 500 | Nil |
| **Income tax payable** | | | | |
| 30 June | Balance | | | 13 000 Cr |
| | Income tax expense (adjustment) | | 14 500 | 27 500 Cr |
| **Profit and loss** | | | | |
| 30 June | Sales | | 500 000 | 500 000 Cr |
| | Cost of goods sold | 120 000 | | 380 000 Cr |
| | Wages | 50 000 | | 30 000 Cr |
| | Depreciation | 20 000 | | 310 000 Cr |
| | Directors' fees | 15 000 | | 295 000 Cr |
| | Operating expenses | 60 000 | | 235 000 Cr |
| | Dividends received | | 15 000 | 250 000 Cr |
| | Impairment loss – shop fittings | 20 000 | | 230 000 Cr |
| | Impairment loss – goodwill | 30 000 | | 200 000 Cr |
| | Impairment loss – investment | 50 000 | | 150 000 Cr |
| | Income tax expense | 64 500 | | 85 500 Cr |

The current liabilities section of the Statement of Financial Position at the end of the financial year would include the income tax payable amount as follows:

**Bart Ltd**
**Statement of financial position**
**at 30 June (extract)**

| Current liabilities | |
|---|---|
| Income tax payable | $ 27 500 |

# Question 5.7

The income tax accounts of Drever Ltd from question 5.5 are shown in the workbook. The accountant has determined the company's income tax liability to be $600 000.

You are required to:

a   prepare the general journal entry to record the income tax adjustment at 30 June;

b   prepare the journal entry to transfer expenses to the profit and loss account;

c   post the adjusting entry to the general ledger accounts; and

d   show the tax liability in the statement of financial position at 30 June.

## Question 5.8

The income tax and profit loss accounts of Strang Ltd are shown in the workbook. The tax accountant has determined that the following expenses cannot be claimed as tax deductions:

Impairment loss – goodwill          $30 000

Impairment loss – investments       $100 000

You are required to:

**a**   prepare the general journal entries to record the income tax adjustment at 30 June and transfer income tax expense to the profit and loss account;

**b**   post the entries to the general ledger accounts; and

**c**   show the tax liability in the statement of financial position at 30 June.

Note: The rate of income tax is 30%.

### Overstated income tax

When a company has expensed income tax during the year under the PAYG system which is higher than the tax liability calculated on its taxable income, it will need to make an adjustment to decrease its income tax expense and income tax liability as income tax has been overstated.

 **Illustration**

Juno Ltd's accounts for the year ended 30 June included the following:

**General ledger – Juno Ltd**

| Date | Details | Debit $ | Credit $ | Balance $ |
|---|---|---|---|---|
| **Income tax expense** | | | | |
| 30 June | Balance | | . | 100 000  Dr |
| **Income tax payable** | | | | |
| 30 June | Balance | | | 30 000  Cr |
| **Profit and loss** | | | | |
| 30 June | Sales | | 800 000 | 800 000  Cr |
| | Cost of goods sold | 300 000 | | 500 000  Cr |
| | Operating expenses | 200 000 | | 300 000  Cr |
| | Impairment loss – goodwill | 20 000 | | 280 000  Cr |
| | Impairment loss – investment | 80 000 | | 200 000  Cr |

The accounts reveal that:
*   income tax expensed during the year of $100 000 of which $30 000 remains payable to the ATO, and a profit (before tax) of $200 000.

- The tax accountant has determined for income tax purposes the impairment losses on goodwill and investments are not deductible.

When these non-deductible expenses are excluded from the profit calculation the resulting accounting profit for AASB112: Income Tax purposes and the taxable income for *Income Tax Assessment Act* purposes is as follows:

**Taxation calculation worksheet**

|  | $ | $ |
|---|---|---|
| Profit (before tax) |  | 200 000 |
| Adjusted for permanent differences |  |  |
| Add back non-deductible expenses |  |  |
|    Impairment loss – goodwill | 20 000 |  |
|    Impairment loss – investments | 80 000 | 100 000 |
| Accounting profit and taxable income |  | 300 000 |
| Multiplied by the tax rate |  | × 30% |
| Income tax expense and income tax payable |  | 90 000 |
| Less income tax expensed as PAYG |  | 100 000 |
| Income tax adjustment |  | (10 000) |

This worksheet reveals that under the PAYG system the company has incurred income tax of $100 000; however, the income tax amount payable on the company's taxable income is $10 000 lower at $90 000. Hence income tax has been overstated under the PAYG system and an adjusting entry is required to reduce income tax expense and reduce the income tax liability owing to the ATO.

The adjusting entry and the entry to transfer income tax expense to profit and loss would appear in the general journal and the accounts as follows:

**General journal – Juno Ltd**

| Date | Particulars | Debit | Credit |
|---|---|---|---|
|  |  | $ | $ |
| 30 June | Income tax payable | 10 000 |  |
|  |    Income tax expense |  | 10 000 |
|  | *Adjustment for overstated PAYG income tax* |  |  |
|  | Profit and loss | 90 000 |  |
|  |    Income tax expense |  | 90 000 |
|  | *Transferred account balance* |  |  |

**General ledger – Juno Ltd**

| Date | Details | Debit $ | Credit $ | Balance $ |
|------|---------|--------:|---------:|----------:|
| **Income tax expense** | | | | |
| 30 June | Balance | | | 100 000  Dr |
| | Income tax payable (adjustment) | | 10 000 | 90 000  Dr |
| | Profit and loss | | 90 000 | Nil |
| **Income tax payable** | | | | |
| 30 June | Balance | | 30 000 | 30 000  Cr |
| | Income tax expense (adjustment) | 10 000 | | 20 000  Cr |
| **Profit and loss** | | | | |
| 30 June | Sales | | 800 000 | 800 000  Cr |
| | Cost of goods sold | 300 000 | | 500 000  Cr |
| | Operating expenses | 200 000 | | 300 000  Cr |
| | Impairment loss – goodwill | 20 000 | | 280 000  Cr |
| | Impairment loss – investment | 80 000 | | 200 000  Cr |
| | Income tax expense | 90 000 | | 110 000  Cr |

The current liabilities section of the statement of financial position at the end of the financial year would include the income tax payable amount as follows:

**Juno Ltd**
**Statement of financial position**
**at 30 June (extract)**

| Current liabilities | |
|---------------------|---:|
| Income tax payable | $ 20 000 |

# Question 5.9

The income tax accounts of Lumo Ltd are shown in the workbook. The tax accountant has determined the company's taxable income for the year ended 30 June was $500 000 and that its annual tax liability for the year was $150 000.

You are required to:
a   prepare the general journal entry to record the income tax adjustment at 30 June;
b   prepare the journal entry to transfer expenses to the profit and loss account;
c   post the adjusting and closing entry to the general ledger accounts; and
d   show the tax liability in the statement of financial position at 30 June.

# Question 5.10

Sparta Ltd has provided you with the following unadjusted trial balance and additional information for the year ended 30 June. From this information you are required to prepare the profit and loss account for the year.

### Trial balance at 30 June

| Account name | Debit $ | Credit $ |
|---|---|---|
| Bank | 25 000 | |
| Stock | 20 000 | |
| Debtors | 60 000 | |
| Allowance for doubtful debts | | 10 000 |
| Equipment | 400 000 | |
| Accumulated depreciation – equipment | | 50 000 |
| Machinery | 250 000 | |
| Investment on Lark Ltd | 180 000 | |
| Accumulated impairment – investment in Lark Ltd | | 30 000 |
| Goodwill | 200 000 | |
| Accounts payable | | 60 000 |
| Income tax payable | | 10 000 |
| GST payable | | 12 000 |
| Debenture loan | | 140 000 |
| Ordinary shares (75 400) | | 754 000 |
| Calls in arrears (6 000) | 30 000 | |
| Sales | | 1 000 000 |
| Cost of goods sold | 600 000 | |
| Advertising | 65 000 | |
| Bad debts | 5 000 | |
| Wages and salaries | 150 000 | |
| Equipment repairs | 20 000 | |
| Dividends received | | 9 000 |
| Interest expense | 20 000 | |
| Income tax expense | 50 000 | |
| | 2 075 000 | 2 075 000 |

### Accounting adjustments

1   The investment in Lark Ltd has a recoverable amount of $140 000.
2   During the year an entity was acquired comprising machinery with a fair value of $250 000. The machinery now has a replaceable value of $225 000 and goodwill has been impaired by $50 000.

### Taxation adjustments

1   For income tax purposes the tax accountant has determined that impairment losses of investments and goodwill are not tax deductible.
2   The company income tax rate is 30%.

# Comprehensive Assessment Activity

From the following information provided by Yea Ltd you are required to:

a   prepare general journals to account for the additional information;
b   prepare the profit and loss account for the year; and
c   prepare a statement of financial position at 30 June.

### Trial balance at 30 June

| Account name | Debit | Credit |
|---|---|---|
| | $ | $ |
| Accounts payable | | 40 000 |
| Accounts receivable | 50 000 | |
| Accumulated depreciation – fixtures and fittings | | 104 000 |
| Accumulated impairment – investment in Karta Ltd | | 20 000 |
| Advertising | 80 000 | |
| Allowance for doubtful debts | | 2 000 |
| Bank | | 174 000 |
| Cost of goods sold | 720 000 | |
| Debenture loan | | 360 000 |
| Dividends income | | 15 000 |
| Equipment | 750 000 | |
| Fixtures and fittings | 500 000 | |
| Goodwill | 400 000 | |
| GST payable | | 15 000 |
| Income tax expense | 150 000 | |
| Income tax payable | | 16 000 |
| Interest expense | 36 000 | |
| Inventory | 100 000 | |
| Investment on Karta Ltd | 510 000 | |
| Ordinary shares ($100 each) | | 1 000 000 |
| Sales | | 1 800 000 |
| Wages and salaries | 250 000 | |
| | 3 546 000 | 3 546 000 |

## Additional information

1.  During the year Yea Ltd purchased Maffra Ltd for $1 150 000 and acquired equipment with a fair value of $750 000. At 30 June the equipment has a replaceable value of $600 000 and the acquisition is now valued at $900 000.
2.  The investment in Karta Ltd is to be revalued at $460 000.
3.  The company income tax rate is 30%. For income tax purposes impairments of goodwill and investments are not deductible.

# Assessment Checklist

Complete the following checklist to identify if you consider yourself capable of being assessed against each of the following outcomes.

| I can: | Chapter reference | Check ✓ |
|---|---|---|
| impair goodwill in accordance with AASB136: Impairment of Assets | 5.3 | |
| impair investments in accordance with AASB136: Impairment of Assets | 5.3 | |
| account for company income tax under the PAYG system | 5.4 | |
| explain how AASB112: Income Taxes affects income tax expense | 5.5 | |
| adjust income tax to comply with the *Income Tax Assessment Act* | 5.5 | |
| prepare a profit and loss account including impairment losses | 5.1–5.5 | |

# CHAPTER 6

## ACCOUNTING FOR COMPANY INCOME TAX

## WHAT YOU WILL LEARN IN THIS CHAPTER

Upon satisfactory completion of this chapter you should be able to:
- identify and account for taxable temporary differences;
- identify and account for deductible temporary differences;
- account for reversal of temporary differences; and
- account for taxation on losses.

**Are you already competent at these tasks?**
If you have already accomplished these tasks as a result of your recent workplace or training experiences you may wish to proceed to the Comprehensive Assessment Activity at the end of this chapter to assess your skills in these areas.

## 6.1  INTRODUCTION

A company's income tax is recorded during the year in accordance with the Pay As You Go (PAYG) instalment system which calculates income tax expense and income tax liability as a percentage of revenue (income) earned.

At the end of the financial year the company uses the *Income Tax Assessment Act 1997* to determine its taxable income to derive the true amount of income tax liability. If the amount differs from the amount calculated under the PAYG system an adjusting entry is made.

In addition a company must comply with Accounting Standard AASB112: Income Taxes, which requires income tax expense to be calculated on its income tax liability plus adjustments for temporary differences.

This chapter examines how AASB112: Income Taxes identifies, calculates and records deferred taxes and how it impacts on taxation expense and income tax payable.

## 6.2  AASB112: INCOME TAXES

AASB112 prescribes how a reporting entity accounts for income taxes in the current year and incorporates the effect of taxation that has been deferred to a future period.

The standard requires:
- income tax payable (referred to as current tax) to be calculated on an entity's taxable income (referred to as taxable profit) for a period; and
- income tax expense to be calculated as the aggregate amount of current tax and deferred tax for the period.

This is shown in Figure 6.1, which illustrates how taxable income is used to calculate income tax payable and how this amount is adjusted for deferred taxes to derive income tax expense.

**Figure 6.1**  Calculating income tax expense

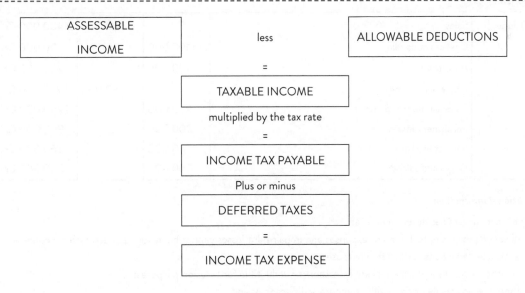

To identify the existence of deferred taxes AASB112 requires the carrying amounts and tax base valuations of specific assets and liabilities to be calculated and compared to identify differences that will impact on taxation outcomes in the future.

The carrying amount of an asset or liability refers to the book value or written down value of an asset or liability on the entity's statement of financial position. The tax base of an asset or liability is the amount attributed to that asset or liability for taxation purposes.

The difference between the carrying amount and the tax base of an asset or liability will arise from temporary differences in valuations which AASB112 describes as either:
- **taxable temporary differences** (referred to as deferred tax liabilities), or
- **deductible temporary differences** (referred to as deferred tax assets).

## Question 6.1

Answer each of the following True or False questions:

1  Revenue less expenses equals taxable income.
2  Taxable income = assessable income less allowable deductions.
3  Income tax payable is calculated on taxable income.
4  Income tax expense is calculated on profit.
5  Income tax expense will equal income tax payable where no deferred taxes exist.
6  Deferred taxes cause income tax payable to equal income tax expense.
7  Income tax expense is the aggregate of income tax payable and deferred taxes.
8  A taxable temporary difference will result in a deferred tax asset.
9  A deferred tax liability is caused by a deductible temporary difference.
10  Deferred taxes are measured as the difference between the carrying amount and the tax base of specific assets and liabilities.

## Question 6.2

Using the following information provided by Ono Ltd you are required to calculate income tax expense for the year.

**General ledger of Ono Ltd**

| Date | Particulars | Debit $ | Credit $ | Balance $ |
|------|-------------|---------|----------|-----------|
| **Profit and loss** | | | | |
| 30 June | Sales | | 2 400 000 | 2 400 000 Cr |
| | Cost of goods sold | 1 100 000 | | 1 300 000 Cr |
| | Advertising | 100 000 | | 1 200 000 Cr |
| | Dividends income | | 50 000 | 1 250 000 Cr |
| | Entertainment expenses | 50 000 | | 1 200 000 Cr |
| | Impairment losses | 300 000 | | 900 000 Cr |
| | Interest expense | 40 000 | | 860 000 Cr |
| | Wages and salaries | 360 000 | | 500 000 Cr |

*Additional information*

The tax accountant has determined that:

- dividend income, entertainment expenses and impairment losses cannot be included as assessable income or allowable deductions for taxation purposes;
- all other revenues and expenses are assessable or deductible for taxation purposes;
- there are no taxable or deductible temporary differences; and
- the tax rate is 30%.

## 6.3  TEMPORARY DIFFERENCES RESULTING IN A DEFERRED TAX LIABILITY

A deferred (future) tax liability will arise when income tax payable in the current year is deferred to a future year.

This will occur when taxable income does not recognise assessable income in the current period or brings to account allowable deductions in advance. Consequently taxable income in the current period will be reduced and income tax payable deferred to a future period; that is, a deferred tax liability is created in the current year.

In future periods, when income that was not reported as assessable income in a previous year is reported as assessable, or where expenses that were previously claimed as tax deductible can no longer be claimed as deductible, future taxable income will increase resulting in larger tax liabilities; that is, the deferred tax liability is paid.

The differences in the timing of the recognition of assessable income and allowable deductions result in a lower taxable income in the current period but larger taxable income in future periods, in which case taxation payable in the current period is deferred to a future period.

When the calculation of taxable income includes either:
- assessable income that differs from the amount of revenue included in the calculation of profit, or
- allowable deductions which are not the same amount expensed in the calculation of profit,

then differences in the carrying amount and tax base valuations of assets and liabilities will result.

AASB112 requires a deferred tax liability to be recognised in the current period if in the future the recovery of an asset's carrying amount will result in future tax payments being **larger**. This will occur when an asset's carrying amount exceeds its tax base valuation.

Assets:    Carrying amount > tax base = Deferred tax liability

An asset's carrying amount will be greater than its tax base where a tax deduction is claimed in advance which reduces the current year's income tax payable, but defers the tax payment to a future period.

AASB112 defines the tax base of an asset as:

> ... the amount that will be deductible for tax purposes against any taxable economic benefits that will flow to an entity when it recovers the carrying amount of the asset. If those economic benefits will not be taxable, the tax base of the asset is equal to its carrying amount.[1]

Taxable economic benefits for an asset include revenue earned from using the asset or profit derived from its future sale. Hence where an asset generates future taxable income, expenses related to that asset can be claimed as tax deductible in future periods, such as depreciation.

A difference in the carrying amount and the tax base will occur when the tax base valuation adopts an accelerated depreciation amount that differs from the amount used in the carrying amount valuation.

The following steps are recommended in identifying, measuring and accounting for deferred taxes arising from accelerated taxation depreciation claims for taxation purposes.

**Step 1**    Calculate the carrying amount and tax base of the asset to determine the difference in valuations, then apply the tax rate to calculate the deferred tax liability.

**Step 2**    Calculate income tax payable and adjust the amount for the deferred tax to determine income tax expense amount.

**Step 3**    Prepare a journal entry to record annual income tax adjustments.

## Illustration

For the year ended 30 June HY Ltd reported a profit and taxable income (before depreciation) of $580 000.

At the start of the year equipment was purchased costing $160 000 which was estimated to have a four-year useful life with a scrap value of $10 000 at the end of its life.

The asset will be depreciated:
- for accounting purposes at 25% per annum using the straight-line method; and
- for taxation purposes at 50% using the reducing-balance method.

The respective depreciation amounts in the first year would be:

|  | Straight line | Reducing balance | Difference |
|---|---|---|---|
| Depreciation | $37 500 | $80 000 | $42 500 |

**Step 1**    Calculate the carrying amount and tax base of the asset to determine the difference in valuations, then apply the tax rate to calculate the deferred tax liability.

---

1   AASB112: Income Taxes

| Equipment valuations | Balance at start | Depreciation | Balance at end | | |
|---|---|---|---|---|---|
| Carrying amount | $160 000 | ($37 500) | $122 500 | | |
| Less tax base amount | $160 000 | ($80 000) | $80 000 | | |
| Deferred tax liability | | | $42 500 | × 30% = | $12 750  Cr |

This calculation shows the deferred tax liability increasing in Year 1 by $12 750 as a result of a $42 500 difference in depreciation amounts used in the calculation of profit and taxable income. The deferred tax liability account at the end of Year 1 would be as follows:

### Deferred tax liability

| Date | Particulars | Debit $ | Credit $ | Balance $ |
|---|---|---|---|---|
| Year 1 | Income tax expense | | 12 750 | 12 750  Cr |

**Step 2**   Calculate income tax payable and adjust the amount for the deferred tax liability to determine the income tax expense.

The annual income tax payable amount should be determined from the entity's taxable income and this amount adjusted for the deferred tax liability to determine the income tax expense.

The following table shows the effect on taxation incorporating the annual changes in the deferred income tax liability. (Note: the company had expensed $145 000 in income tax under the PAYG system during the year.)

| Taxation adjustments | Year 1 $ |
|---|---|
| Taxable income (before depreciation) | 580 000 |
| Less tax deductible depreciation | (80 000) |
| Taxable income | 500 000 |
| Multiplied by the tax rate | × 30% |
| Estimated income tax payable | 150 000  Cr |
| Less PAYG income tax expensed (see Note p.89) | (145 000)  Dr |
| Income tax payable adjustment | 5 000  Cr |
| Plus deferred tax liability | 12 750  Cr |
| Equals income tax expense adjustment | 17 750  Dr |

**Step 3**   Prepare a journal entry to record income tax adjustments.

The journal entries to record income tax adjustments for Year 1 and transfer income tax expense to profit and loss would be as follows:

### General journal

| Date | Details | Debit $ | Credit $ |
|---|---|---|---|
| Year 1 | | | |
| 30 June | Income tax expense | 17 750 | |
| |    Income tax payable | | 5 000 |
| |    Deferred tax liability | | 12 750 |
| | *Taxation adjustments* | | |
| | Profit and loss | 162 750 | |
| |    Income tax expense (see Note p.89) | | 162 750 |
| | *Transfer of income tax expense* | | |

(Note: Income tax expense = PAYG income tax expense $145 000 + income tax expense adjustment $17 750.)

The profit and loss account after the inclusion of income tax expense would be as follows:

**Profit and loss**

| Date | Particulars | Debit $ | Credit $ | Balance $ |
|------|-------------|---------|----------|-----------|
| 30 June | Profit (before depreciation) | | | 580 000 Cr |
| | Depreciation expense | 37 500 | | 542 500 Cr |
| | Income tax expense | 162 750 | | 379 750 Cr |

On the assumption that the profit (before tax) does not include any permanent differences the income tax expense amount can be reconciled by multiplying the profit (before tax) by 30% as follows:

| Income tax expense reconciliation schedule | Year 1 $ |
|---------------------------------------------|----------|
| Profit (before tax) | 542 500 |
| Adjusted for permanent differences | Nil |
| Accounting profit | 542 000 |
| Multiplied by the tax rate | × 30% |
| Income tax expense | 162 750 |

## Question 6.3

Jasper Ltd has provided the following information relating to its profit and income tax for the year ended 30 June.

From this information you are required to:

a   prepare a general journal entry at 30 June to adjust the income tax accounts;

b   prepare an income tax expense reconciliation schedule; and

c   complete the profit and loss account for the year ended 30 June to include income tax expense.

**Profit and loss**

| Date | Particulars | Debit $ | Credit $ | Balance $ |
|------|-------------|---------|----------|-----------|
| 30 June | Service income | | 750 000 | 750 000 Cr |
| | Operating expenses | 300 000 | | 450 000 Cr |
| | Depreciation expense | 40 000 | | 410 000 Cr |

*Additional information*

• The company purchased machinery on 1 July for $400 000.

• For accounting purposes the asset is being depreciated over 10 years using the straight-line method of depreciation and the reducing-balance method for taxation purposes. The respective depreciation amounts in the first year would be:

| | Straight line | Reducing balance |
|--|---------------|------------------|
| Depreciation | $40 000 | $80 000 |

- Income tax expensed under the PAYG system for the year totalled $110 000.
- There are no permanent differences and the tax rate is 30%.

## Question 6.4

Using the following information provided by Barma Ltd you are required to:

a  calculate the taxation adjustments for the Year 1;

b  prepare a reconciliation of income tax schedule;

c  prepare journal entries in to adjust taxation outcomes and transfer income tax to profit and loss; and

d  show the profit and loss account after the adjustments.

The company reported the following information in its calculation of profit for the year ended 30 June:

**Profit and loss**

| Date | Particulars | Debit $ | Credit $ | Balance $ |
|------|-------------|---------|----------|-----------|
| 30 June | Sales | | | 950 000  Cr |
| | Entertainment expense | 50 000 | | 900 000  Cr |
| | Depreciation expense | 26 000 | | 874 000  Cr |

- At the start of the year the company purchased equipment costing $81 000 which has a useful life of three years.
- For accounting purposes the asset will be depreciated using the straight-line method at 33.33% p.a. and have a residual value of $3000.
- For taxation purposes depreciation will use the reducing-balance method at the rate of 66.66% p.a.
- Income tax has been expensed under the PAYG system totalling $240 000.
- Income tax is applied at 30% and entertainment expenses are not tax deductible.

## 6.4  TEMPORARY DIFFERENCES RESULTING IN A DEFERRED TAX ASSET

A deferred tax asset, also referred to as a future tax benefit, will arise when an expense cannot be claimed as an allowable tax deduction in the current year, but may be allowed in a future period.

In the current year this has the effect of increasing taxable income and income tax payable with a tax deduction being deferred; that is, a deferred tax asset brought to account. However, in a future year when the expense is claimed as a tax deduction, taxable income will fall and income tax payable will be smaller.

When the calculation of taxable income defers an expense used in the calculation of profit to a future period the carrying amount and tax base valuations of assets and liabilities will differ resulting in the recognition of a deferred tax asset.

AASB112 requires a deferred tax asset to be recognised in the current period if in the future:

- the recovery of an asset's carrying amount, or
- the payment of a liability's carrying amount

will result in future tax payments being **smaller**.

When comparing carrying costs of assets and liabilities to their tax base valuations a deferred tax asset will occur in the following circumstances:

**Assets**          Tax base > carrying amount

**Liabilities**     Carrying amount > tax base

The following steps are recommended when accounting for deferred taxes and recording of taxation outcomes:

**Step 1**  Calculate the carrying amount and tax base of the asset (or liability) to determine the difference in valuations, then apply the tax rate to calculate the deferred tax asset.

**Step 2**    Calculate income tax payable and adjust the amount for the deferred tax to determine the income tax expense amount.

**Step 3**    Prepare a journal entry to record annual income tax adjustments.

## Deferred tax asset arising from debtors

In relation to assets, AASB 112 defines the tax base of an asset as:

> ... the amount that will be deductible for tax purposes against any taxable economic benefits that will flow to an entity when it recovers the carrying amount of the asset.[2]

The carrying amount of an asset will be less than its tax base when the carrying amount includes estimates for deductions which will not be recognised in the tax base valuation until the deduction is realised. This will occur in relation to debtors when the carrying amount identifies doubtful debts which cannot be recognised for taxation purposes in the tax base valuation of debtors until the amount is identified as a bad debt.

When the tax base of debtors precludes the doubtful debt in its valuation the entity will be able to obtain a *deductible temporary difference* in the future if the doubtful debt eventuates in a bad debt. Hence a deferred tax asset shall be brought to account.

If the bad debt eventuates in a future year this will reduce taxable income and the resulting income tax payable will be made smaller, in which case the deferred tax asset will be reversed.

## Illustration

For the year ended 30 June, Saga Ltd reported a profit (and taxable income) of $120 000 before the inclusion of bad and doubtful debts.

At 30 June debtors owed $220 000. Bad debts of $20 000 were yet to be deducted from this amount. In addition $10 000 was estimated as doubtful debts.

**Step 1**    Calculate the carrying amount and tax base of the asset to determine the difference in valuations, and then apply the tax rate to calculate the deferred tax asset.

The comparisons of the tax base and carrying amount of debtors over these two years and the resulting difference would be as follows:

| Debtor's valuations | Balance at start | Bad debts | Doubtful debts | Balance at end | | |
|---|---|---|---|---|---|---|
| Tax base amount | $220 000 | ($20 000) | 0 | $200 000 | | |
| Less carrying amount | $220 000 | ($20 000) | ($10 000) | $190 000 | | |
| Deferred tax asset | | | | $10 000 | × 30% = | $3 000  Dr |

The deferred tax asset account would appear as follows:

**Deferred tax asset**

| Date | Particulars | Debit | Credit | Balance |
|---|---|---|---|---|
| Year 1 | | $ | $ | $ |
| 30 June | Income tax expense | 3 000 | | 3 000  Dr |

**Step 2**    Calculate income tax payable and adjust the amount for the deferred tax asset to determine the income tax expense amount.

---

2   AASB 112: Income Taxes

The following table shows the calculation of adjustments to income tax to determine taxable income and income tax payable and the effect of the deferred tax asset on the calculation of income tax expense.

| Taxation adjustments | Year 1<br>$ |
|---|---|
| Taxable income (before bad debts) | 120 000 |
| Less tax deductible bad debts | (20 000) |
| Taxable income | 100 000 |
| Multiplied by the tax rate | × 30% |
| Estimated income tax payable | 30 000  Cr |
| *Less PAYG income tax expensed | (25 000)  Dr |
| Income tax payable adjustment | 5 000  Cr |
| Less deferred tax asset | 3 000  Dr |
| Equals income tax expense adjustment | 2 000  Dr |

*Note: Income tax expensed under the PAYG system was $25 000.

**Step 3**   Prepare a journal entry to record annual income tax adjustments.

The journal entries to record the income tax adjustment for Year 1 and the transfer of income tax expense would be as follows:

**General journal**

| Date | Details | Debit<br>$ | Credit<br>$ |
|---|---|---|---|
| 30 June | Income tax expense | 2 000 | |
| | Deferred tax asset | 3 000 | |
| | Income tax payable | | 5 000 |
| | *Taxation adjustments* | | |
| | Profit and loss | 27 000 | |
| | *Income tax expense | | 27 000 |
| | *Transfer of taxation expense* | | |

*Note: Income tax expense = PAYG income tax expense $25 000 + income tax expense adjustment $2000.

The profit and loss account after the inclusion of income tax expense would be as follows:

**Profit and loss**

| Date | Particulars | Debit<br>$ | Credit<br>$ | Balance<br>$ |
|---|---|---|---|---|
| 30 June | Profit (before adjustments) | | | 120 000  Cr |
| | Bad debts | 20 000 | | 100 000  Cr |
| | Doubtful debts | 10 000 | | 90 000  Cr |
| | Income tax expense | 27 000 | | 63 000  Cr |

On the assumption that the profit (before tax) does not include any permanent differences the income tax expense amount can be reconciled by multiplying the profit (before tax) by 30% as follows:

| Income tax expense reconciliation schedule | Year 1 |
|---|---|
| | $ |
| Profit (before tax) | 90 000 |
| Adjusted for permanent differences | Nil |
| Accounting profit | 90 000 |
| Multiplied by the tax rate | × 30% |
| Income tax expense | 27 000 |

## Question 6.5

Using the following information provided by WOO Ltd you are required to:

a   identify and calculate any deferred taxes;

b   calculate the taxation adjustments at 30 June and prepare a journal entry;

c   prepare an income tax expense reconciliation schedule; and

d   record income tax expense in the profit and loss account.

**Profit and loss**

| Date | Particulars | Debit $ | Credit $ | Balance $ |
|---|---|---|---|---|
| 30 June | Sales | | 800 000 | 800 000  Cr |
| | Cost of sales | 300 000 | | 500 000  Cr |
| | Wages | 100 000 | | 400 000  Cr |
| | Bad debts | 30 000 | | 370 000  Cr |
| | Doubtful debts | 10 000 | | 360 000  Cr |

The tax accountant has determined the following:

- Debtors owed $300 000 at 30 June (**before** writing off $30 000 in bad debts).
- An allowance for doubtful debts account was created of $10 000.
- All items in the profit and loss account are assessable or deductible for taxation purposes with the exception of doubtful debts.
- PAYG income tax expensed during the year is $110 000.
- The income tax rate is 30%.

## Deferred tax asset arising from leave liability

AASB112 defines the tax base of a liability as:

> ... the carrying amount, less any amount that will be deductible for tax purposes in respect of that liability in future periods.[3]

When a liability's carrying amount is greater than its tax base valuation a deferred tax asset will be recognised as the liability will provide a tax deduction in a future period when it is paid.

---

3   ASB112: Income Taxes

The carrying amount of a liability will exceed its tax base when the carrying amount includes estimates which are not tax deductible in the same period. This will occur in relation to the accrual of employee leave entitlements and warranty provisions.

Consequently the tax base of a liability will normally be zero on the basis that the carrying amount represents a future tax deductible amount when the leave is paid to employees or a warranty claim is paid to a customer.

## Illustration

In its first year of operation Pace Ltd reported a profit (and taxable income) before annual leave of $110 000.

During the year the company provided for leave expense of $40 000 of which $10 000 was paid to employees during the year.

**Step 1**    Calculate the carrying amount of the liability and its tax base to determine the difference in valuations, then apply the tax rate to calculate the deferred tax asset.

The following table shows the carrying amount balance at end (after adjustments for leave expensed and paid). This amount will normally be fully deductible for tax purposes in future periods, thereby resulting in a tax base valuation of zero. Hence the deferred asset is equal to the liability's carrying amount.

| Leave liability valuations | Balance at start | Leave expensed | Leave paid | Balance at end | | |
|---|---|---|---|---|---|---|
| Carrying amount | Nil | $40 000 | ($10 000) | $30 000 | | |
| Less tax base amount | | | | $0 | | |
| Deferred tax asset | | | | $30 000 | × 30% = | $9 000 Dr |

The deferred tax asset account would appear as follows:

**Deferred tax asset**

| Date | Particulars | Debit $ | Credit $ | Balance $ |
|---|---|---|---|---|
| Year 1 | Income tax expense | | 9 000 | 9 000 Dr |

**Step 2**    Calculate income tax payable and adjust the amount for the deferred tax asset to determine the income tax expense amount.

The following table shows the effect on taxation incorporating the annual changes in the deferred tax asset.

| Taxation adjustments | Year 1 $ |
|---|---|
| Taxable income (before leave) | 110 000 |
| Less tax deductible annual leave paid | (10 000) |
| Taxable income | 100 000 |
| Multiplied by the tax rate | × 30% |
| Estimated income tax payable | 30 000  Cr |
| *Less PAYG income tax expensed | (10 000)  Dr |
| Income tax payable adjustment | 20 000  Cr |
| Less deferred tax asset | 9 000  Dr |
| Equals income tax expense adjustment | 11 000  Dr |

*Note: Income tax expensed under the PAYG system was $10 000.

**Step 3** Prepare a journal entry to record annual income tax adjustments.
The journal entry to record income tax adjustments would be as follows:

**General journal**

| Date | Details | Debit | Credit |
|---|---|---|---|
| | | $ | $ |
| 30 June | Income tax expense | 11 000 | |
| | Deferred tax asset | 9 000 | |
| | Income tax payable | | 20 000 |
| | *Taxation adjustments* | | |
| | Profit and loss | 21 000 | |
| | Income tax expense | | 21 000 |
| | *Transferred tax expense* | | |

The profit and loss account after the inclusion of income tax expense would be as follows:

**Profit and loss**

| Date | Particulars | Debit | Credit | Balance |
|---|---|---|---|---|
| | | $ | $ | $ |
| 30 June | Profit (before adjustments) | | | 110 000  Cr |
| | Annual leave expense | 40 000 | | 70 000  Cr |
| | Income tax expense | 21 000 | | 49 000  Cr |

On the assumption that the profit (before tax) does not include any permanent differences the income tax expense amount can be reconciled by multiplying the profit (before tax) by 30% as follows:

| Income tax expense reconciliation schedule | Year 1 |
|---|---|
| | $ |
| Profit (before tax) | 70 000 |
| Multiplied by the tax rate | × 30% |
| Income tax expense | 21 000 |

# Question 6.6

Chalm Ltd is in its first year of operation and has provided the following profit and loss account and additional information for the year ended 30 June.

**Profit and loss**

| Date | Particulars | Debit | Credit | Balance |
|---|---|---|---|---|
| | | $ | $ | $ |
| 30 June | Sales | | 1 800 000 | 1 800 000 Cr |
| | Cost of sales | 700 000 | | 1 100 000 Cr |
| | Wages | 500 000 | | 600 000 Cr |
| | Leave expense | 100 000 | | 500 000 Cr |

*Additional information*

- Profit includes leave expensed of $100 000 during the year.
- During the year $40 000 in leave was paid to employees.
- During the year income tax expensed under the PAYG system was $130 000.

You are required to:

a  identify and calculate any deferred taxes;

b  calculate the taxation adjustments at 30 June and prepare a journal entry;

c  prepare an income tax expense reconciliation schedule; and

d  record income tax expense in the profit and loss account.

# 6.5  COMBINING TEMPORARY DIFFERENCES

Taxable temporary differences will result in a deferred tax liability whilst a deferred tax asset arises from a deductible temporary difference.

Deferred taxes can be identified by comparing the differences in the carrying amount and the tax base of specific assets and liabilities which occur when their respective valuations include different amounts.

The following table shows examples of causes of differences in asset and liability valuations and their impact on deferred taxes.

| Deferred tax liability | | |
|---|---|---|
| Assets | Carrying amount > tax base | Caused by accelerated tax depreciation |
| **Deferred tax asset** | | |
| Assets | Tax base > carrying amount | Caused by non-deductible doubtful debts |
| Liabilities | Carrying amount > tax base | Caused by non-deductible provisions for leave expense and warranty expense |

## Illustration

For the year ended 30 June Lark Ltd reported the following information for accounting and taxation purposes:
- Profit (before tax) of $353 000 with taxable income of $350 000.
- Temporary differences were identified in the following asset and liability valuations:

| | Accounting values | | Taxation values | |
|---|---|---|---|---|
| | Carrying amount (before expenses) | Amount expensed | Tax base (before deductions) | Tax deductible amount |
| Equipment | $100 000 | $20 000 | $100 000 | $40 000 |
| This was acquired during the year and is being depreciated over 4 years using the straight-line method for accounting purposes at 25% p.a. and 50% for taxation purposes using the reducing-balance method. | | | | |
| Debtors | $80 000 | $12 000 | $80 000 | $5 000 |
| During the year debtors totalling $5 000 were written off as bad debts and an additional $7 000 declared doubtful. | | | | |
| Leave liability | $0 | $40 000 | $0 | $30 000 |
| Leave totalling $40 000 was expensed during the year with $30 000 paid out. | | | | |

The deferred taxes arising from these differences is as follows:

| Equipment valuations | Balance at start | Depreciation | Balance at end | | |
|---|---|---|---|---|---|
| Carrying amount | $100 000 | ($20 000) | $80 000 | | |
| Less tax base amount | $100 000 | ($40 000) | $60 000 | | |
| **Deferred tax liability** | | | **$20 000** | × 30% = | **$6 000  Cr** |

| Debtors' valuations | Balance at start | Bad debts | Doubtful debts | Balance at end | | |
|---|---|---|---|---|---|---|
| Tax base amount | $80 000 | ($5 000) | Nil | $75 000 | | |
| Less tax base amount | $80 000 | ($5 000) | ($7 000) | $68 000 | | |
| **Deferred tax asset** | | | | **$7 000** | × 30% = | **$2 100  Dr** |

| Leave liability valuations | Balance at start | Leave expensed | Leave paid | Balance at end | | |
|---|---|---|---|---|---|---|
| Carrying amount | Nil | $40 000 | ($30 000) | $10 000 | | |
| Less tax base amount | | | | 0 | | |
| **Deferred tax asset** | | | | **$10 000** | × 30% = | **$3 000  Dr** |

The following table shows the combined effects of the movements in the deferred taxes:

| | | Deferred tax liability $ | Deferred tax asset $ |
|---|---|---|---|
| Assets | Equipment | 6 000  Cr | |
| | Debtors | | 2 100  Dr |
| Liabilities | Leave liability | | 3 000  Dr |
| **Deferred tax result** | | **6 000  Cr** | **5 100  Dr** |

The taxation adjustment for the current year can be calculated as follows:

| | $ |
|---|---|
| Profit (before tax) | 353 000 |
| Less understated tax deductible depreciation | (20 000) |
| Add back non-deductible doubtful debts | 7 000 |
| Add back overstated leave expense | 10 000 |
| Taxable income | 350 000 |
| Multiplied by the tax rate | × 30% |
| Income tax payable | 105 000  Cr |
| *Less PAYG income tax expensed | (80 000)  Dr |
| Income tax payable adjustment | 25 000  Cr |
| Add deferred tax liability | 6 000  Cr |
| Less deferred tax asset | 5 100  Dr |
| Equals income tax expense adjustment | 25 900  Dr |

*Note: PAYG income tax expensed during the year is $80 000.

The resulting general journal would be as follows:

### General journal of Lark Ltd

| Date | Details | Debit | Credit |
|------|---------|-------|--------|
|      |         | $     | $      |
| 30 June | Income tax expense | 25 900 | |
|      | Deferred tax asset | 5 100 | |
|      | Income tax payable | | 25 000 |
|      | Deferred tax liability | | 6 000 |
|      | Adjustments for income tax | | |

The profit and loss account showing the income tax expense amount would be as follows:

### Profit and loss

| Date | Particulars | Debit | Credit | Balance |
|------|-------------|-------|--------|---------|
|      |             | $     | $      | $       |
| 30 June | Balance (profit before tax) | | | 353 000  Cr |
|      | Income tax expense | 105 900 | | 247 100  Cr |

Proof of the income tax expense amount can be determined as follows:

| Income tax expense reconciliation schedule | $ |
|--------------------------------------------|---|
| Profit (before tax) | 353 000 |
| Multiplied by the tax rate | × 30% |
| Income tax expense | 105 900 |

# Question 6.7

For the year ended 30 June Parka Ltd reported the following information:
- Profit (before tax) of $628 000 with taxable income of $560 000.
- Temporary differences were identified in the following assets and liability information:

| | Accounting values | | Taxation values | |
|---|---|---|---|---|
| | Carrying amount (before expenses) | Amount expensed | Tax base (before deductions) | Tax deductible amount |
| | $ | $ | $ | $ |
| Equipment | 400 000 | 80 000 | 400 000 | 160 000 |
| Debtors | 200 000 | 12 000 | 200 000 | 10 000 |
| Leave liability | 0 | 55 000 | 0 | 45 000 |

- **Machinery:** This was acquired during the year and is being depreciated over five years using the straight-line method for accounting purposes at 20% p.a. and 40% for taxation purposes.
- **Debtors:** During the year $10 000 in bad debts were brought to account and an additional $2000 in doubtful debts were recognised.
- **Leave liability:** In the current year $55 000 was accrued with $45 000 paid to employees.
- PAYG income tax expensed during the year is $175 000.

Using this information you are required to:

a   identify and calculate temporary differences;

b   prepare a journal entry to record adjustments to income tax; and

c   show the profit and loss account after including income tax.

# Question 6.8

Using the following information provided by Freo Ltd you are required to:

a   identify and calculate any deferred taxes;

b   calculate the taxation adjustments at 30 June and prepare an adjusting journal entry;

c   prepare a taxation expense reconciliation schedule; and

d   show the profit and loss account inclusive of income tax.

### Profit and loss

| Date | Particulars | Debit $ | Credit $ | Balance $ |
|------|-------------|---------|----------|-----------|
| 30 June | Sales | | 1 800 000 | 1 800 000  Cr |
| | Operating expenses | 900 000 | | 900 000  Cr |
| | Doubtful debts | 20 000 | | 880 000  Cr |
| | Bad debts | 10 000 | | 870 000  Cr |
| | Depreciation – vehicles | 50 000 | | 820 000  Cr |
| | Leave expense | 20 000 | | 800 000  Cr |
| | Warranty expense | 30 000 | | 770 000  Cr |
| | Impairment loss – investments | 20 000 | | 750 000  Cr |

### Additional information provided by the tax accountant included the following

The tax accountant has determined that all amounts included in the profit and loss account will be used in the calculation of taxable income with the following exceptions:

- **Impairment loss:** Investments is a non-deductible permanent difference for taxation purposes.
- **Debtors:** Debtors at 30 June have a carrying amount of $80 000 after writing off bad debts of $10 000 and providing for doubtful debts of $20 000. Doubtful debts will not be allowed as a tax deduction in the current year.
- **Vehicles:** The vehicle was purchased in the current year at a cost of $500 000 and will provide tax deductible depreciation of $100 000.
- **Leave expense:** Not tax deductible in the current year. No leave was paid during the year.
- **Warranty:** Not tax deductible in the current year. Tax deductible warranty payments totalling $10 000 were paid during the year.
- PAYG income tax expensed during the year is $231 000.
- The tax rate is 30%.

# Question 6.9

Cisco Ltd has provided you with its draft income statement and taxation return for the year ended 30 June. Using these drafts and the additional information provided you are required to:

a   identify and calculate any deferred taxes;

b   calculate the taxation adjustments at 30 June;

c   prepare a journal entry to adjust income tax; and

d   show the income statement after income tax.

| Income statement | $ | $ |
|---|---|---|
| Services | | 2 400 000 |
| Operating expenses | 1 400 000 | |
| Entertainment expense | 15 000 | |
| Leave expense | 20 000 | |
| Warranty expense | 45 000 | |
| Depreciation expense | 200 000 | |
| Bad debts | 20 000 | |
| Doubtful debts | 10 000 | 1 710 000 |
| Profit (before income tax) | | 690 000 |

| Taxation return | $ | $ |
|---|---|---|
| Services | | 2 400 000 |
| Operating expenses | 1 400 000 | |
| Entertainment expense | 0 | |
| Leave expense | 15 000 | |
| Warranty expense | 10 000 | |
| Depreciation expense | 400 000 | |
| Bad debts | 20 000 | |
| Doubtful debts | 0 | 1 845 000 |
| Taxable income | | 555 000 |

**Additional information at 30 June**

- Entertainment expenses are a non-deductible permanent difference for taxation purposes.
- Temporary taxation differences (after expenses and deductions) arise due to the following accounts:

| Account | Carrying amount $ | Tax base $ |
|---|---|---|
| Equipment | 600 000 | 400 000 |
| Debtors | 70 000 | 80 000 |
| Leave liability | 5 000 | 0 |
| Warranty liability | 35 000 | 0 |

- PAYG income tax expensed during the year is $200 000;
- The tax rate is 30%.

# 6.6 REVERSING TEMPORARY DIFFERENCES

Deferred taxes will arise when an entity identifies a difference in an asset or liability's carrying amount and tax base. This difference can arise when the entity includes different amounts in the calculation of profit than in the calculation of taxation payable in the same year.

In the years following the creation of a deferred tax liability or deferred tax asset the amount that gave rise to the deferred tax may become deductible or assessable for taxation purposes which will increase or decrease taxable income. When this occurs the deferred tax will reduce in value. This reduction is referred to as a 'reversal of a deferred tax'.

## Reversing a deferred tax liability

A deferred (future) tax liability will initially occur in relation to depreciation when an entity identifies a greater amount of depreciation on an asset for taxation purposes than the amount included as an expense in the calculation of profit.

In the early years of the asset's life the higher amount of tax depreciation will cause the carrying amount of the asset to be greater than its tax base, resulting in a deferred tax liability. The accumulated deferred tax liability will increase in the initial years in which the liability will be credited.

In the later years of the asset's life when the tax deductibility of depreciation falls below the amount expensed in the calculation of profit, the accumulated deferred tax liability will reduce; that is, be debited.

The following steps are recommended in identifying, measuring and accounting for deferred taxes caused by depreciation over the life of the asset.

**Step 1**   Calculate the carrying amount and tax base of the asset and determine the difference in valuations.

**Step 2**   Using the difference in valuations calculate the yearly change in the deferred tax liability.

**Step 3**   Calculate income tax payable and add (or subtract) taxation deferrals to determine income tax expense amount.

**Step 4**   Prepare a journal entry to record annual income tax adjustments.

## Illustration

HY Ltd purchased equipment on 1 July costing $160 000 with an estimated useful life of four years and scrap value of $10 000.

The asset will be depreciated:
- for taxation purposes at 50% using the reducing-balance method; and
- for accounting purposes at 25% per annum using the straight-line method.

The differences in depreciation for taxation and accounting purposes are shown in the following table:

|  | Year 1 $ | Year 2 $ | Year 3 $ | Year 4 $ |
|---|---|---|---|---|
| Taxation depreciation | 80 000 | 40 000 | 20 000 | 10 000 |
| Accounting depreciation | 37 500 | 37 500 | 37 500 | 37 500 |
| Difference in depreciation | 42 500 | 2 500 | (17 500) | (27 500) |

**Step 1**   Calculate the carrying amount and tax base of the asset and determine the difference in valuations.

| Equipment – carrying amount valuation | Year 1 $ | Year 2 $ | Year 3 $ | Year 4 $ |
|---|---|---|---|---|
| Carrying amount (at start) | 160 000 | 122 500 | 85 000 | 47 500 |
| Less depreciation expense | 37 500 | 37 500 | 37 500 | 37 500 |
| Carrying amount (at end) | 122 500 | 85 000 | 47 500 | 10 000 |
| **Equipment – tax base valuation** |  |  |  |  |
| Tax base (at start) | 160 000 | 80 000 | 40 000 | 20 000 |
| Less depreciation expense | 80 000 | 40 000 | 20 000 | 10 000 |
| Tax base (at end) | 80 000 | 40 000 | 20 000 | 10 000 |
| Difference in valuation | 42 500 | 45 000 | 27 500 | Nil |

**Step 2**   Using the difference in valuations calculate the changes in the deferred tax liability.

The difference in valuations from year to year multiplied by the tax rate will reveal the accumulated balance in the deferred tax liability account. The change in the liability account represents the adjustment for the year.

When the deferred tax liability increases a credit adjustment is required. When the liability falls a debit adjustment is required as the deferral is reversing.

The following table shows the change in the annual deferred tax liability.

| | Year 1 $ | Year 2 $ | Year 3 $ | Year 4 $ |
|---|---|---|---|---|
| Difference in valuation | 42 500 | 45 000 | 27 500 | Nil |
| Multiplied by the tax rate | × 30% | × 30% | × 30% | × 30% |
| Deferred tax liability | 12 750 Cr | 13 500 Cr | 8 250 Cr | Nil |
| Change in deferred tax liability | 12 750 Cr | 750 Cr | (5 250) Dr | (8 250) Dr |

These calculations show the deferred tax liability increasing in Years 1 and 2 but falling (reversing) in Years 3 and 4. The deferred tax liability over the life of the asset would appear as follows:

### Deferred tax liability

| Date Year | Particulars | Debit $ | Credit $ | Balance $ |
|---|---|---|---|---|
| 1 | Income tax expense | | 12 750 | 12 750 Cr |
| 2 | Income tax expense | | 750 | 13 500 Cr |
| 3 | Income tax expense | 5 250 | | 8 250 Cr |
| 4 | Income tax expense | 8 250 | | Nil |

**Step 3** Calculate income tax payable and add (or subtract) deferred tax liability to determine income tax expense.

The following table shows the effect on taxation incorporating the annual changes in the deferred income tax liability. The table assumes, in each of the four years, taxable income of $500 000* and income tax expensed under the PAYG system of $160 000**.

| Taxation adjustments | Year 1 $ | Year 2 $ | Year 3 $ | Year 4 $ |
|---|---|---|---|---|
| Taxable income* | 500 000 | 500 000 | 500 000 | 500 000 |
| Multiplied by the tax rate | × 30% | × 30% | × 30% | × 30% |
| Estimated income tax payable | 165 000 Cr | 165 000 Cr | 165 000 Cr | 165 000 Cr |
| Less PAYG income tax expensed** | 160 000 Dr | 160 000 Dr | 160 000 Dr | 160 000 Dr |
| Income tax payable adjustment | 5 000 Cr | 5 000 Cr | 5 000 Cr | 5 000 Cr |
| Add (subtract) deferred tax liability | 12 750 Cr | 750 Cr | 5 250 Dr | 8 250 Dr |
| Equals income tax expense adjustment | 17 750 Dr | 5 750 Dr | 250 Cr | 3 250 Cr |

**Step 4** Prepare a journal entry to record income tax adjustments.

The journal entries to record income tax adjustments for Years 1 and 2 would be as follows:

### General journal

| Date | Details | Debit $ | Credit $ |
|---|---|---|---|
| Year 1 | | | |
| 30 June | Income tax expense | 17 750 | |
| | Income tax payable | | 5 000 |
| | Deferred tax liability | | 12 750 |
| | *Taxation adjustments* | | |

### General journal

| Date | Details | Debit $ | Credit $ |
|---|---|---|---|
| Year 2 | | | |
| 30 June | Income tax expense | 5 750 | |
| | Deferred tax liability | | 750 |
| | Income tax payable | | 5 000 |
| | *Taxation adjustments* | | |

The journal entries to record income tax adjustments for Years 3 and 4 would be as follows:

**General journal**

| Date | Details | Debit $ | Credit $ |
|------|---------|---------|----------|
| Year 3 | | | |
| 30 June | Deferred tax liability | 5 250 | |
| | Income tax payable | | 250 |
| | Income tax payable | | 5 000 |
| | *Taxation adjustments* | | |

**General journal**

| Date | Details | Debit $ | Credit $ |
|------|---------|---------|----------|
| Year 4 | | | |
| 30 June | Deferred tax liability | 8 250 | |
| | Income tax expense | | 3 250 |
| | Income tax expense | | 5 000 |
| | *Taxation adjustments* | | |

## Question 6.10

From the following information provided by Barma Ltd you are required to:
a calculate the taxation adjustments for the life of the asset; and
b prepare journal entries in each of the three years to adjust taxation outcomes.
The company purchased equipment on 1 July costing $81 000 which has a useful life of three years.
- For accounting purposes the asset will be depreciated using the straight-line method at 33.33% p.a. and have a scrap value of $3000.
- For taxation purposes depreciation will use the reducing-balance method at the rate of 66.66% p.a.
The company has provided the following future estimates for taxable income and PAYG income tax.

| Estimates | Year 1 $ | Year 2 $ | Year 3 $ |
|-----------|----------|----------|----------|
| Taxable income | 800 000 | 850 000 | 900 000 |
| PAYG income tax expense | 240 000 | 250 000 | 260 000 |

## Question 6.11

Parker Ltd has provided the following information relating to its profit and income tax for the year ended 30 June.
From this information you are required to:
a identify and calculate any deferred taxes;
b prepare a general journal entry at 30 June to adjust the income tax accounts; and
c record the income tax expense in the income statement.

| Income statement (profit and loss) | $ | $ |
|-------------------------------------|---|---|
| Sales income | | 1 200 000 |
| Operating expenses | 800 000 | |
| Depreciation expense | 200 000 | 1 000 000 |
| Profit (before income tax) | | 200 000 |

| Income tax return amounts | $ | $ |
|----------------------------|---|---|
| Sales income | | 1 200 000 |
| Operating expenses | 800 000 | |
| Depreciation expense | 150 000 | 950 000 |
| Taxable income | | 250 000 |

*Additional information*

| Account | Carrying amount (after adjustments) $ | Tax base (after adjustments) $ | Deferred tax liability (start of year) $ |
|---------|----------------------------------------|---------------------------------|-------------------------------------------|
| Equipment | 400 000 | 210 000 | 72 000 |

- Income tax expensed under the PAYG system for the year totalled $60 000.
- The tax rate is 30%.

## Reversing a deferred tax asset

A deferred tax asset will result when an expense included in the calculation of profit cannot be claimed as a tax deduction in the same year, but can be claimed in a future period when the expense is paid. This temporary difference causes the carrying amount of an asset or liability to differ to the tax base valuation.

A deferred tax asset will reverse when the expense causing the taxation deferral becomes deductible for taxation purposes in a following period.

When a deferred tax asset increases the asset will be debited. When it reverses the deferred tax asset will be credited.

To identify a deferred tax asset movement the following steps can be applied.

**Step 1** Calculate the tax base and carrying amount of the asset or liability and determine the difference.
**Step 2** Using the difference in valuations calculate the annual changes in the deferred tax asset.
**Step 3** Calculate income tax payable and add (or subtract) taxation deferrals to determine income tax expense amount.
**Step 4** Prepare a journal entry to record annual income tax adjustments.

### Reversing a deferred tax asset arising from debtors

When an entity includes doubtful debts expense in the calculation of profit but cannot claim the expense as a tax deduction in the same year, a deferred tax asset will be brought to account as the tax base of the asset exceeds its carrying amount. Hence the deferred tax asset increases or is debited.

If the doubtful debt eventuates in a bad debt in a future year resulting in a tax deduction, taxable income and the resulting income tax payable will fall and the deferred tax asset will be reversed; that is, credited.

## Illustration

At 30 June Year 1, Saga Ltd's debtors owed $200 000, of which $10 000 was considered doubtful debts.

At 30 June Year 2 the doubtful debts identified in Year 1 eventuated in a bad debt for taxation purposes.

**Step 1** Calculate the tax base and carrying amount of the asset and determine the difference.

The comparisons of the tax base and carrying amount of debtors over these two years and the resulting difference would be as follows:

| Debtors | Year 1 | Year 2 |
|---|---|---|
| | $ | $ |
| **Tax base valuation** | | |
| Tax base (at start) | 200 000 | 200 000 |
| Less bad debts identified in year | 0 | 10 000 |
| **Tax base (at end)** | 200 000 | 190 000 |
| **Less carrying amount valuation** | | |
| Carrying amount (at start) | 200 000 | 190 000 |
| Less estimated doubtful debts | 10 000 | 0 |
| **Carrying amount (at end)** | 190 000 | 190 000 |
| **Difference in valuations** | 10 000 | 0 |

**Step 2** Using the difference in valuations calculate the changes in the deferred tax asset.

The deferred tax asset can be calculated by multiplying the difference in valuation by the tax rate. The change in the deferred tax asset from year to year represents the adjustment required in each year.

If the deferred tax asset is increasing a debit adjustment is required. If it reduces, the deferred tax asset will be credited as it is reversing.

The following table shows the deferred tax asset increasing in Year 1 but reducing (reversing) in Year 2 to bring the asset to a nil balance.

| Debtors | Year 1 $ | Year 2 $ |
|---|---|---|
| Difference in valuations | 10 000 | 0 |
| Multiplied by the tax rate | × 30% | × 30% |
| Deferred tax asset | 3 000 | Nil |
| Change in deferred tax asset | 3 000  Dr | (3 000)  Cr |

The deferred tax asset account would appear as follows over the two years:

**Deferred tax asset**

| Date Year | Particulars | Debit $ | Credit $ | Balance $ |
|---|---|---|---|---|
| 1 | Income tax expense | 3 000 | | 3 000  Dr |
| 2 | Income tax expense | | 3 000 | Nil |

**Step 3** Calculate income tax payable (current tax) and add (or subtract) the deferred tax asset to determine income tax expense amount.

The following table shows the effect on taxation incorporating the annual changes in the deferred tax asset. The table assumes taxable income of $100 000* in Year 1 and $90 000 in Year 2 with income tax expensed under the PAYG system of $20 000**.

| Taxation adjustments | Year 1 $ | Year 2 $ |
|---|---|---|
| *Taxable income | 100 000 | 90 000 |
| Multiplied by the tax rate | × 30% | × 30% |
| Estimated income tax payable | 30 000  Cr | 27 000  Cr |
| **Less PAYG income tax expensed | 20 000  Dr | 20 000  Dr |
| Income tax payable adjustment | 10 000  Cr | 7 000  Cr |
| Add (subtract) deferred tax asset | 3 000  Dr | 3 000  Cr |
| Equals income tax expense adjustment | 7 000  Dr | 10 000  Dr |

**Step 4** Prepare a journal entry to record annual income tax adjustments.

The journal entries to record the income tax adjustments for Years 1 and 2 would be as follows:

| General journal | | Year 1 | | Year 2 | |
|---|---|---|---|---|---|
| Date | Details | Debit $ | Credit $ | Debit $ | Credit $ |
| 30 June | Income tax expense | 7 000 | | 10 000 | |
| | Deferred tax asset | 3 000 | | | 3 000 |
| | Income tax payable | | 10 000 | | 7 000 |
| | Taxation adjustments | | | | |

## Question 6.12

Ram Ltd has provided you with the following profit and income tax information. Using this information you are required to:

a    identify and calculate any deferred taxes;

b    calculate the taxation adjustments at 30 June and prepare a journal entry; and

c    record income tax expense in the profit and loss account.

The accountant has provided the following profit account:

### Profit and loss

| Date | Particulars | Debit $ | Credit $ | Balance $ |
|------|-------------|---------|----------|-----------|
| 30 June | Sales | | 900 000 | 900 000  Cr |
| | Cost of sales | 400 000 | | 500 000  Cr |
| | Wages | 200 000 | | 300 000  Cr |
| | Doubtful debts | 10 000 | | 290 000  Cr |

The tax accountant also provided the following tax related information:

| Income tax return – calculations | $ | $ |
|----------------------------------|-----|-----|
| Sales income | | 900 000 |
| Cost of sales | 400 000 | |
| Wages | 200 000 | |
| Bad debts | 30 000 | 630 000 |
| Taxable income | | 270 000 |

| Account | Carrying amount (before adjustments) $ | Tax base (before adjustments) $ | Deferred asset (start of year) $ |
|---------|-----------------|-----------|-----------------|
| Debtors | 210 000 | 240 000 | 30 000 |

- In the previous year the company brought to account $30 000 in doubtful debts that were not deductible in that year.
- In the current year the doubtful debts from the previous year were declared bad debts and written off.
- An additional $10 000 has been identified as doubtful debts in the current year.
- PAYG income tax expensed during the year is $80 000.
- The tax rate is 30%.

## Reversing a deferred tax asset arising from a liability

A deferred tax asset will be recognised when a liability's carrying amount is less than its tax base valuation.

This will occur when the carrying amount includes estimates which are not tax deductible in the same period. This will occur when leave or warranty expenses are included in the calculation of profit and cannot be taken as a tax deduction as they have not been paid. In such cases the deferred tax asset will increase; that is, be debited.

A deferred tax asset resulting from increases in liabilities will reverse in subsequent years when the payment of the liability reduces taxable income and income tax payable. When this occurs the deferred tax asset will be credited as it is reversing.

## Illustration

At 30 June Year 1, Pace Ltd's leave liability account had a carrying amount of nil. This balance had to be adjusted to provide for leave owing to employees of $40 000. Leave was not paid in this year.

During Year 2 leave liability of $40 000 was paid to employees and an additional $30 000 was accrued.

**Step 1**  Calculate the carrying amount and tax base of the liability and determine the difference.

The comparisons of the carrying amount and tax base of leave liability and the resulting differences over these two years would be as follows:

| Leave liability | Year 1 | Year 2 |
|---|---|---|
| | $ | $ |
| Carrying amount valuation | | |
|    Carrying amount (at start) | 0 | 40 000 |
|    Add estimated leave provision | 40 000 | 30 000 |
| | | 70 000 |
|    Less leave paid | 0 | (40 000) |
| Carrying amount (at end) | 40 000 | 30 000 |
| Tax base valuation | | |
|    Carrying amount (at end of year) | 40 000 | 30 000 |
|    Less future deductible leave | (40 000) | (30 000) |
| Tax base (at end) | 0 | 0 |
| Difference in valuation | 40 000 | 30 000 |

**Step 2**  Using the difference in valuations calculate the change in the deferred tax asset.

The deferred tax asset amount can be ascertained by multiplying the difference in valuation by the tax rate. If the deferred tax asset increases from year to year a debit adjustment is required. When the deferred tax asset falls a credit adjustment is required.

The following table shows the deferred tax asset increasing in Year 1 but falling (reversing) in Year 2.

| Taxation deferral | Year 1 | Year 2 |
|---|---|---|
| | $ | $ |
| Difference in valuation | 40 000 | 30 000 |
| Multiplied by the tax rate | × 30% | × 30% |
| Deferred tax liability | 12 000  Dr | 9 000  Dr |
| Change in deferred tax liability | 12 000  Dr | (3 000)  Cr |

The deferred tax asset account would appear as follows over the two years:

**Deferred tax asset**

| Date Year | Particulars | Debit $ | Credit $ | Balance $ |
|---|---|---|---|---|
| 1 | Income tax expense | 12 000 | | 12 000  Dr |
| 2 | Income tax expense | | 3 000 | 9 000  Dr |

**Step 3**  Calculate income tax payable (current tax) and aggregate deferred tax asset to determine income tax expense amount.

The following table shows the effect on taxation incorporating the annual changes in the deferred tax asset. The table assumes taxable income of $100 000* in Year 1 and $60 000 in Year 2 with income tax expensed under the PAYG system of $10 000**.

| Taxation adjustments | Year 1 $ | Year 2 $ |
|---|---|---|
| *Taxable income | 100 000 | 60 000 |
| Multiplied by the tax rate | × 30% | × 30% |
| Estimated income tax payable | 30 000  Cr | 18 000  Cr |
| **Less PAYG income tax expensed | 10 000  Dr | 10 000  Dr |
| Income tax payable adjustment | 20 000  Cr | 8 000  Cr |
| Add (subtract) deferred tax asset | 12 000  Dr | 12 000  Cr |
| Equals income tax expense adjustment | 8 000  Dr | 20 000  Dr |

**Step 4** Prepare a journal entry to record annual income tax adjustments.

The journal entry to record income tax adjustments for Years 1 and 2 would be as follows:

| General journal | | Year 1 | | Year 2 | |
|---|---|---|---|---|---|
| Date | Details | Debit $ | Credit $ | Debit $ | Credit $ |
| 30 June | Income tax expense | 8 000 | | 20 000 | |
| | Deferred tax asset | 12 000 | | | 12 000 |
| | Income tax payable | | 20 000 | | 8 000 |
| | *Taxation adjustments* | | | | |

# Question 6.13

Using the following information provided by Chalm Ltd in its second year of operation you are required to:

**a** identify and calculate any deferred taxes;

**b** calculate the taxation adjustments at 30 June and prepare a journal entry; and

**c** record income tax expense in the profit and loss account.

### Profit and loss

| Date | Particulars | Debit $ | Credit $ | Balance $ |
|---|---|---|---|---|
| 30 June | Sales | | 2 000 000 | 2 000 000  Cr |
| | Cost of sales | 800 000 | | 1 200 000  Cr |
| | Wages | 550 000 | | 650 000  Cr |
| | Leave expense | 80 000 | | 570 000  Cr |

### Taxable income

| | $ | $ |
|---|---|---|
| Sales | | 2 000 000 |
| Cost of sales | 800 000 | |
| Wages | 550 000 | |
| Leave paid | 120 000 | 1 470 000 |
| Taxable income | | 530 000 |

*Additional information*

- At the end of the previous year the leave liability account was $100 000 which attracted a deferred tax asset of $30 000.
- An additional $80 000 was accrued in leave in the current year.
- During the year $120 000 in leave was paid.
- During the year income tax expensed under the PAYG system was $160 000.

# 6.7   COMBINING TEMPORARY DIFFERENCES WITH REVERSALS

Taxable temporary differences will result in a deferred tax liability whilst a deferred tax asset arises from a deductible temporary difference.

Deferred taxes can be identified by comparing the differences in the carrying amount and the tax base of specific assets and liabilities which occur when their respective valuations include different amounts.

The following table shows examples of causes of differences in asset and liability valuations and their impact on deferred taxes.

| Deferred tax liability | | |
|---|---|---|
| Assets | Carrying amount > tax base | Caused by accelerated tax depreciation |
| Deferred tax asset | | |
| Assets | Tax base > carrying amount | Caused by non-deductible doubtful debts |
| Liabilities | Carrying amount > tax base | Caused by non-deductible provisions for leave expense and warranty expense |

The identification of an increasing or decreasing taxation deferral can be made by analysing the movement in the respective deferred liability or deferred asset from year to year. The analysis will assist in determining if the deferral is increasing or decreasing. The following table summarises the accounting treatment for movements in deferred taxes.

|  | Debit | Credit |
|---|---|---|
| Deferred liability | Decreasing | Increasing |
| Deferred asset | Increasing | Decreasing |

## Illustration

For the year ended 30 June Lark Ltd reported the following information:

| Income statement | $ | Taxation return | $ |
|---|---|---|---|
| Income | 800 000 | Income | 800 000 |
| Less operating expenses | (240 000) | Less operating expenses | (240 000) |
| Equipment depreciation | (20 000) | Equipment depreciation | (40 000) |
| Machinery depreciation | (100 000) | Machinery depreciation | (50 000) |
| Doubtful debts | (5 000) | Bad debts | (20 000) |
| Leave expense | (40 000) | Leave paid | (30 000) |
| Impairment loss – goodwill | (10 000) | Taxable income | 420 000 |
| **Profit (before income tax)** | **385 000** | | |

Temporary differences were identified in the following accounts:

| | Carrying amount | Tax base |
|---|---|---|
| Equipment | $80 000 | $60 000 |

This was acquired during the year and is being depreciated over four years using the straight-line method for accounting purposes at 25% p.a. and 50% for taxation purposes. Being the first year of the asset's use there was no taxation deferral on this asset at the start of the year.

| | Carrying amount | Tax base |
|---|---|---|
| Machinery | $100 000 | $50 000 |

This was acquired 3three years earlier and is being depreciated on the straight-line method for accounting purposes and the reducing-balance method for taxation purposes. At the start of the year depreciation differences over the asset's life had resulted in a deferred tax liability of $30 000.

| | Carrying amount | Tax base |
|---|---|---|
| Debtors | $75 000 | $80 000 |

In the previous year doubtful debts of $20 000 were expensed, resulting in a deferred tax asset of $6 000. These doubtful debts were written off as bad debts in the current year and claimed as a tax deduction. An additional $5 000 of debtors were identified as doubtful debts expense in the current year.

| | Carrying amount | Tax base |
|---|---|---|
| Leave liability | $10 000 | $0 |

In the previous year $30 000 leave was expensed but not paid, resulting in a deferred tax asset of $9 000. The liability was paid in the current year and an additional $40 000 has been expensed.

A comparison and explanation of how these amounts affect the carrying amount and tax base valuations and resulting deferred tax follows:

- **Equipment:** As the carrying amount is greater than the assets tax base a deferred liability must be brought to account as calculated in the following table.

| Equipment | | | | |
|---|---|---|---|---|
| Carrying amount | $80 000 | | | |
| Less tax base valuation | $60 000 | | | |
| Deferred tax liability (at end of year) | $20 000 Cr | × 30% = | $6 000 Cr | |
| Less deferred liability (from previous year) | | | Nil | |
| Change in deferred tax liability | | | $6 000 Cr | |

- **Machinery:** The deferred tax liability at the start of the year on this asset was $30 000. The following calculations show a comparison of the asset's carrying amount and tax base revealing a fall in the deferred tax liability to $15 000, indicating a decline in the liability; that is, a reversal of the liability.

| Machinery | | | | |
|---|---|---|---|---|
| Carrying amount | $100 000 | | | |
| Less tax base valuation | $50 000 | | | |
| Deferred tax liability (at end of year) | $50 000 Cr | × 30% = | $15 000 Cr | |
| Less deferred liability (from previous year) | | | ($30 000) Cr | |
| Change in deferred tax liability | | | ($15 000) Dr | |

- **Debtors:** This asset had an existing deferred tax asset of $6000. Comparison of the carrying amount and the tax base in the current year results in the deferred asset falling to $1500 indicating a fall in the asset, that is, a reversal of the asset.

| Debtors | | | |
|---|---|---|---|
| Tax base valuation | $80 000 | | |
| Less carrying amount | $75 000 | | |
| Deferred tax asset (at end of year) | $5 000  Cr | × 30% = | $1 500  Cr |
| Less deferred asset (from previous year) | | | ($6 000)  Cr |
| Change in deferred tax asset | | | ($4 500)  Dr |

- **Leave liability:** The following calculations reveal the liability's carrying amount to be $40 000 greater than its tax base, resulting in a deferred asset. Consequently the deferred tax asset is $12 000, which is $3000 more than the assets $9000 balance at the start of the year. Hence the deferred tax asset is increasing.

| Leave liability | | | |
|---|---|---|---|
| Carrying amount | $40 000 | | |
| Tax base | 0 | | |
| Deferred tax asset (at end of year) | $40 000  Dr | × 30% = | $12 000  Dr |
| Less deferred asset (from previous year) | | | ($9 000)  Dr |
| Change in deferred tax asset | | | $3 000  Dr |

The following table shows the combined effects of the movements in the deferred taxes:

| Temporary differences | | Deferred tax liability $ | Deferred tax asset $ |
|---|---|---|---|
| Assets | Equipment (increase) | 6 000  Cr | |
| | Machinery (reversal) | 15 000  Dr | |
| | Debtors (reversal) | | 4 500  Cr |
| Liabilities | Leave liability (increase) | | 3 000  Dr |
| Change in deferred tax | | 9 000  Dr | 1 500  Cr |

The taxation adjustment for the current year can be calculated as follows.

| | | |
|---|---|---|
| Income tax payable on taxable income | $420 000 × 30% = | $126 000  Cr |
| *Less PAYG income tax expensed | | $120 000  Dr |
| Income tax payable adjustment | | $6 000  Cr |
| Less deferred tax liability (reversal) | | ($9 000)  Dr |
| Add deferred tax asset (reversal) | | $1 500  Cr |
| Equals income tax expense adjustment | | $1 500  Cr |

*Note: PAYG income tax expensed during the year was $120 000.

The resulting general journal entry would be as follows:

### General journal of Lark Ltd

| Date | Particulars | Debit $ | Credit $ |
|---|---|---|---|
| 30 June | Deferred tax liability | 9 000 | |
| | Income tax expense | | 1 500 |
| | Income tax payable | | 6 000 |
| | Deferred tax asset | | 1 500 |
| | *Adjustments for income tax* | | |
| | Profit and loss | 118 500 | |
| | Income tax expense | | 118 500 |
| | *Transferred tax expense* | | |

The profit and loss account showing the income tax expense amount would be as follows:

### Profit and loss

| Date | Particulars | Debit $ | Credit $ | Balance $ |
|---|---|---|---|---|
| 30 June | Balance (profit before tax) | | | 385 000  Cr |
| | Income tax expense | 118 500 | | 266 500  Cr |

Proof of the income tax expense amount can be determined as follows:

| Income tax expense reconciliation schedule | $ |
|---|---|
| Profit (before tax) | 385 000 |
| Adjusted for permanent difference – impaired goodwill | 10 000 |
| Adjusted profit | 395 000 |
| Multiplied by the tax rate | × 30% |
| Income tax expense | 118 500 |

# Question 6.14

Using the following information provided by BBQ Ltd you are required to prepare a journal entry at 30 June to adjust the income tax accounts.

- Taxable income $600 000.
- Income tax expensed under the PAYG system $170 000.
- Temporary differences and associated taxation deferrals were identified in the following accounts:

| Account | | Carrying amount (at 30 June) $ | Tax base (at 30 June) $ | Deferred tax asset (previous year) $ | Deferred tax liability (previous year) $ |
|---|---|---|---|---|---|
| Assets | Debtors | 120 000 | 130 000 | 10 000 | |
| | Vehicle | 60 000 | 40 000 | | 0 |
| | Equipment | 400 000 | 200 000 | | 72 000 |
| Liabilities | Warranty liability | 10 000 | 0 | 2 000 | |
| | Leave liability | 30 000 | 0 | 12 000 | |

# Question 6.15

Fargo Ltd has provided you with its draft income statement and taxation return for the year ended 30 June. Using these drafts and the additional information provided you are required to:

**a** calculate the taxation adjustments;

**b** prepare a journal entry to adjust income tax; and

**c** complete the income statement to show profit (after tax).

| Income statement | $ | $ |
|---|---|---|
| Services | | 2 400 000 |
| Operating expenses | 1 325 000 | |
| Doubtful debts | 50 000 | |
| Leave expense | 20 000 | |
| Warranty expense | 5 000 | |
| Depreciation – equipment | 200 000 | |
| Depreciation – machinery | 200 000 | 1 800 000 |
| Profit (before income tax) | | 600 000 |

| Income tax return amounts | $ | $ |
|---|---|---|
| Services | | 2 400 000 |
| Operating expenses | 1 325 000 | |
| Bad debts | 20 000 | |
| Leave paid | 15 000 | |
| Warranty paid | 10 000 | |
| Depreciation – equipment | 150 000 | |
| Depreciation – machinery | 200 000 | 1 720 000 |
| Taxable income | | 680 000 |

Additional information provided by the tax accountant included the following:

| Account | Carrying amount (at 30 June) | Tax base (at 30 June) | Deferred tax asset (previous year) | Deferred tax liability (previous year) |
|---|---|---|---|---|
| | $ | $ | $ | $ |
| Debtors | 750 000 | 790 000 | 3 000 | |
| Leave liability | 50 000 | 0 | 13 500 | |
| Warranty liability | 20 000 | 0 | 7 500 | |
| Equipment | 200 000 | 150 000 | | 30 000 |
| Machinery | 400 000 | 200 000 | | 60 000 |

- PAYG income tax expensed during the year is $180 000.
- The tax rate is 30%.

## 6.8 ACCOUNTING FOR TAXATION ON LOSSES

In some years companies may incur a taxation loss as a result of allowable taxation deductions exceeding assessable income.

AASB112: Income Taxes allows an entity to record a deferred tax asset in respect of tax losses in the current period, provided that the entity is likely to derive taxable income in future periods against which the deferred tax asset can be offset.

Where a company is permitted to apportion taxation losses against future years' taxable income, it effectively reduces the amount of income tax that would fall due in the future. As a result of the taxation loss the company therefore derives a future benefit (deferred tax asset) in the period in which the tax loss arises.

In addition, a company may record an accounting loss, as expenses exceed revenues. Where this occurs the company will record an income tax credit (revenue item), which will result in a reduced accounting loss.

## Illustration

For the year ended 30 June XYZ Ltd reported an accounting loss and consequent tax loss of $60 000. In addition income tax of $100 000 was incurred under the PAYG system which has been paid. The accounts at 30 June were as follows:

### General ledger of XYZ Ltd

| Date | Particulars | Debit $ | Credit $ | Balance $ |
|------|-------------|---------|----------|-----------|
| **Profit and loss** | | | | |
| June 30 | Sales income | | 1 200 000 | 1 200 000  Cr |
| | Operating expenses | 1 260 000 | | 60 000  Dr |
| **Income tax expense** | | | | |
| June 30 | Balance | | | 100 000  Dr |
| **Income tax payable** | | | | |
| June 30 | Balance | | | Nil |

As a tax loss of $60 000 has been made the company can bring to account a deferred tax asset of $18 000. In addition, the income tax expensed during the year must be reversed and an income tax credit brought to account and included in the income statement.

The following calculations show the amounts that will give rise to the adjustments.

| | | |
|---|---|---|
| Income tax on taxable income (deferred tax asset) | ($60 000 × 30%) = | $18 000  Dr |
| Add PAYG income tax expensed (refund) | | $100 000  Dr |
| Equals income tax expense adjustment | | $118 000  Cr |

The journal entries recording the tax adjustments and transferring the income tax credit to the profit and loss account would be as follows:

### General journal of XYZ Ltd

| Date | Particulars | Debit $ | Credit $ |
|------|-------------|---------|----------|
| 30 June | | | |
| | Income tax payable | 100 000 | |
| | Deferred tax asset | 18 000 | |
| |     Income tax expense | | 118 000 |
| | *Adjustments for income tax* | | |
| | Income tax credit | 18 000 | |
| |     Profit and loss | | 18 000 |
| | *Transferred balance to profit and loss* | | |

These adjustments would be posted to the general ledger as follows:

### General ledger of XYZ Ltd

| Date | Particulars | Debit $ | Credit $ | Balance $ |
|------|-------------|---------|----------|-----------|
| **Income tax expense** | | | | |
| 30 June | Balance | | | 100 000 Dr |
| | Income tax (adjustment) | | 118 000 | 18 000 Cr |
| | Profit and loss | 18 000 | | Nil |
| **Income tax refund** | | | | |
| 30 June | Balance | | | Nil |
| | Income tax (adjustment) | 100 000 | | 100 000 Dr |
| **Deferred tax asset** | | | | |
| 30 June | Income tax payable | 18 000 | | 18 000 Dr |
| **Profit and loss** | | | | |
| 30 June | Sales income | | 1 200 000 | 1 200 000 Cr |
| | Operating expenses | 1 260 000 | | 60 000 Dr |
| | Income tax credit | | 18 000 | 42 000 Dr |

These accounts reveal that:
- the company has a deferred tax asset of $18 000 that it will be able to claim against future income tax payable when it returns a future taxable income;
- the income tax payable account has a balance of $100 000 debit representing the amount refundable when the company lodges its taxation return with the ATO; and
- the loss before tax of $60 000 has fallen to $42 000 as a result of an income tax credit which arose from the deferral of tax.

# Question 6.16

From the following information about Jongo Ltd you are required to:

**a**  prepare the general journal entry to adjust income tax outcomes at 30 June;

**b**  record the adjustments in the accounts; and

**c**  finalise the profit and loss account to include income tax.

### General ledger of Jongo Ltd

| Date | Particulars | Debit | Credit | Balance |
|------|-------------|-------|--------|---------|
| **Profit and loss** | | | | |
| | | $ | $ | $ |
| 30 June | Sales income | | 2 500 000 | 2 500 000  Cr |
| | Cost of goods sold | 1 300 000 | | 1 200 000  Cr |
| | Wages | 250 000 | | 950 000  Cr |
| | Other expenses | 1 050 000 | | 100 000  Dr |
| **Income tax expense** | | | | |
| 30 June | Balance | | | 200 000  Dr |
| **Income tax payable (receivable)** | | | | |
| 30 June | Balance | | | 40 000  Cr |

*Additional information*

- The income tax rate is 30%.

# Question 6.17

From the following information provided by Fargo Ltd for the year ended 30 June you are required to:

a   identify and calculate any deferred taxes;

b   calculate the taxation adjustments at 30 June;

c   prepare a journal entry to adjust income tax; and

d   show the profit and loss account inclusive of income tax.

### Profit and loss account

| Date | Particulars | Debit $ | Credit $ | Balance $ |
|------|-------------|---------|----------|-----------|
| 30 June | Services | | 1 300 000 | 1 300 000  Cr |
| | Operating expenses | 1 000 000 | | 300 000  Cr |
| | Depreciation – machinery | 250 000 | | 50 000  Cr |

| Income tax return amounts | $ | $ |
|---------------------------|---|---|
| Services | | 1 300 000 |
| Operating expenses | 1 000 000 | |
| Depreciation – machinery | 500 000 | 1 500 000 |
| Tax loss | | (200 000) |

Additional information provided by the tax accountant included the following:

| Account | Carrying amount $ | Tax base $ | Deferred liability (start of year) $ |
|---------|-------------------|------------|--------------------------------------|
| Machinery | 500 000 | 250 000 | Nil |

- PAYG income tax expensed during the year is $120 000.
- The tax rate is 30%.

# Comprehensive Assessment Activity

From the following information provided by Seemore Ltd you are required to:

a   identify and calculate the deferred taxes;

b   prepare a journal entry to adjust income tax outcomes; and

c   show the profit and loss account inclusive of income tax.

**Profit and loss**

| Date | Particulars | Debit $ | Credit $ | Balance $ | |
|------|-------------|---------|----------|-----------|---|
| 30 June | Sales | | 3 000 000 | 3 000 000 | Cr |
| | Operating expenses | 1 600 000 | | 1 400 000 | Cr |
| | Impairment of investments | 250 000 | | 1 150 000 | Cr |
| | Dividends income | | 50 000 | 1 200 000 | Cr |
| | Doubtful debts | 10 000 | | 1 190 000 | Cr |
| | Bad debts | 20 000 | | 1 170 000 | Cr |
| | Depreciation – vehicles | 80 000 | | 1 090 000 | Cr |
| | Depreciation – equipment | 40 000 | | 1 050 000 | Cr |
| | Leave expenses | 20 000 | | 1 030 000 | Cr |
| | Warranty expense | 15 000 | | 1 015 000 | Cr |

## Additional information provided by the tax accountant

The following amounts are to be included in the company's taxation return:

| | |
|---|---|
| Sales | $3 000 000 |
| Operating expenses | $1 600 000 |
| Impairment of investments | Nil  Not deductible |
| Dividends income | Nil  Not assessable |
| Bad debts | $35 000 |
| Depreciation – vehicles | $160 000 |
| Depreciation – equipment | $35 000 |
| Leave paid | $15 000 |
| Warranty paid | $25 000 |

* The carrying amounts and tax base valuations of tax related assets and liabilities were as follows:

| Account | Carrying amount (30 June) $ | Tax base (30 June) $ | Deferred asset (start of year) $ | Deferred liability (start of year) $ |
|---------|------------------|----------|----------------|--------------------|
| Debtors | 100 000 | 110 000 | 4 500 | |
| Vehicles | 720 000 | 640 000 | | Nil |
| Equipment | 200 000 | 130 000 | | 22 500 |
| Leave liability | 15 000 | 0 | 3 000 | |
| Warranty liability | 20 000 | 0 | 9 000 | |

* PAYG income tax expensed during the year is $350 000.
* The tax rate is 30%.

# Assessment Checklist

Complete the following checklist to identify if you consider yourself capable of being assessed against each of the following outcomes.

| I can: | Chapter reference | Check ✓ |
|---|---|---|
| explain how deferred taxes impact on the calculation of income tax | 6.2 | |
| identify and account for taxable temporary differences | 6.3 & 6.5 | |
| identify and account for deductible temporary differences | 6.4 & 6.5 | |
| identify and account for reversals of temporary differences | 6.6 & 6.7 | |
| account for taxation on losses | 6.8 | |

# CHAPTER 7

## DISTRIBUTING SHAREHOLDERS' WEALTH

## WHAT YOU WILL LEARN IN THIS CHAPTER

Upon satisfactory completion of this chapter you should be able to account for:
- the payment of dividends to shareholders;
- the transfer of profits to revenue reserves;
- the revaluation of property, plant and equipment; and
- the issue of bonus shares.

**Are you already competent at these tasks?**
If you have already accomplished these tasks as a result of your recent workplace or training experiences you may wish to proceed to the Comprehensive Assessment Activity at the end of this chapter to assess your skills in these areas.

## 7.1    INTRODUCTION

Generally shareholders invest in companies to obtain a return on their investment in the form of dividends or an increase in the value of their investment. This chapter examines how shareholder wealth is increased through the distribution of profits and the revaluation of company assets.

## 7.2    DISTRIBUTING PROFITS

When a company earns profits it can choose to make dividend payments to its shareholders or retain the profits for future use. The distribution of profit includes:
1  transferring profit to retained profits;
2  providing for interim and final dividends; and
3  transferring profit to revenue reserves.

### Transferring profits

Once a company has determined its profit after tax it should then transfer the amount to an account called retained profits. This account is used to distribute profits to shareholders as dividends or appropriate profits to reserves. Where profits are not distributed the balance of the retained profits account represents undistributed profits and is included under shareholders' equity in the statement of financial position.

 **Illustration**

The following accounts of Solo Ltd for the year ended 30 June show:
- a profit and loss account with a profit (after tax) of $70 000 which has been transferred to the retained profits account; and
- a retained profits account with a balance at the start of the current year of $400 000 representing undistributed profits plus the transfer of the current year's profit.

**General ledger (extract) – Solo Ltd**

| Date | Particulars | Debit $ | Credit $ | Balance $ |
|---|---|---|---|---|
| **Profit and loss** | | | | |
| 30 June | Service income | | 300 000 | 300 000  Cr |
| | Operating expenses | 200 000 | | 100 000  Cr |
| | Income tax expense | 30 000 | | 70 000  Cr |
| | Retained profits | 70 000 | | Nil |
| **Retained profits** | | | | |
| 1 July | Balance | | | 100 000  Cr |
| 30 June | Profit and loss | | 70 000 | 170 000  Cr |

The general journal entry to transfer the profit (after tax) from the profit and loss account to the retained profits account would be as follows:

**General journal – Solo Ltd**

| Date | Particulars | Debit $ | Credit $ |
|---|---|---|---|
| 30 June | Profit and loss | 70 000 | |
| |     Retained profits | | 70 000 |
| | *Transfer of profit (after tax)* | | |

## Interim dividends

In return for their investment in the company, shareholders receive a distribution of profit in the form of dividends. A company's dividends policy will dictate how dividends are calculated and when they are paid.

Dividend payouts will depend on the type of share and their dividend rights and may be calculated using a number of methods including the following:

1  Stable dividend per share: This policy provides for a dividend expressed in cents per share, for example, ABC Ltd pays out a dividend of 20 cents per share on its 500 000 shares. The dividend would total $100 000 (500 000 shares × $0.20 per share).

2  Constant dividend payout ratio: This policy pays a dividend as a percentage of profits; for example, XYZ Ltd pays 60% of its profits as dividends. If profits totalled $100 000 the dividend amount would be $60 000. If share capital consisted of 200 000 shares the dividend equates to $60 000 (200 000 shares or $0.30 per share).

A company's constitution may allow a dividend to be paid during the year. This is referred to as an interim dividend as it occurs before the end of the year accounts are finalised.

When an interim dividend is made the dates associated with its declaration and payment will give rise to the following accounting entries:

1  **Dividend declaration date:** When the directors declare an interim dividend a liability is created payable to the company's shareholders as follows:

| | | |
|---|---|---|
| Interim dividend | Dr | |
| Dividends payable (or provision for dividend) | | Cr |

2  **Dividend payment date:** When the dividend is paid the liability is reduced as follows:

| | | |
|---|---|---|
| Dividends payable (or provision for dividend) | Dr | |
| Bank | | Cr |

3  **Transfer date:** At the end of the year the interim dividend account, which represents a distribution of profits to shareholders, must be transferred to the retained profits account as follows:

| | | |
|---|---|---|
| Retained profits | Dr | |
| Interim dividend | | Cr |

 **Illustration**

Solo Ltd has a share capital consisting of 500 000 ordinary shares at $1.00 each. On 10 January the directors declared that each share was to be paid a dividend of $0.08 per share – that is, $40 000 (500 000 shares @ $0.08) – and that the dividend would be paid on 1 March.

The entries to record the declaration and the payment of this interim dividend would be as follows:

**General journal**

| Date | Particulars | Debit | Credit |
|---|---|---|---|
| | | $ | $ |
| 10 Jan | Interim dividend | 40 000 | |
| | Dividends payable | | 40 000 |
| | *Declaration of interim dividend* | | |
| 1 Mar | Dividends payable | 40 000 | |
| | Bank | | 40 000 |
| | *Payment of interim dividend* | | |

At the end of the year the interim dividend would be transferred to the retained profits account as follows:

**General journal**

| Date | Particulars | Debit | Credit |
|------|-------------|-------|--------|
| | | $ | $ |
| 30 June | Retained profits | 40 000 | |
| |     Interim dividend | | 40 000 |
| | *Transfer of interim dividend* | | |

The general ledger of Solo Ltd showing these transactions would appear as follows:

**General ledger (extract) – Solo Ltd**

| Date | Particulars | Debit | Credit | Balance |
|------|-------------|-------|--------|---------|
| | | $ | $ | $ |
| **Interim dividend** | | | | |
| 10 Jan | Dividends payable | 40 000 | | 40 000  Dr |
| 30 June | Retained profits | | 40 000 | Nil |
| **Dividends payable** | | | | |
| 10 Jan | Interim dividend | | 40 000 | 40 000  Cr |
| 1 Mar | Bank | 40 000 | | Nil |
| **Retained profits** | | | | |
| 1 July | Balance | | | 100 000  Cr |
| 30 June | Profit and loss | | 70 000 | 170 000  Cr |
| | Interim dividend | 40 000 | | 130 000  Cr |

# Final dividends

Final dividends are normally declared at the end of the company's annual reporting period when profits for the year are known.

However, unlike an interim dividend which is paid in the year, a final dividend may need to be approved by shareholders at the company's annual general meeting (AGM) which is held in the following accounting period.

Hence the accounting treatment for the declaration of a final dividend in the year in which it is declared will include the following:

1 **Dividend declaration date:** When the directors declare a final dividend a liability is created payable to the company's shareholders as follows:

    Final dividend          Dr

        Dividends payable (or provision for dividend)          Cr

2 **Transfer date:** The final dividend account, which represents a distribution of profits to shareholders, must be transferred to the retained profits account as follows:

    Retained profits          Dr

        Final dividend          Cr

3 **Dividend payment date:** In the following year after the AGM of shareholders has accepted the dividend, the entry to record the payment is as follows:

Dividends payable (or provision for dividend)     Dr

    Bank               Cr

## Illustration

On 20 June the directors of Solo Ltd declared a final dividend of $50 000.

The entries to record the declaration and the distribution of this final dividend would be as follows:

### General journal

| Date | Particulars | Debit | Credit |
|------|-------------|-------|--------|
|  |  | $ | $ |
| 20 June | Final dividend | 50 000 |  |
|  |    Dividends payable |  | 50 000 |
|  | *Declaration of interim dividend* |  |  |
| 30 June | Retained profits | 50 000 |  |
|  |    Final dividend |  | 50 000 |
|  | *Transfer of final dividend* |  |  |

The general ledger of Solo Ltd showing these transactions would appear as follows:

### General ledger (extract) – Solo Ltd

| Date | Particulars | Debit | Credit | Balance |
|------|-------------|-------|--------|---------|
|  |  | $ | $ | $ |
| **Final dividend** |  |  |  |  |
| 20 June | Dividends payable | 50 000 |  | 50 000 Dr |
| 30 June | Retained profits |  | 50 000 | Nil |
| **Dividends payable** |  |  |  |  |
| 20 June | Final dividend |  | 50 000 | 50 000 Cr |
| **Retained profits** |  |  |  |  |
| 1 July | Balance |  |  | 100 000 Cr |
| 30 June | Profit and loss |  | 70 000 | 170 000 Cr |
|  | Interim dividend | 40 000 |  | 130 000 Cr |
|  | Final dividend | 50 000 |  | 80 000 Cr |

The dividends payable account at the end of the financial year would be included as a current liability in the statement of financial position.

### Solo Ltd
### Statement of financial position
### at 30 June (extract)

| Liabilities | $ |
|-------------|---|
|    Current liability: dividends payable | 50 000 |

## Question 7.1

Sharp Ltd's general ledger accounts at 30 June appear in the workbook. You are required to prepare the accounts at 30 June taking into consideration the following transactions:

1   An interim dividend of $32 000 was declared on 31 December and paid on 1 February.
2   A final dividend of $16 000 is to be provided on 30 June and will be paid on 1 September after the AGM.

## Question 7.2

Live Ltd has provided the following information for the year ended 30 June. You are required to:

a   prepare general journal entries arising from the information; and
b   complete the retained profits account after recording the transactions.

• The company has reported a profit of $76 000 for the year.
• An interim dividend of $16 000 was declared on 31 March and paid on 1 May.
• The directors have declared a final dividend on 28 June of $0.06 per share on all fully paid shares. The accounts show the following in relation to share capital.

| Ordinary shares (@ $1.00 each) | $1 000 000 | |
| Less calls in arrears (@ $0.50 each) | $50 000 | $950 000 |

## Revenue reserves

In addition to using profits to make dividend payments, companies may also transfer profits to reserve accounts thereby setting profits aside for future use. These reserves are classified as 'revenue reserves'; that is, profit (revenue) has been transferred.

A revenue reserve may be established for a specific purpose such as a dividend reserve which sets current profits aside to provide for future dividends in years when profits are low. Retained profits can also be transferred to a general reserve that has not been set up for any specific purpose.

When revenue reserves are decreased amounts are transferred back to the retained profits account for appropriation to shareholders as dividends.

Balances in revenue reserve accounts and the retained profits account are classified as shareholders' equity and are included with share capital in the statement of financial position.

## Illustration

On 30 June, the directors of Solo Ltd resolved to:
• create a dividend reserve of $20 000 from existing profits; and
• reduce the existing general reserve from $30 000 to $25 000.
The following entries would be required to record the directors' resolutions.

**General journal**

| Date | Particulars | Debit | Credit |
|---|---|---|---|
| | | $ | $ |
| 30 June | Retained profits | 20 000 | |
| | Dividend reserve | | 20 000 |
| | Creation of a dividend reserve | | |
| | General reserve | 5 000 | |
| | Retained profits | | 5 000 |
| | Reduction in general reserve | | |

These revenue reserve transfers would be posted to the general ledger as follows:

**General ledger (extract) – Solo Ltd**

| Date | Particulars | Debit $ | Credit $ | Balance $ | |
|------|------------|---------|----------|-----------|---|
| **General reserve** | | | | | |
| 1 July | Balance | | | 30 000 | Cr |
| 30 June | Retained profits | 5 000 | | 25 000 | Cr |
| **Dividend reserve** | | | | | |
| 30 June | Retained profits | | 20 000 | 20 000 | Cr |
| **Retained profits** | | | | | |
| 1 July | Balance | | | 100 000 | Cr |
| 30 June | Profit and loss | | 70 000 | 170 000 | Cr |
| | Interim dividend | 40 000 | | 130 000 | Cr |
| | Final dividend | 50 000 | | 80 000 | Cr |
| | Dividend reserve | 20 000 | | 60 000 | Cr |
| | General reserve | | 5 000 | 65 000 | Cr |

As Solo Ltd has a share capital of 500 000 $1.00 ordinary shares, the company's statement of financial position would show the following for shareholders' equity.

**Solo Ltd**
**Statement of financial position**
**at 30 June (extract)**

| Shareholders' equity | $ | $ |
|----------------------|---|---|
| Share capital | | |
| Ordinary shares (500 000 shares @ $1.00 each) | | 500 000 |
| Reserves | | |
| General reserve | 25 000 | |
| Dividend reserve | 20 000 | |
| Retained profits | 65 000 | 110 000 |
| Total shareholders' equity | | 610 000 |

## Question 7.3

From the following information relating to Jumbuck Ltd you are required to prepare the retained profits account for the year ended 30 June.

- Retained profits account balance at start of period: $50 000 Cr.
- Profit and loss account closing balance: $850 000 Cr.
- An interim dividend of $250 000 was paid during the year.
- A final dividend of $500 000 has been declared at 30 June.
- The dividend reserve is to be increased from $300 000 to $400 000.
- The general reserve is to be reduced by $50 000.

## Question 7.4

From the following information provided by Rocket Ltd for the year ended 30 June you are required to:

a  prepare the journal entries to finalise the profit and loss account and the retained profits account; and

b  prepare the retained profits account for the year.

**Rocket Ltd**
**Trial balance at 30 June (extract)**

| Account name | Debit | Credit |
|---|---|---|
| | $ | $ |
| Share capital – ordinary shares (200 000 shares) | | 400 000 |
| Calls in arrears – ordinary shares (10 000 shares) | 5 000 | |
| Dividend reserve | | 18 000 |
| General reserve | | 45 000 |
| Interim dividend | 50 000 | |
| Profit and loss (after income tax) | | 150 000 |
| Retained profits (1 July) | | 20 000 |

**Additional information at 30 June**

- The general reserve is to be reduced by $25 000.
- The dividend reserve is to be increased by $20 000.
- All fully paid shares are to receive a final dividend of $0.50 per share. Shareholders who have not paid for the call are not to receive the dividend.

# Question 7.5

From the following information relating to the accounts of Yonder Ltd you are required to prepare:

**a** the profit and loss account for the year ended 30 June;

**b** the retained profits account for the year ended 30 June; and

**c** the shareholders' equity section of the statement of financial position at 30 June.

**Yonder Ltd**
**Trial balance at 30 June**

| Account name | Debit | Credit |
|---|---|---|
| | $ | $ |
| Sales | | 480 000 |
| Cost of sales | 260 000 | |
| Operating expenses | 115 000 | |
| Income tax expense | 30 000 | |
| Bank | 190 000 | |
| Accounts payable | | 10 000 |
| Accounts receivable | 100 000 | |
| Buildings | 280 000 | |
| Income tax payable | | 15 000 |
| Retained profits (1 July) | | 30 000 |
| Interim dividend | 30 000 | |
| General reserve | | 40 000 |
| Share capital – ordinary shares (@ $1.00 each) | | 550 000 |
| Stock | 120 000 | |
| | 1 125 000 | 1 125 000 |

**Additional information**

- The income tax rate is 30%.
- A final dividend of 6% of ordinary shares is to be declared but not paid until the AGM.
- The general reserve is to be decreased to $25 000.
- A dividend reserve is to be created at $50 000.

## 7.3   REVALUATION OF PROPERTY, PLANT AND EQUIPMENT

Accounting standard AASB116: Property, Plant and Equipment requires property, plant and equipment to be measured at their purchase price (cost of purchase).

After the initial recording of the cost price of the asset, a company is then required to value the asset using either the cost price or the revaluation model.

Where the cost model is adopted the asset is valued at its cost price less depreciation. The cost price less accumulated depreciation is called the 'carrying amount' of the asset.

If a company chooses to adopt the revaluation model the asset must be valued at its fair value, commonly referred to as its 'market value', and revaluations shall be carried out regularly to ensure that the asset's carrying cost does not differ significantly from its fair value.

In the case of a revaluation of a building AASB116 requires any accumulated depreciation to be offset against the asset before the asset is revalued.

### Increasing an asset's value

When an asset's carrying amount is increased in value AASB116 requires a 'revaluation reserve' to be created. The revaluation reserve is classified as a 'capital reserve' as its value represents an increase in shareholder wealth and is supported by assets that have a higher value.

Unlike revenue reserves which are used to pay dividends resulting from profits, the capital reserve cannot be used to pay cash dividends but can be used to distribute bonus shares to shareholders.

**Illustration**

On 30 June Solo Ltd directors determined that land and buildings were being carried in the accounts below their market values, as shown in the following table, and decided to revalue both assets.

| | | Carrying cost | Fair value |
|---|---|---|---|
| Land | | $800 000 | $1 000 000 |
| Buildings | $450 000 | | |
| Less accumulated depreciation on buildings | $50 000 | $400 000 | $500 000 |

The journal entries to revalue each asset would be as follows:

**General journal**

| Date | Particulars | Debit | Credit |
|---|---|---|---|
| | | $ | $ |
| 30 June | Land | 200 000 | |
| | Asset revaluation reserve | | 200 000 |
| | *Revalued land upwards to its fair value* | | |
| | Accumulated depreciation – buildings | 50 000 | |
| | Buildings | | 50 000 |
| | *Offset accumulated depreciation during building revaluation* | | |
| | Building | 100 000 | |
| | Asset revaluation reserve | | 100 000 |
| | *Revalued land upwards to its fair value* | | |

These entries would be recorded in the accounts as follows:

**General ledger (extract) – Solo Ltd**

| Date | Particulars | Debit $ | Credit $ | Balance $ |
|---|---|---|---|---|
| **Land** | | | | |
| 30 June | Balance | | | 800 000 Dr |
| | Asset revaluation reserve | 200 000 | | 1 000 000 Dr |
| **Buildings** | | | | |
| 30 June | Balance | | | 450 000 Dr |
| | Accumulated depreciation | | 50 000 | 400 000 Dr |
| | Asset revaluation reserve | 100 000 | | 500 000 Dr |
| **Accumulated depreciation – buildings** | | | | |
| 30 June | Balance | | | 50 000 Cr |
| | Buildings | 50 000 | | Nil |
| **Asset revaluation reserve** | | | | |
| 30 June | Land | | 200 000 | 200 000 Cr |
| | Buildings | | 100 000 | 300 000 Cr |

An extract of the company's statement of financial position would show these accounts as follows:

**Solo Ltd**
**Statement of financial position**
**at 30 June (extract)**

| Shareholders' equity | $ | $ |
|---|---|---|
| Share capital | | |
| Ordinary shares (500 000 shares @ $1.00 each) | | 500 000 |
| Reserves | | |
| General reserve | 25 000 | |
| Dividend reserve | 20 000 | |
| Retained profits | 65 000 | |
| Asset revaluation reserve | 300 000 | 410 000 |
| Total shareholders' equity | | 910 000 |
| Assets | | |
| Land (at independent valuation) | 1 000 000 | |
| Buildings (at independent valuation) | 500 000 | 1 500 000 |

## Question 7.6

Storm Ltd has provided the following trial balance extract at 30 June.

**Storm Ltd**
**Trial balance (extract) at 30 June**

| Account name | Debit | Credit |
|---|---|---|
| | $ | $ |
| Buildings | 1 200 000 | |
| Accumulated depreciation – buildings | | 400 000 |
| Land | 3 000 000 | |

Using this information you are required to prepare journal entries to revalue buildings at $1 000 000 and land at $3 200 000.

## Question 7.7

Using the following information relating to Bronco Ltd's land and buildings you are required to prepare the accounts showing the revaluation of assets from their carrying costs to their fair values at 30 June.

| | Carrying cost | | Fair value |
|---|---|---|---|
| Buildings | $900 000 | | |
| Less accumulated depreciation on buildings | $250 000 | $650 000 | $750 000 |
| Land | | $680 000 | $800 000 |

## Decreasing an asset's value

Where the revaluation model is used and the fair market value of property, plant and equipment fall below their carrying costs the assets will need to be devalued. A downward revaluation can be brought about in the following ways:

a where an asset has been previously revalued upwards and an asset revaluation reserve created, the devaluation shall be debited to the reserve account to reverse the revaluation; and/or

b where an asset has not been previously revalued the decrease in value shall be recorded as an expense and recorded in the calculation of profit.

## Illustration

The directors of Yahoo Ltd on 30 June decided to devalue their buildings to $550 000. In the previous year the value of the buildings had been increased from $600 000 to $700 000.
   The general journal entries to record this decrement would be as follows:

**General journal**

| Date | Particulars | Debit | Credit |
|---|---|---|---|
| | | $ | $ |
| 30 June | Asset revaluation reserve | 100 000 | |
| | Impairment loss – buildings | 50 000 | |
| | Buildings | | 350 000 |
| | *Downward revaluation of buildings* | | |
| | Profit and loss | 50 000 | |
| | Impairment loss – buildings | | 50 000 |
| | *Transfer account balance* | | |

These entries would be recorded in the accounts as follows:

**General ledger (extract) – Yahoo Ltd**

| Date | Particulars | Debit | Credit | Balance |
|------|-------------|-------|--------|---------|
| | | $ | $ | $ |
| **Buildings** | | | | |
| 30 June | Balance | | | 700 000  Dr |
| | Asset revaluation reserve | | 100 000 | 600 000  Dr |
| | Impairment loss – buildings | | 50 000 | 550 000  Dr |
| **Asset revaluation reserve** | | | | |
| 30 June | Balance | | | 100 000  Cr |
| | Buildings | 100 000 | | Nil |
| **Impairment loss – buildings** | | | | |
| 30 June | Buildings | 50 000 | | 50 000  Dr |
| | Profit and loss | | 50 000 | Nil |
| **Profit and loss** | | | | |
| 30 June | Impairment loss – buildings | 50 000 | | 50 000  Dr |

## Question 7.8

Ru Ltd revalues its land and buildings at market value every year. The carrying costs of land and buildings and the asset revaluation reserve arising from previous revaluations are shown in the following trial balance extract.

**Ru Ltd**
**Trial balance (extract) at 30 June**

| Account name | Debit | Credit |
|--------------|-------|--------|
| | $ | $ |
| Asset revaluation reserve | | 200 000 |
| Buildings (at independent valuation) | 600 000 | |
| Land (at independent valuation) | 750 000 | |

Using this information you are required to prepare journal entries to:
a   revalue buildings at $500 000 (note: buildings have an original cost price of $540 000); and
b   revalue land at $800 000.

## 7.4   ISSUING BONUS SHARES

An asset revaluation reserve reflects increased shareholder wealth as the entity has increased the value of its assets. To return this wealth to existing shareholders the company constitution may permit the directors to issue free shares, commonly referred to as 'bonus shares', to existing shareholders on the basis of the number of shares each shareholder currently holds.

A bonus share issue has the following advantages:
• existing shareholder wealth increases as shareholders receive additional shares at no cost; and
• company liquidity is not affected as shares are issued from the asset revaluation reserve.

The procedure for declaring and issuing a bonus share is as follows:

1   **Dividend declaration date:** When the directors declare a bonus share dividend a liability is created payable to the company's shareholders as follows:

| | |
|---|---|
| Bonus share dividend | Dr |
| Dividends payable (or provision for dividend) | Cr |

2   **Transfer date:** As the bonus share dividend has been sourced from the asset revaluation reserve it must be transferred to the reserve account as follows:

| | |
|---|---|
| Asset revaluation reserve | Dr |
| Bonus share dividend | Cr |

3   **Dividend payment date:** When the shares are issued the liability is reduced and share capital increases as follows:

| | |
|---|---|
| Dividends payable (or provision for dividend) | Dr |
| Share capital – ordinary shares | Cr |

## Illustration

Solo Ltd's statement of financial position extract is shown below:

**Solo Ltd**
**Statement of financial position**
**at 30 June (extract)**

| Shareholders' equity | $ | $ |
|---|---|---|
| Share capital | | |
| Ordinary shares (500 000 shares @ $1.00 each) | | 500 000 |
| Reserves | | |
| General reserve | 25 000 | |
| Dividend reserve | 20 000 | |
| Retained profits | 65 000 | |
| Asset revaluation reserve | 300 000 | 410 000 |
| Total shareholders' equity | | 910 000 |

The accounts reveal an asset revaluation reserve of $300 000 and 500 000 ordinary shares at $1.00 each. On 30 June the directors decided to issue one bonus share for every two shares held; that is, a one-for-four bonus share issue. The dividend will be presented to the AGM on 30 September for shareholder ratification.

To calculate the bonus share amount the following formula can be applied:

$$\text{Bonus share dividend} = \frac{\text{No. of existing shares}}{\text{No. of shares held}} \times \text{Share price}$$

Therefore:

$$\text{Bonus share dividend} = \frac{500\ 000 \text{ shares}}{4 \text{ shares held}} \times \$1.00$$

Bonus share dividend = $125 000

In the year ended 30 June the bonus share would be recorded as follows:

### General journal

| Date | Particulars | Debit | Credit |
|---|---|---|---|
| | | $ | $ |
| 1 June | Bonus share dividend | 125 000 | |
| |     Dividends payable | | 125 000 |
| | *Declaration of bonus share dividend* | | |
| 30 June | Asset revaluation reserve | 125 000 | |
| |     Bonus dividend | | 125 000 |
| | *Allocation of bonus share dividend* | | |

If the bonus share is ratified at the AGM the journal entry issuing the shares would be as follows:

### General journal

| Date | Particulars | Debit | Credit |
|---|---|---|---|
| | | $ | $ |
| 30 Sept | Dividends payable | 125 000 | |
| |     Ordinary shares | | 125 000 |
| | *Issue of bonus share dividend* | | |

The general ledger after the bonus share acceptance would appear as follows:

### General ledger (extract) – Solo Ltd

| Date | Particulars | Debit $ | Credit $ | Balance $ |
|---|---|---|---|---|
| **Bonus share dividend** | | | | |
| 30 June | Dividends payable | 125 000 | | 125 000 Dr |
| | Asset revaluation reserve | | 125 000 | Nil |
| **Dividends payable** | | | | |
| 30 June | Bonus share dividend | | 125 000 | 125 000 Cr |
| 30 Sep | Share capital – ordinary shares | 125 000 | | Nil |
| **Asset revaluation reserve** | | | | |
| 30 June | Balance | | | 300 000 Cr |
| | Bonus share dividend | 125 000 | | 175 000 Cr |
| **Share capital – ordinary shares** | | | | |
| 30 June | Balance | | | 500 000 Cr |
| 30 Sep | Dividends payable | | 125 000 | 625 000 Cr |

Solo Ltd's statement of financial position extract after the bonus share would be as follows:

### Solo Ltd
### Statement of financial position
### at 30 September (extract)

| Shareholders' equity | $ | $ |
|---|---|---|
| Share capital | | |
|   Ordinary shares (625 000 shares @ $1.00 each) | | 625 000 |
|   General reserve | 25 000 | |
|   Dividend reserve | 20 000 | |
|   Retained profits | 65 000 | |
|   Asset revaluation reserve | 175 000 | 285 000 |
| Total shareholders' equity | | 910 000 |

# Question 7.9

Blight Ltd's shareholders' equity is shown in the following extract of its statement of financial position:

**Blight Ltd**
**Statement of financial position**
**at 1 June (extract)**

| Shareholders' equity | $ | $ |
|---|---|---|
| Share capital | | |
|    Ordinary shares (500 000 shares @ $2.00 each) | | 1 000 000 |
| Reserves | | |
|    Retained profits | 100 000 | |
|    Asset revaluation reserve | 200 000 | 300 000 |
| Total shareholders' equity | | 1 300 000 |

On 20 June the directors decided to issue bonus shares at the rate of one for every five shares held, payable after the AGM on 20 September.

You are required to:

a  prepare the journal entries for the year ended 30 June to declare and account for the bonus share dividend;

b  prepare the journal entry at 20 September after shareholders accept the dividend; and

c  show the shareholders' equity section of the statement of financial position after the AGM.

# Question 7.10

From the following trial balance of Marks Ltd you are required to:

a  prepare journal entries to account for the directors recommendations at 30 June; and

b  prepare a statement of financial position at 30 June.

**Trial balance at 30 June**

| Account name | Debit | Credit |
|---|---|---|
| | $ | $ |
| Buildings | 1 000 000 | |
| Accumulated depreciation – buildings | | 300 000 |
| Share capital – 400 000 ordinary shares | | 600 000 |
| Asset revaluation reserve | | 100 000 |

**Directors' recommendations on 30 June**

1  Revalue land and buildings at the fair value of $800 000.

2  Declare a bonus shares at the rate of one for every four shares held. This will be paid after AGM approval in August.

# Comprehensive Assessment Activity

The following information has been provided by Jonah Ltd for the year ended 30 June.

**Jonah Ltd**
**Trial balance at 30 June (extract)**

| Account name | Debit | Credit |
|---|---|---|
| | $ | $ |
| Buildings (at valuation) | 1 200 000 | |
| Accumulated depreciation – buildings | | 500 000 |
| Share capital – ordinary shares (250 000 shares) | | 1 000 000 |
| Calls in arrears – ordinary shares (20 000 shares) | 40 000 | |
| Asset revaluation reserve | | 100 000 |
| Dividend reserve | | 60 000 |
| Interim dividend | 100 000 | |
| Profit and loss (after income tax) | | 120 000 |
| Retained profits (1 July) | | 30 000 |

Using this information you are required to:
a prepare journal entries to record the transactions listed;
b prepare the retained profits account for the year; and
c prepare the liabilities and shareholders' equity sections of the statement of financial position at 30 June.

## Transactions to be recorded

1 A final dividend of $0.30 per share is to be declared at 30 June, payable to all shareholders. The dividend will be paid after ratification at the AGM in September.
2 The dividend reserve is to be reduced to $10 000.
3 A general reserve of $20 000 is to be created.
4 Buildings are to be revalued at $800 000.
5 A bonus share dividend of one share for every five fully paid shares is to be declared. The dividend will be paid after ratification at the AGM in September.

# Assessment Checklist

Complete the following checklist to identify if you consider yourself capable of being assessed against each of the following outcomes.

| I can: | Chapter reference | Check ✓ |
|---|---|---|
| explain the purpose of the retained profits account | 7.2 | |
| transfer profit to retained profits | 7.2 | |
| account for payment of interim dividends to shareholders | 7.2 | |
| account for payment of final dividends to shareholders | 72 | |
| account for transfer of profits to and from revenue reserves | 7.2 | |
| account for the revaluation of property, plant and equipment | 7.3 | |
| account for the issue of bonus shares | 7.4 | |

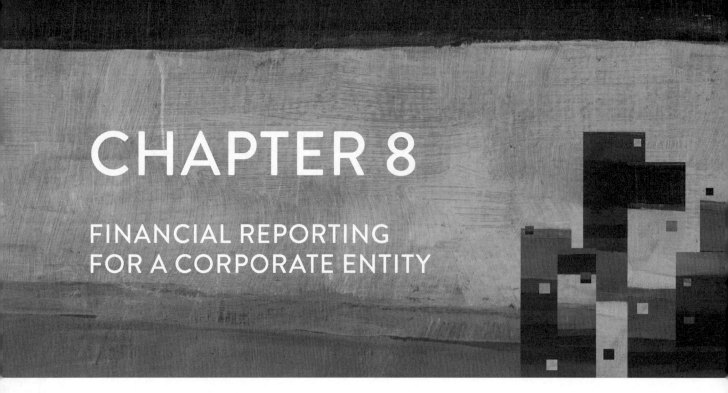

# CHAPTER 8

## FINANCIAL REPORTING FOR A CORPORATE ENTITY

## WHAT YOU WILL LEARN IN THIS CHAPTER

Upon satisfactory completion of this chapter you should be able to:
- list the financial reporting responsibilities of company directors; and
- prepare a complete set of financial statements that comply with the Australian Accounting Standards.

**Are you already competent at these tasks?**
If you have already accomplished these tasks as a result of your recent workplace or training experiences you may wish to proceed to the Comprehensive Assessment Activity at the end of this chapter to assess your skills in these areas.

# 8.1 INTRODUCTION

The *Corporations Act 2001* (Cwlth) requires directors to present to an annual general meeting of shareholders financial statements that give a true and fair view. These financial statements and their disclosure notes are prescribed in the accounting standards.

This chapter examines the preparation of the income statement, statement of changes in equity and the statement of financial position for a corporate entity that meet the requirements of the Australian Accounting Standards.

# 8.2 FINANCIAL REPORTING REQUIREMENTS

The requirement for an entity to prepare financial reports is influenced by the entity's need to report to dependent users and on its corporate identity.

Statement of Accounting Concepts 1 (SAC1) requires an entity (with users who are dependent on financial information provided by the entity to assist them in making decisions) to prepare general-purpose financial statements in accordance with the Accounting Standards.

General-purpose financial statements are designed to provide information for dependent users by complying with the minimum presentation and disclosure requirements required by the accounting standards.

In addition, the *Corporations Act 2001* requires corporate entities to prepare financial reports that consist of:
- the financial statements;
- the notes to the financial statements (comprising regulatory disclosures, notes required by the accounting standards and other information necessary to give a true and fair view); and
- the directors' declaration in respect of the statements and notes (stating that the statements comply with the accounting standards, that they give a true and fair view, and that the company can pay its debts when they become due and payable).

The Corporations Act requires corporate entities to:
- hold an AGM within four months after the end of the financial year and provide shareholders with a copy of the financial reports at least 21 days before the meeting is held; and
- lodge the financial reports with ASIC within four months after the end of the financial year.

Consequently Australian companies are required to prepare financial statements that comply with the Australian Accounting Standards and provide the statements to dependent users at an AGM conducted in accordance with the Corporations Act.

These financial reporting requirements apply to public companies and large private companies. Small proprietary companies only need to issue financial reports if shareholders with 5% of the share capital require a report or ASIC directs the company to issue financial reports.

## Financial reporting and the accounting standards

Accounting Standards AASB101: Presentation of Financial Statements and AASB134: Interim Financial Reporting prescribe the content and presentation of general-purpose financial statements (referred to as 'financial statements'). These standards require reporting entities to present annual financial statements consisting of:
- a statement of profit and loss and other comprehensive income;
- a statement of changes in equity;
- a statement of financial position;
- a statement of cash flows; and
- notes to the accounts describing accounting policies on which the financial statements are based, information required by the accounting standards and other information that will assist dependent users in understanding the financial statements.

The accounting and auditing standards also require reporting entities to state in the notes:
- whether the financial reports have been prepared in accordance with the Australian Accounting Standards; and
- if the statements presented are general-purpose financial reports or special-purpose financial reports.

Where an entity prepares financial statements in accordance with the accounting standards the statements are referred to as general-purpose financial statements. These statements provide dependent users with the minimum presentation and disclosure requirements required by the accounting standards.

In addition to preparing general-purpose financial statements, entities may be required to prepare financial statements that provide more information than that disclosed in general-purpose financial statements. These statements, referred to as specific-purpose financial statements, provide specific interested users with specific information required by the user. These users may be lenders of finance such as banks, where the entity is dependent on the lender for finance and must provide specific financial information requested by the lender to be extended the finance.

# 8.3   STATEMENT OF PROFIT AND LOSS AND OTHER COMPREHENSIVE INCOME

Accounting Standard AASB101: Presentation of Financial Statements sets out the reporting and disclosure requirements of the statement of profit and loss and other comprehensive income (commonly referred to as a 'profit and loss statement').

This is a two-part statement that the standard permits to be presented as a single statement or as two separate statements.

The first part of the statement includes information relating to profit and loss with the standard requiring the following amounts to be reported as line items on the statement:

- revenue;
- finance costs; and
- tax expense.

The second part of the statement relates to other 'comprehensive' income attributable to shareholders including:

- income derived from associated investments and joint ventures accounted for using the equity method of accounting; and
- other items required by the accounting standards such as AASB116: Property, Plant and Equipment which requires increases in asset values resulting in an increase in a reserve (asset revaluation reserve account) to be reported as 'other comprehensive income'.

Whilst AASB101 does not specify a specific format for the presentation of the statement of profit and loss and other comprehensive income, it does state that expenses should be classified as to their *nature* or *function* so as to provide information that is reliable and more relevant to users of the statement.

AASB101 also requires the following information to be disclosed:

- the name of the reporting entity;
- whether the financial statements are of the individual entity or a group of entities;
- the date of the end of the reporting period;
- the presentation currency;
- comparison amounts for the previous period; and
- the level of rounding used in presenting amounts in the financial statements.

Whilst AASB101 encourages the use of a prescribed format these examples are not mandatory. When presenting a financial statement a company should ensure that it meets the needs of dependent users who are not in a position to require an entity to prepare reports tailored to their particular information needs; that is, a general-purpose financial report.

## Reporting and disclosure using the functional expense analysis

When preparing the statement of profit and loss and other comprehensive income that:

a   discloses the line items required to be included on the statement; and
b   discloses additional information to be attached to the statement explaining aggregate amounts included on the statement,

a reporting entity will need to structure the statement so that it complies with AASB101 and other accounting standards.

AASB101 stipulates the following:

- the statement of profit and loss and other comprehensive income can be presented as one report;
- specific information must be presented on the face of the statement; and
- the disclosure of expenses using either the 'nature' or 'function' format is encouraged.

A suitable format for the statement of profit and loss and other comprehensive income disclosing the *functional* analysis of expenses could be presented as follows:

**Statement of profit and loss and other comprehensive income
for the year ended 30 June**

|  | $ |
|---|---|
| Revenue | XX |
| *Less* cost of sales | (XX) |
| Gross profit | XX |
| *Add* other income | XX |
| *Less* | |
| Distribution costs | (XX) |
| Administrative expenses | (XX) |
| Finance costs | (XX) |
| Other expenses | (XX) |
| Profit (before tax) | XX |
| *Less* Income tax expense | (XX) |
| Profit (after tax) | XX |
| *Add* other comprehensive income | XX |
| Profit and loss and other comprehensive income | **XX** |

## Illustration

For the year ended 30 June Challenge Ltd's accounts included the following information:

**Profit and loss account**

| Date | Particulars | Debit $ | Credit $ | Balance $ |
|---|---|---|---|---|
| 30 June | Sales | | 900 000 | 900 000 Cr |
| | Profit on sale of assets | | 50 000 | 950 000 Cr |
| | Cost of sales | 300 000 | | 650 000 Cr |
| | Loss on sale of vehicles | 5 000 | | 645 000 Cr |
| | Advertising | 60 000 | | 585 000 Cr |
| | Wages and employee benefits | 120 000 | | 465 000 Cr |
| | Depreciation | 80 000 | | 385 000 Cr |
| | Rent expense | 70 000 | | 315 000 Cr |
| | Electricity and heating | 30 000 | | 285 000 Cr |
| | Auditors' remuneration | 40 000 | | 245 000 Cr |
| | Directors' remuneration | 60 000 | | 185 000 Cr |
| | Bad and doubtful debts | 20 000 | | 165 000 Cr |
| | Impairment of investments | 30 000 | | 135 000 Cr |
| | Interest expense | 20 000 | | 115 000 Cr |
| | Income tax expense | 43 500 | | 71 500 Cr |

**Additional information**

The asset revaluation reserve increased by $200 000 during the year.

An analysis of the costs by functionality allocated expenses as follows:

### Functional expense analysis

| Expense | Amount $ | Distribution $ | Administration $ | Other $ |
|---|---|---|---|---|
| Loss on sale of vehicles | 5 000 | 5 000 | | |
| Advertising | 60 000 | 60 000 | | |
| Wages and employee benefits | 120 000 | 88 000 | 32 000 | |
| Depreciation | 80 000 | 48 000 | 32 000 | |
| Rent expense | 70 000 | 42 000 | 28 000 | |
| Electricity and heating | 30 000 | 20 000 | 10 000 | |
| Auditors' remuneration | 40 000 | | | 40 000 |
| Directors' remuneration | 60 000 | | | 60 000 |
| Bad and doubtful debts | 20 000 | | | 20 000 |
| Impairment of assets | 30 000 | | | 30 000 |
| **Total functional expenses** | 515 000 | 263 000 | 102 000 | 150 000 |

This information could be reported on the statement as follows:

### Challenge Ltd
### Statement of profit and loss and other comprehensive income
### for the year ended 30 June

| | $ |
|---|---|
| Revenue | 900 000 |
| *Less* cost of sales | (300 000) |
| Gross profit | 600 000 |
| *Add* other income | 50 000 |
| *Less* | |
| Distribution costs | (263 000) |
| Administrative expenses | (102 000) |
| Finance costs | (20 000) |
| Other expenses | (150 000) |
| Profit (before tax) | 115 000 |
| *Less* income tax expense | (43 500) |
| Profit (after tax) | 71 500 |
| *Add* other comprehensive income | 200 000 |
| **Profit and loss and other comprehensive income** | 271 500 |

## Question 8.1

Sapphire Ltd has provided the following profit related information for the year ended 30 June.

You are required to prepare the statement of profit and loss and comprehensive income for the year that complies with AASB101: Presentation of Financial Statements based on the **functional** method of reporting expenses.

| | Total $ | Functional expense analysis | | |
| --- | --- | --- | --- | --- |
| | | Distribution $ | Administration $ | Other $ |
| **Revenues** | | | | |
| Sales | 1 200 000 | | | |
| Dividends received | 55 000 | | | |
| **Expenses** | | | | |
| Non-functional expenses | | | | |
| Cost of sales | 480 000 | | | |
| Interest expense | 40 000 | | | |
| Income tax expense | 57 000 | | | |
| **Functional expenses** | | | | |
| Audit expenses | 50 000 | | | 50 000 |
| Depreciation expense | 70 000 | 35 000 | 35 000 | |
| Depreciation – buildings | 30 000 | 21 000 | 9 000 | |
| Directors' fees | 60 000 | | | 60 000 |
| Discount expense | 5 000 | | | 5 000 |
| Employee benefits | 10 000 | 6 000 | 4 000 | |
| Lease expenses | 50 000 | 20 000 | 30 000 | |
| Marketing costs | 90 000 | 90 000 | | |
| Sales commissions | 10 000 | 10 000 | | |
| Utility costs | 40 000 | 28 000 | 12 000 | |
| Wages and salaries | 160 000 | 96 000 | 64 000 | |
| **Net profit** | 103 000 | | | |

*Additional information*

The asset revaluation reserve increased by $100 000 during the year.

## Question 8.2

From the following information provided by Ruby Ltd you are required to prepare the statement of profit and loss and comprehensive income for the year that complies with AASB101: Presentation of Financial Statements based on the **functional** method of reporting expenses.

**Profit and loss**

| Date | Details | Debit | Credit | Balance |
|---|---|---|---|---|
| 30 June | | $ | $ | $ |
| | Sales | | 1 500 000 | 1 500 000 Cr |
| | Cost of sales | 750 000 | | 750 000 Cr |
| | Interest received | | 25 000 | 775 000 Cr |
| | Selling costs | 120 000 | | 655 000 Cr |
| | Sales commissions | 10 000 | | 645 000 Cr |
| | Depreciation | 90 000 | | 555 000 Cr |
| | Lease expenses | 40 000 | | 515 000 Cr |
| | Utility expenses | 40 000 | | 475 000 Cr |
| | Wages and employee entitlements | 200 000 | | 275 000 Cr |
| | Interest expense | 30 000 | | 245 000 Cr |
| | Audit expenses | 20 000 | | 225 000 Cr |
| | Entertainment expenses | 30 000 | | 195 000 Cr |
| | Directors' fees | 25 000 | | 170 000 Cr |
| | Bad debts | 6 000 | | 164 000 Cr |
| | Income tax expense | 58 200 | | 105 800 Cr |

**Additional information**

- Costs associated with distribution and administration functions are allocated equally between the two functions. These costs include depreciation, lease expenses, utility expenses and employee entitlements.
- The asset revaluation reserve increased by $250 000 during the year.

## Reporting using the nature of expense analysis

An alternative to the disclosure of expenses by function is the disclosure of expenses by **nature**. A suitable format for the statement of profit and loss and other comprehensive income that complies with the AASB101 line item disclosures reporting expenses by **nature** could be presented as follows:

**Statement of profit and loss and other comprehensive income for year ended 30 June**

| | $ |
|---|---|
| Revenue | XX |
| *Add* other income | XX |
| Total income | XX |
| *Less* expenses | |
| Changes in inventories | (XX) |
| Cost of materials and consumables used | (XX) |
| Employee benefits expense | (XX) |
| Depreciation and asset impairments expense | (XX) |
| Financial costs | (XX) |
| Other expenses | (XX) |
| Total expenses | (XX) |
| Profit before tax | XX |
| *Less* income tax expense | (XX) |
| Profit (after tax) | XX |
| *Add* other comprehensive income | XX |
| Profit and loss and other comprehensive income | XX |

## Illustration

For the year ended 30 June Challenge Ltd's accounts included the following information:

### Profit and loss account

| Date | Particulars | Debit $ | Credit $ | Balance $ |
|---|---|---|---|---|
| 30 June | Sales | | 900 000 | 900 000 Cr |
| | Profit on sale of assets | | 50 000 | 950 000 Cr |
| | Cost of sales | 300 000 | | 650 000 Cr |
| | Loss on sale of vehicles | 5 000 | | 645 000 Cr |
| | Advertising | 60 000 | | 585 000 Cr |
| | Wages and employee benefits | 120 000 | | 465 000 Cr |
| | Depreciation | 80 000 | | 385 000 Cr |
| | Rent expense | 70 000 | | 315 000 Cr |
| | Electricity and heating | 30 000 | | 285 000 Cr |
| | Auditors' remuneration | 40 000 | | 245 000 Cr |
| | Directors' remuneration | 60 000 | | 185 000 Cr |
| | Bad and doubtful debts | 20 000 | | 165 000 Cr |
| | Impairment of investments | 30 000 | | 135 000 Cr |
| | Interest expense | 20 000 | | 115 000 Cr |
| | Income tax expense | 43 500 | | 71 500 Cr |

### Additional information

• The stock on hand account includes the following:

### Stock on hand account

| Date | Particulars | Debit $ | Credit $ | Balance $ |
|---|---|---|---|---|
| 1 June | Balance | | | 40 000 Dr |
| 30 June | Purchases of materials | 310 000 | | 350 000 Dr |
| | Cost of sales | | 300 000 | 50 000 Dr |

• The asset revaluation reserve increased by $200 000 during the year.

This financial statement disclosing expenses by **nature** and notes of disclosure would be presented as follows:

### Challenge Ltd
### Statement of profit and loss and other comprehensive income
### for year ended 30 June

| | $ |
|---|---|
| Revenue | 900 000 |
| *Add* other income | 50 000 |
| Total income | 950 000 |
| *Less* expenses | |
| Changes in inventories | 10 000 |
| Cost of materials and consumables used | (310 000) |
| Employee benefits expense | (120 000) |
| Depreciation and asset impairments expense | (115 000) |
| Finance costs | (20 000) |
| Other expenses | (280 000) |
| Total expenses | 835 000 |
| Profit before tax | 115 000 |
| *Less* income tax expense | (43 500) |
| Profit (after tax) | 71 500 |
| *Add* other comprehensive income | 200 000 |
| Profit and loss and other comprehensive income | 271 500 |

## Question 8.3

Sapphire Ltd has provided the following profit related information for the year ended 30 June.

You are required to prepare the statement of profit and loss and comprehensive income for the year that complies with AASB101: Presentation of Financial Statements, reporting expenses by their **nature**.

| | $ | $ |
|---|---:|---:|
| **Revenues** | | |
| Sales | 1 200 000 | |
| Less cost of sales (refer below) | 480 000 | |
| **Gross profit** | | 720 000 |
| Add dividends received | | 55 000 |
| | | 775 000 |
| **Less expenses** | | |
| Wages and salaries | 160 000 | |
| Sales commissions | 10 000 | |
| Employee benefits | 10 000 | |
| Depreciation expense | 70 000 | |
| Depreciation – buildings | 30 000 | |
| Interest expense | 40 000 | |
| Audit expenses | 50 000 | |
| Directors' fees | 60 000 | |
| Discount expense | 5 000 | |
| Lease expenses | 50 000 | |
| Marketing costs | 90 000 | |
| Utility costs | 40 000 | |
| Income tax expense | 57 000 | 672 000 |
| Net profit | | 103 000 |

### Additional information

#### Stock on hand account

| Date | Particulars | Debit $ | Credit $ | Balance $ |
|---|---|---:|---:|---|
| 1 June | Balance | | | 85 000  Dr |
| 30 June | Purchases of materials | 495 000 | | 580 000  Dr |
| | Cost of sales | | 480 000 | 100 000  Dr |

The asset revaluation reserve increased by $100 000 during the year.

## Question 8.4

The following information for Ruby Ltd was used in question 8.2 to prepare a profit and loss statement disclosing expenses by function.

You are now required to use this information to prepare a statement of profit and loss and comprehensive income for the year that complies with AASB101: Presentation of Financial Statements, disclosing the **nature** of expenses.

**Profit and loss**

| Date | Details | Debit $ | Credit $ | Balance $ |
|------|---------|---------|----------|-----------|
| 30 June | Sales | | 1 500 000 | 1 500 000 Cr |
| | Cost of sales (refer below) | 750 000 | | 750 000 Cr |
| | Wages and employee entitlements | 200 000 | | 550 000 Cr |
| | Depreciation | 90 000 | | 460 000 Cr |
| | Interest expense | 30 000 | | 430 000 Cr |
| | Interest received | | 25 000 | 455 000 Cr |
| | Selling costs | 120 000 | | 335 000 Cr |
| | Sales commissions | 10 000 | | 325 000 Cr |
| | Lease expenses | 40 000 | | 285 000 Cr |
| | Utility expenses | 40 000 | | 245 000 Cr |
| | Audit expenses | 20 000 | | 225 000 Cr |
| | Entertainment expenses | 30 000 | | 195 000 Cr |
| | Directors' fees | 25 000 | | 170 000 Cr |
| | Bad debts | 6 000 | | 164 000 Cr |
| | Income tax expense | 58 200 | | 105 800 Cr |

*Additional information*

The stock on hand account includes the following:

**Stock on hand account**

| Date | Particulars | Debit $ | Credit $ | Balance $ |
|------|-------------|---------|----------|-----------|
| 1 June | Balance | | | 100 000 Dr |
| 30 June | Purchases of materials | 770 000 | | 870 000 Dr |
| | Cost of sales | | 750 000 | 120 000 Dr |

- The asset revaluation reserve increased by $250 000 during the year.

## Disclosure requirements

To provide users of the statement of profit and loss and other comprehensive income with more information about the line item amounts included on the statement, AASB101 requires notes of disclosure to be attached to the statement.

AASB101 also requires revenue and expense items that are considered significant or material due to their nature and amount to be disclosed separately. The decision to specifically disclose or not to disclose an item of revenue or expense may depend on the amount of the item, the effect that it has on the accounts and the regularity of the transactions that give rise to the amount.

Disclosure of material items of revenue or expense in the accounts will vary from entity to entity. Bad debts of $50 000, for example, may be considered material if the sales revenue of the business is $250 000 and the bad debt relates to one debtor. On the other hand, $50 000 in bad debts may be considered immaterial if sales revenue is $2 500 000.

Generally, an item should be disclosed if its individual reporting will assist the user of the reports to obtain more information, from which they will be able to make an informed decision. Items of revenue or expense cited in AASB101 that may warrant separate disclosure include:
- writedowns of inventories to net realisable value (that is, stock writedowns);
- adjustments made to property, plant and equipment to their recoverable amount (that is, impairment of assets);
- disposals of items of property, plant and equipment (that is, profits and losses on asset disposals);

- disposals of investments (that is, profits and losses on investment disposals); and
- litigation settlements (that is, significant legal costs or gains).

  In addition to the disclosures required by AASB101, other accounting standards require disclosure as follows:

| Accounting standard | | Disclosure requirement (if material) |
|---|---|---|
| AASB102: | Inventories | Amount of stock expensed in the year |
| AASB112: | Income Taxes | Disclosure of a range of tax-related information and reconciliations relating to the calculation of income tax expense |
| AASB116: | Property, Plant and Equipment | Depreciation expense and impairment losses associated with property, plant and equipment |
| AASB117: | Leases | Disclosure of amounts expensed relating to lease agreements |
| AASB118: | Revenues | Revenue derived from sale of goods, provision of services, interest revenue, dividends revenue and income from royalties |
| AASB119: | Employee Benefits | Amounts set aside as employee benefits expense including wages, salaries and leave expenses |
| AASB132: | Financial Instruments | Interest revenue and interest expense associated with financial instruments |
| AASB136: | Impairment of Assets | Impairment losses expensed in the year |
| AASB137 | Provisions and Contingent Assets and Liabilities | Amounts set aside for uncertain assets and liabilities |
| AASB138: | Intangible Assets | Amounts expensed as impairment losses of assets |
| AASB1046: | Director and Executives | Amounts paid to directors and executive officers |
| AASB1054: | Australian Additional Disclosures | Audit fees expensed |

The following is a summary of the accounting standards relating to the disclosure of material revenues and expenses included in profit and loss.

| Note of disclosure | Accounting standard |
|---|---|
| Cost of sales | AASB101 and AASB102 |
| Depreciation of assets | AASB116 |
| Employee entitlements | AASB101, AASB119 and AASB137 |
| Impairment of assets | AASB101, AASB116, AASB136 and AASB138 |
| Income tax expense | AASB101 and AASB112 |
| Interest and finance costs | AASB101 and AASB132 |
| Lease rental expenses | AASB117 |
| Legal and litigation costs | AASB101 |
| Profit (loss) on sale of assets | AASB101 |
| Remuneration of auditors | AASB1054 |
| Remuneration of executive officers | AASB1046 |
| Research and development expenses | AASB138 |
| Sales and other revenue | AASB101 and AASB118 |

## Reconciliation of income tax

AASB112: Income Taxes requires disclosure of a range of tax related transactions including a reconciliation of how the income tax expense reconciles to the profit before tax (accounting profit).

Where permanent differences (non-tax deductible expenses or non-tax assessable income) have been recorded in the calculation of profit before tax the resulting income tax expense calculation will not be based on the profit before tax but instead on the profit adjusted for permanent differences.

The AASB112 reconciliation will disclose the effect of permanent differences in the calculation of income tax expense.

## Illustration

Challenge Ltd's profit and loss account from the previous illustration follows:

### Profit and loss account

| Date | Details | Debit $ | Credit $ | Balance $ | |
|------|---------|---------|----------|-----------|---|
| 30 June | Sales | | 900 000 | 900 000 | Cr |
| | Profit on sale of assets | | 50 000 | 950 000 | Cr |
| | Cost of sales | 300 000 | | 650 000 | Cr |
| | Loss on sale of vehicles | 5 000 | | 645 000 | Cr |
| | Advertising | 60 000 | | 585 000 | Cr |
| | Wages and employee benefits | 120 000 | | 465 000 | Cr |
| | Depreciation | 80 000 | | 385 000 | Cr |
| | Rent expense | 70 000 | | 315 000 | Cr |
| | Electricity and heating | 30 000 | | 285 000 | Cr |
| | Auditors' remuneration | 40 000 | | 245 000 | Cr |
| | Directors' remuneration | 60 000 | | 185 000 | Cr |
| | Bad and doubtful debts | 20 000 | | 165 000 | Cr |
| | Impairment of investments | 30 000 | | 135 000 | Cr |
| | Interest expense | 20 000 | | 115 000 | Cr |
| | Income tax expense | 43 500 | | 71 500 | Cr |

### Additional information

- The asset revaluation reserve increased by $200 000 during the year.
- Impairment of investments is not a tax deductible item.

An analysis of the revenue and expense items appearing in the account reveal the following amounts that will need to be reported in the disclosure notes presented with the statement of profit and loss and other comprehensive income.

| | $ | Individual disclosure required if considered material |
|---|---|---|
| Sales | 900 000 | Yes | AASB101 and AASB118 |
| Profit on sale of assets | 50 000 | Yes | AASB101 |
| Cost of sales | 300 000 | Yes | AASB101 and AASB102 |
| Loss on sale of vehicles | 5 000 | Yes | AASB101, AASB116, AASB136 and AASB138 |
| Advertising | 60 000 | No | |
| Wages and employee benefits | 120 000 | Yes | AASB101 and AASB119 |
| Depreciation | 80 000 | Yes | AASB116 |
| Rent expense | 70 000 | No | |
| Electricity and heating | 30 000 | No | |
| Auditors' remuneration | 40 000 | Yes | AASB1054 |
| Directors' remuneration | 60 000 | Yes | AASB1046 |
| Bad and doubtful debts | 20 000 | No | |
| Impairment of investments | 30 000 | Yes | AASB101, AASB116, AASB136 and AASB138 |
| Interest expense | 20 000 | Yes | AASB101 and AASB132 |
| Income tax expense | 43 500 | Yes | AASB101 and AASB112 |

This financial statement disclosing expenses by **function** and notes of disclosure would be presented as follows:

**Challenge Ltd**
**Statement of profit and loss and other comprehensive income**
**for year ended 30 June**

| | Note | $ |
|---|---|---|
| Revenue | 1 | 900 000 |
| Less cost of sales | | (300 000) |
| Gross profit | | 600 000 |
| Add other income | 1 | 50 000 |
| Less    Distribution costs | 2 | (263 000) |
|            Administrative expenses | 2 | (102 000) |
|            Finance costs | | (20 000) |
|            Other expenses | 2 & 3 | (150 000) |
| Profit (before tax) | | 115 000 |
| Less income tax expense | 4 | (43 500) |
| Profit (after tax) | | 71 500 |
| Add other comprehensive income | 5 | 200 000 |
| Profit and loss and other comprehensive income | | 271 500 |

Notes of disclosure accompanying this report

| | | $ |
|---|---|---|
| **Note 1: Revenue and other income includes:** | | |
| Sales | | 900 000 |
| Profit on sale of assets | | 50 000 |
| **Note 2: Expenses include:** | | |
| Loss on sale of vehicles | | 5 000 |
| Wages and employee benefits | | 120 000 |
| Depreciation | | 80 000 |
| Auditors' remuneration | | 40 000 |
| Impairment of investments | | 30 000 |
| **Note 3: Directors' remunerations:** | | |
| Amounts paid to directors | | 60 000 |
| **Note 4: Income tax expense reconciliation:** | | |
| Income tax on profit before tax | ($115 000 × 30%) | 34 500 |
| Adjusted for income tax on permanent differences | | |
| Impairment of investments | ($30 000 × 30%) | 9 000 |
| Income tax expense | | 43 500 |
| **Note 5: Other comprehensive income** | | |
| Increase in asset revaluation reserve | | 200 000 |

This financial statement disclosing expenses by **nature** and notes of disclosure would be presented as follows:

**Challenge Ltd**
**Statement of profit and loss and other comprehensive income**
**for year ended 30 June**

|  | Note | $ |
|---|---|---|
| Revenue | 1 | 900 000 |
| *Add* other income | 1 | 50 000 |
| Total income |  | 950 000 |
| *Less* expenses |  |  |
| Changes in inventories |  | 10 000 |
| Cost of materials and consumables used |  | (310 000) |
| Employee benefits expense |  | (120 000) |
| Depreciation and asset impairments expense | 2 | (115 000) |
| Finance costs |  | (20 000) |
| Other expenses | 2 & 3 | (280 000) |
| Total expenses |  | 835 000 |
| Profit before tax |  | 115 000 |
| *Less* income tax expense | 4 | (43 500) |
| Profit (after tax) |  | 71 500 |
| *Add* other comprehensive income | 5 | 200 000 |
| Profit and loss and other comprehensive income |  | 271 500 |

**Notes of disclosure accompanying this report**

| Note 1: Revenue and other income includes: |  | $ |
|---|---|---|
| Sales |  | 900 000 |
| Profit on sale of assets |  | 50 000 |
| **Note 2: Expenses include:** |  |  |
| Loss on sale of vehicles |  | 5 000 |
| Depreciation |  | 80 000 |
| Impairment of investments |  | 30 000 |
| Auditors' remuneration |  | 40 000 |
| **Note 3: Directors' remunerations:** |  |  |
| Amounts paid to directors |  | 60 000 |
| **Note 4: Income tax expense reconciliation:** |  |  |
| Income tax on profit before tax | ($115 000 × 30%) | 34 500 |
| Adjusted for income tax on permanent differences |  |  |
| Impairment of investments | ($30 000 × 30%) | 9 000 |
| Income tax expense |  | 43 500 |
| **Note 5: Other comprehensive income** |  |  |
| Increase in asset revaluation reserve |  | 200 000 |

## Question 8.5

The statement of profit and loss and comprehensive income for Sapphire Ltd from question 8.1 is shown in the workbook showing expenses reported by function.

Using this statement and the information that gave rise to this statement shown below, you are required to prepare the disclosure notes required by the accounting standards that would accompany the statement.

### Profit and loss account

| Date | Details | Debit $ | Credit $ | Balance $ |
|------|---------|--------:|---------:|----------:|
| 30 June | Sales | | 1 200 000 | 1 200 000 Cr |
| | Dividends received | | 55 000 | 1 255 000 Cr |
| | Cost of sales | 480 000 | | 775 000 Cr |
| | Interest expense | 40 000 | | 735 000 Cr |
| | Audit expenses | 50 000 | | 685 000 Cr |
| | Depreciation expense | 70 000 | | 615 000 Cr |
| | Depreciation – buildings | 30 000 | | 585 000 Cr |
| | Directors' fees | 60 000 | | 525 000 Cr |
| | Discount expense | 5 000 | | 520 000 Cr |
| | Employee benefits | 10 000 | | 510 000 Cr |
| | Lease expenses | 50 000 | | 460 000 Cr |
| | Marketing costs | 90 000 | | 370 000 Cr |
| | Sales commissions | 10 000 | | 360 000 Cr |
| | Utility costs | 40 000 | | 320 000 Cr |
| | Wages and salaries | 160 000 | | 160 000 Cr |
| | Income tax expense | 57 000 | | 103 000 Cr |

*Additional information*

- The asset revaluation reserve increased by $100 000 during the year.
- Depreciation on buildings is not a tax-deductible amount.

## Question 8.6

The information that follows was used in question 8.2 to prepare the statement of profit and loss and other comprehensive income for Ruby Ltd reporting expenses by function.

Using this information and the financial statement in the workbook you are required to prepare the disclosure notes required by the accounting standards that would accompany the statement.

**Profit and loss**

| Date | Details | Debit $ | Credit $ | Balance $ |
|---|---|---|---|---|
| 30 June | Sales | | 1 500 000 | 1 500 000  Cr |
| | Cost of sales | 750 000 | | 750 000  Cr |
| | Interest received | | 25 000 | 775 000  Cr |
| | Selling costs | 120 000 | | 655 000  Cr |
| | Sales commissions | 10 000 | | 645 000  Cr |
| | Depreciation | 90 000 | | 555 000  Cr |
| | Lease expenses | 40 000 | | 515 000  Cr |
| | Utility expenses | 40 000 | | 475 000  Cr |
| | Wages and employee entitlements | 200 000 | | 275 000  Cr |
| | Interest expense | 30 000 | | 245 000  Cr |
| | Audit expenses | 20 000 | | 225 000  Cr |
| | Entertainment expenses | 30 000 | | 195 000  Cr |
| | Directors' fees | 25 000 | | 170 000  Cr |
| | Bad debts | 6 000 | | 164 000  Cr |
| | Income tax expense | 58 200 | | 105 800  Cr |

*Additional information*

Entertainment expenses are not tax deductible.

# Question 8.7

The following information for Ruby Ltd was used in question 8.4 to prepare a profit and loss statement disclosing expanses by function.

You are now required to use this information to prepare a statement of profit and loss and comprehensive income for the year that complies with AASB101: Presentation of Financial Statements disclosing the **nature** of expenses with supporting notes of disclosure.

**Profit and loss**

| Date | Details | Debit $ | Credit $ | Balance $ |
|---|---|---|---|---|
| 30 June | Sales | | 1 500 000 | 1 500 000  Cr |
| | Cost of sales (refer below) | 750 000 | | 750 000  Cr |
| | Wages and employee entitlements | 200 000 | | 550 000  Cr |
| | Depreciation | 90 000 | | 460 000  Cr |
| | Interest expense | 30 000 | | 430 000  Cr |
| | Interest received | | 25 000 | 455 000  Cr |
| | Selling costs | 120 000 | | 335 000  Cr |
| | Sales commissions | 10 000 | | 325 000  Cr |
| | Lease expenses | 40 000 | | 285 000  Cr |
| | Utility expenses | 40 000 | | 245 000  Cr |
| | Audit expenses | 20 000 | | 225 000  Cr |
| | Entertainment expenses | 30 000 | | 195 000  Cr |
| | Directors' fees | 25 000 | | 170 000  Cr |
| | Bad debts | 6 000 | | 164 000  Cr |
| | Income tax expense | 58 200 | | 105 800  Cr |

### Additional information

The stock on hand account includes the following:

### Stock on hand account

| Date | Particulars | Debit $ | Credit $ | Balance $ | |
|---|---|---|---|---|---|
| 1 June | Balance | | | 100 000 | Dr |
| 30 June | Purchases of materials | 770 000 | | 870 000 | Dr |
| | Cost of sales | | 750 000 | 120 000 | Dr |

- Entertainment expenses are not tax deductible.
- The asset revaluation reserve increased by $250 000 during the year.

## Question 8.8

Silver Ltd has provided the following information for the year ended 30 June. You are required to:

**a** prepare the statement of profit and loss and other comprehensive income using the nature of expense analysis method of disclosing expenses; and

**b** prepare the disclosure notes to accompany the statement.

### Profit and loss

| Date | Details | Debit $ | Credit $ | Balance $ | |
|---|---|---|---|---|---|
| 30 June | Sales | | 2 000 000 | 2 000 000 | Cr |
| | Stock on hand (start of year) | 60 000 | | 1 940 000 | Cr |
| | Purchases of stock | 1 290 000 | | 650 000 | Cr |
| | Stock on hand (end of year) | | 50 000 | 700 000 | Cr |
| | Services income | | 400 000 | 1 100 000 | Cr |
| | Dividends received | | 10 000 | 1 110 000 | Cr |
| | Audit expenses | 25 000 | | 1 085 000 | Cr |
| | Depreciation expense | 120 000 | | 965 000 | Cr |
| | Building depreciation | 60 000 | | 905 000 | Cr |
| | Directors' fees | 100 000 | | 805 000 | Cr |
| | Bad debts | 15 000 | | 790 000 | Cr |
| | Interest expense | 20 000 | | 770 000 | Cr |
| | Lease expenses | 30 000 | | 740 000 | Cr |
| | Sales and marketing expenses | 60 000 | | 680 000 | Cr |
| | Communications expenses | 50 000 | | 630 000 | Cr |
| | Utility expenses | 30 000 | | 600 000 | Cr |
| | Employee entitlements | 250 000 | | 350 000 | Cr |
| | Income tax expense | 120 000 | | 230 000 | Cr |

### Additional information

- Non-tax assessable/deductible amounts: Dividends income and building depreciation.
- The asset revaluation reserve increased by $270 000 during the year.

# Question 8.9

From the following information provided by Gold Ltd for the year ended 30 June you are required to:

**a** prepare the statement of profit and loss and other comprehensive income using the functional analysis method of disclosing expenses; and

**b** prepare the disclosure notes to accompany the statement.

**Profit and loss**

| Date | Details | Debit $ | Credit $ | Balance $ |
|------|---------|---------|----------|-----------|
| 30 June | Sales | | 1 800 000 | 1 800 000 Cr |
| | Commission received | | 50 000 | 1 850 000 Cr |
| | Cost of sales | 800 000 | | 1 050 000 Cr |
| | Employee entitlements | 215 000 | | 835 000 Cr |
| | Audit expenses | 30 000 | | 805 000 Cr |
| | Depreciation expense | 60 000 | | 745 000 Cr |
| | Impairment of investments | 50 000 | | 695 000 Cr |
| | Directors' fees | 50 000 | | 645 000 Cr |
| | Bad debts | 15 000 | | 630 000 Cr |
| | Interest expense | 20 000 | | 610 000 Cr |
| | Lease expenses | 20 000 | | 590 000 Cr |
| | Marketing expenses | 60 000 | | 530 000 Cr |
| | Sales commissions | 50 000 | | 480 000 Cr |
| | Power and gas | 30 000 | | 450 000 Cr |
| | Income tax expense | 150 000 | | 300 000 Cr |

*Additional information*

- Functional expenses are listed below. Expenses not listed are to be reported as line items or classified as 'other expenses'.

| Expense | Distribution | Administration |
|---------|-------------|----------------|
| Employee entitlements | 130 000 | 85 000 |
| Depreciation expense | 40 000 | 20 000 |
| Lease expenses | 15 000 | 5 000 |
| Marketing expenses | 60 000 | |
| Sales commissions | 50 000 | |
| Power and gas | 20 000 | 10 000 |

- The asset revaluation reserve increased by $700 000 during the year.
- Impairment of investments is not a tax-deductible amount.

# 8.4 STATEMENT OF CHANGES IN EQUITY

AASB101: Presentation of Financial Statements requires reporting entities to issue a statement of changes in equity when presenting the financial statements.

The purpose of this statement is to provide owners with information relating to the components of equity and how they have changed during the reporting period.

The standard does not prescribe a specific format but requires a reconciliation of the balances at the start and end of the period for each component of equity consisting of:

- profit or loss;
- other comprehensive income; and
- transactions with owners including capital contributions and distributions of equity.

The format of the statement in changes in equity adopted for use in this text is as follows:

**Statement of changes in equity**
**for year ended...**

| Equity | Share capital $ | Reserves $ | Retained profits $ | Total $ |
|---|---|---|---|---|
| Balance (at start of period) | XX | XX | XX | XX |
| Share capital issued | XX | | | XX |
| Calls in arrears | (XX) | | | (XX) |
| Bonus shares issued | XX | (XX) | | XX |
| Asset revaluation increase | | XX | | XX |
| Profit (for the period) | | | XX | XX |
| Transfers from reserves | | (XX) | XX | XX |
| Transfers to reserves | | XX | (XX) | XX |
| Interim dividends | | | (XX) | (XX) |
| Final dividends | | | (XX) | (XX) |
| Balance (at end of period) | XX | XX | XX | XX |

## Illustration

For the year ended 30 June, Challenge Ltd reported the following information relating to shareholders' equity:

| Account balances at 1 July (start of year) | $ |
|---|---|
| Share capital | 200 000 |
| Asset revaluation reserve | 120 000 |
| General reserve | 10 000 |
| Dividend reserve | 70 000 |
| Retained profits | 200 000 |
| Total shareholders' equity | 600 000 |

### Additional information

- The company made a call of $0.50 per share on 300 000 shares totalling $150 000 during the year.
- Calls remain outstanding on 20 000 shares totalling $10 000.
- Land and buildings were revalued upwards during the year by $50 000.

- Bonus shares totalling $100 000 were issued during the year from the asset revaluation reserve.
- The retained profits account for the year was as follows:

### Retained profits

| Date | Particulars | Debit $ | Credit $ | Balance $ |
|------|-------------|---------|----------|-----------|
| 1 July | Balance | | 200 000 | 200 000 Cr |
| 30 June | Profit and loss | | 71 500 | 271 500 Cr |
| | Dividend reserve (transfer from) | | 60 000 | 331 500 Cr |
| | General reserve (transfer to) | 50 000 | | 281 500 Cr |
| | Interim dividend | 100 000 | | 181 500 Cr |
| | Final dividend | 150 000 | | 31 500 Cr |

The completed statement of changes in equity arising from this information would be as follows:

### Challenge Ltd
### Statement of changes in equity
### for year ended 30 June

| Equity | Share capital $ | Reserves $ | Retained profits $ | Total equity $ |
|--------|-----------------|------------|--------------------|----------------|
| Balance (at start of period) | 200 000 | 200 000 | 200 000 | 600 000 |
| Share capital issued | 150 000 | | | 150 000 |
| Calls in arrears | (10 000) | | | (10 000) |
| Bonus shares issued | 100 000 | (100 000) | | Nil |
| Asset revaluation increase | | 50 000 | | 50 000 |
| Profit (for the period) | | | 71 500 | 71 500 |
| Transfers from reserves | | (60 000) | 60 000 | Nil |
| Transfers to reserves | | 50 000 | (50 000) | Nil |
| Interim dividends | | | (100 000) | (100 000) |
| Final dividends | | | (150 000) | (150 000) |
| Balance (at end of period) | 440 000 | 140 000 | 31 500 | 611 500 |

## Question 8.10

Using the following information provided by Sapphire Ltd you are required to prepare the statement of changes in equity for the year ended 30 June.

| Account balances at 1 July (start of year): | |
|---------------------------------------------|--------------|
| | $ |
| Share capital (ordinary shares @ $2.00 each) | 1 000 000 |
| Asset revaluation reserve | 200 000 |
| Dividend reserve | 100 000 |
| Retained profits | 500 000 |
| Total shareholders' equity | 1 800 000 |

### Additional information

- During the year the company issued 100 000 preference shares at $5.00 each.
- Land was revalued upwards during the year by $400 000.

- During the year 250 000 bonus shares were issued from the asset revaluation reserve.
- The retained profits account for the year revealed was as follows:

### Retained profits

| Date | Particulars | Debit $ | Credit $ | Balance $ |
|---|---|---|---|---|
| 1 July | Balance | | 500 000 | 500 000 Cr |
| 30 June | Profit and loss | | 103 000 | 603 000 Cr |
| | General reserve (transfer to) | 40 000 | | 563 000 Cr |
| | Dividend reserve (transfer from) | | 100 000 | 663 000 Cr |
| | Interim dividend | 300 000 | | 363 000 Cr |
| | Final dividend | 300 000 | | 63 000 Cr |

## Question 8.11

From the following information for Ruby Ltd for the year ended 30 June you are required to prepare the statement of changes in equity.

### Retained profits

| Date | Particulars | Debit $ | Credit $ | Balance $ |
|---|---|---|---|---|
| 1 July | Balance | | 100 000 | 100 000 Cr |
| 30 June | Profit and loss | | 105 800 | 205 800 Cr |
| | General reserve (transfer from) | | 50 000 | 255 800 Cr |
| | Dividend reserve (transfer to) | 100 000 | | 155 800 Cr |
| | Interim dividend | 50 000 | | 105 800 Cr |
| | Final dividend | 100 000 | | 5 800 Cr |

| Account balances at 30 June (end of year) | $ |
|---|---|
| Share capital (1 000 000 ordinary shares @ $1.00 each) | 1 000 000 |
| Calls in arrears (50 000 shares @ $0.50 each) | (25 000) |
| Asset revaluation reserve | 800 000 |
| General reserve | 50 000 |
| Dividend reserve | 120 000 |
| Retained profits | 5 000 |
| Total shareholders' equity | 1 950 000 |

**Additional information**

- During the year a call of $0.50 was made on ordinary shares of which 50 000 shares remain unpaid.
- Buildings were revalued upwards during the year by $800 000.

## Question 8.12

JG Ltd has provided the following information for the year ended 30 June from which you are required to prepare:

**a**   a statement of profit and loss and other comprehensive income showing expenses by nature;

**b**   a statement of changes in equity; and

**c**   disclosure notes.

| Account balances at 1 July (start of year) | |
|---|---|
| | **$** |
| Share capital (ordinary shares @ $1.00 each) | 200 000 |
| Dividend reserve | 80 000 |
| Retained profits | 80 000 |
| Total shareholders' equity | 360 000 |

**General ledger (extract)**

| Date | Details | Debit $ | Credit $ | Balance $ |
|---|---|---|---|---|
| **Profit and loss** | | | | |
| 30 June | Sales | | 2 200 000 | 2 200 000 Cr |
| | Stock (1 July) | 50 000 | | 2 150 000 Cr |
| | Cost of goods purchased | 880 000 | | 1 270 000 Cr |
| | Stock (30 June) | | 50 000 | 1 320 000 Cr |
| | Dividends received | | 20 000 | 1 340 000 Cr |
| | Audit expenses | 20 000 | | 1 320 000 Cr |
| | Depreciation expense | 150 000 | | 1 170 000 Cr |
| | Impairment of investments | 50 000 | | 1 120 000 Cr |
| | Directors' fees | 80 000 | | 1 040 000 Cr |
| | Interest expenses | 60 000 | | 980 000 Cr |
| | Distribution expenses | 60 000 | | 920 000 Cr |
| | Administration expenses | 50 000 | | 870 000 Cr |
| | Employee entitlements | 250 000 | | 620 000 Cr |
| | Income tax expense | 195 000 | | 425 000 Cr |
| | Retained profits | 425 000 | | Nil |
| **Retained profits** | | | | |
| 1 July | Balance | | 80 000 | 80 000 Cr |
| 30 June | Profit and loss | | 425 000 | 505 000 Cr |
| | General reserve | 100 000 | | 405 000 Cr |
| | Dividend reserve | | 60 000 | 465 000 Cr |
| | Interim dividend | 150 000 | | 315 000 Cr |
| | Final dividend | 200 000 | | 115 000 Cr |

*Additional information*

- Impairment of investments and dividends received are not deductible or assessable for taxation purposes.
- During the year 400 000 ordinary shares were issued at $2.00 each.
- Buildings were revalued upwards during the year by $800 000.

## Question 8.13

Parker Ltd has provided the following information for the year ended 30 June from which you are required to prepare:

**a** a statement of profit and loss and other comprehensive income showing expenses by function;

**b** a statement of changes in equity; and

**c** disclosure notes.

| Account balances at 30 June (end of year) | |
|---|---|
| Share capital (ordinary shares 250 000 @ $2.00 each) | $500 000 |
| Calls in arrears (ordinary shares 40 000 @ $0.50 each) | $20 000 |
| Share capital (preference shares) | $500 000 |
| General reserve | $50 000 |

**General ledger (extract)**

| Date | Details | Debit $ | Credit $ | Balance $ |
|---|---|---|---|---|
| **Profit and loss** | | | | |
| 30 June | Sales | | 2 500 000 | 2 500 000 Cr |
| | Cost of sales | 1 000 000 | | 1 500 000 Cr |
| | Interest received | | 20 000 | 1 520 000 Cr |
| | Audit expenses | 30 000 | | 1 490 000 Cr |
| | Depreciation expense | 180 000 | | 1 310 000 Cr |
| | Entertainment expenses | 20 000 | | 1 290 000 Cr |
| | Directors' fees | 120 000 | | 1 170 000 Cr |
| | Interest expense | 30 000 | | 1 140 000 Cr |
| | Lease expenses | 40 000 | | 1 100 000 Cr |
| | Distribution expenses | 100 000 | | 1 000 000 Cr |
| | Administration expenses | 160 000 | | 840 000 Cr |
| | Employee entitlements | 300 000 | | 540 000 Cr |
| | Income tax expense | 168 000 | | 372 000 Cr |
| | Retained profits | 372 000 | | Nil |
| **Retained profits** | | | | |
| 1 July | Balance | | | 100 000 Cr |
| 30 June | Profit and loss | | 372 000 | 472 000 Cr |
| | Interim dividends | 200 000 | | 272 000 Cr |
| | Final dividends | 200 000 | | 72 000 Cr |
| | General reserve | 50 000 | | 22 000 Cr |

*Additional information*

- Depreciation, employee benefits and lease expenses are to be apportioned equally between distribution and administration.
- Entertainment expenses are not deductible for taxation purposes.
- During the year a call was made on ordinary shares of $0.50 each.
- Buildings were revalued upwards during the year by $400 000.
- A bonus dividend of $500 000 in preference shares was made during the year from the asset revaluation reserve.

## 8.5   STATEMENT OF FINANCIAL POSITION

AASB101: Presentation of Financial Statements sets out specific requirements for the presentation and disclosure of a statement of financial position. The standard requires disclosure of current and non-current assets and liabilities on the statement and specifies categories to be disclosed as line items on the statement.

A suggested format for this statement that complies with the requirements of AASB101 is as follows:

### Statement of financial position at...

| Assets | Note | $ | $ |
|---|---|---|---|
| **Current assets** | | | |
| Cash and cash equivalents | 6 | XX | |
| Trade receivables | 7 | XX | |
| Inventories | 8 | XX | |
| Other current assets | 9 | XX | |
| Total current assets | | | XX |
| **Non-current assets** | | | |
| Available-for-sale investments | 10 | XX | |
| Financial assets | 11 | XX | |
| Deferred tax assets | 12 | XX | |
| Property, plant and equipment | 13 | XX | |
| Intangible assets | 14 | XX | |
| Total non-current assets | | | XX |
| **Total assets** | | | XX |
| **Liabilities** | | | XX |
| **Current liabilities** | | | |
| Trade and other payables | 15 | XX | |
| Financial liabilities (short term) | 16 | XX | |
| Current tax payable | 17 | XX | |
| Provisions (short term) | 18 | XX | |
| Other current liabilities | 19 | XX | |
| Total current liabilities | | | XX |
| **Non-current liabilities** | | | |
| Financial liabilities (long term) | 20 | XX | |
| Deferred tax liabilities | 21 | XX | |
| Provisions (long term) | 22 | XX | |
| Total non-current liabilities | | | XX |
| **Total liabilities** | | | XX |
| **Net assets** | | | XX |
| **Equity** | | | |
| Share capital | 23 | XX | |
| Reserves | 24 | XX | |
| Retained profits | | XX | |
| **Total equity** | | | XX |

## Reporting and disclosing assets

Assets on the statement of financial position should identify current and non-current assets. AASB101: Presentation of Financial Statements defines current assets and non-current assets as follows:

An asset shall be classified as a current asset when it satisfies any of the following criteria:

a   it is expected to be realised in, or is intended for sale or consumption in, the entity's normal operating cycle;
b   it is held primarily for the purpose of being traded;
c   it is expected to be realised within 12 months after the reporting date; or
d   it is cash or a cash equivalent.

Assets that do not meet one of these criteria shall be classified as non-current.

The following table lists the line items that should be included on the statement of financial position and provides examples of assets associated with each line item and the related accounting standard.

| | Examples | AASB |
|---|---|---|
| **Current assets** | | |
| Cash and cash equivalents | Cash at bank, petty cash, cash in registers, cash on hand and deposits at call and short-term deposits | 107 |
| Trade and other receivables | Debtors, accounts receivable and allowances (provisions) for doubtful debts | |
| Inventories | Stocks of finished goods, raw materials, work in progress | 102 |
| Other current assets | Prepaid expenses, accrued revenues | |
| **Non-current assets** | | |
| Available-for-sale investments | Investments in shares and other assets purchased with the intention of selling the asset | 139 |
| Biological assets | Living animals or plants; for example plantations, crops, fish, cattle, sheep, chickens | 141 |
| Investment property | Property, investments and buildings held in the long term to acquire income from sources other than sales or services such as rental, capital gains purposes, dividends or interest | 140 |
| Intangible assets | Goodwill purchased during a business combination, patents, franchises, licenses and copyrights less any accumulated impairments of these assets | 3 & 138 |
| Financial assets | Loan contracts, financial obligations, derivatives | 132 & 139 |
| Deferred tax assets | Arising from differences in the calculation of income tax expense and income tax payable | 112 |
| Property, plant and equipment | Representing land and buildings, vehicles, machinery and equipment, and other income-generating assets, less any accumulations (provisions) for depreciation | 116 |

# Illustration

The trial balance of Challenge Ltd for the year ended 30 June included the following assets:

**Trial balance at 30 June**

| Account | Debit $ | Credit $ |
|---|---|---|
| Accrued revenues | 10 000 | |
| Equipment | 220 000 | |
| Accumulated depreciation – equipment | | 72 000 |
| Franchise | 200 000 | |
| Cash at bank | 15 000 | |
| Cash on hand | 2 000 | |
| Debtors | 50 000 | |
| Allowance for doubtful debts | | 2 500 |
| Deposits at call | 100 000 | |
| Deferred tax assets | 6 000 | |
| Goodwill | 25 000 | |
| Government bonds (due 1 December 2020) | 30 000 | |
| Land and buildings (independent valuation) | 200 000 | |
| Motor vehicles | 80 000 | |
| Accumulated depreciation – motor vehicles | | 48 000 |
| Patents | 100 000 | |
| Petty cash | 1 000 | |
| Prepaid expenses | 3 500 | |
| Investment in shares in Gold Ltd (held for resale) | 60 000 | |
| Accumulated impairment losses – shares in Gold Ltd | | 6 000 |
| Stock of finished goods | 35 000 | |
| Stock of materials | 40 000 | |

The statement of financial position (assets section) prepared from these accounts to conform to AASB101 could be presented as follows:

**Challenge Ltd**
**Statement of financial position**
**at 30 June**

| | Note | $ | $ |
|---|---|---|---|
| Assets | | | |
| Current assets | | | |
|    Cash | 6 | 118 000 | |
|    Trade receivables | 7 | 47 500 | |
|    Inventories | 8 | 75 000 | |
|    Other | 9 | 13 500 | |
| Total current assets | | | 254 000 |
| Non-current assets | | | |
|    Available for sale investments | 10 | 54 000 | |
|    Financial assets | 11 | 30 000 | |
|    Deferred tax assets | 12 | 6 000 | |
|    Property, plant and equipment | 13 | 380 000 | |
|    Intangibles | 14 | 325 000 | |
| Total non-current assets | | | 795 000 |
| Total assets | | | 1 049 000 |

**Notes to and forming part of the accounts**

| Note | | | $ | $ |
|---|---|---|---|---|
| 6 | Cash | | | |
| | | Cash at bank | 15 000 | |
| | | Cash on hand | 2 000 | |
| | | Petty cash | 1 000 | |
| | | Deposits at call | 100 000 | 118 000 |
| 7 | Trade receivables | | | |
| | | Debtors | 50 000 | |
| | | Allowance for doubtful debts | (2 500) | 47 500 |
| 8 | Inventories | | | |
| | | Stock of finished goods | 35 000 | |
| | | Stock of materials | 40 000 | 75 000 |
| 9 | Other | | | |
| | | Accrued revenues | 10 000 | |
| | | Prepaid expenses | 3 500 | 13 500 |
| 10 | Available for sale investments | | | |
| | | Shares in Gold Ltd | 60 000 | |
| | | Accumulated impairment losses – shares in Gold Ltd | (6 000) | 54 000 |
| 11 | Financial assets | | | |
| | | Government bonds (due 1 December 2020) | | 30 000 |

| Note | | $ | $ |
|---|---|---|---|
| 12 | Deferred tax assets | | 6 000 |
| 13 | Property, plant and equipment | | |
| | Equipment | 220 000 | |
| | Accumulated depreciation – equipment | (72 000) | 148 000 |
| | Motor vehicles | 80 000 | |
| | Accumulated depreciation – motor vehicles | (48 000) | 32 000 |
| | Land and buildings (independent valuation) | | 200 000 |
| | | | 380 000 |
| 14 | Intangibles | | |
| | Goodwill | 25 000 | |
| | Franchise | 200 000 | |
| | Patents | 100 000 | 325 000 |

# Question 8.14

From the following extract of the trial balance of Asean Ltd for the year ended 30 June, you are required to prepare a statement of financial position (assets section) and disclosure notes that conform to the requirements of AASB101.

### Trial balance (extract) at 30 June

| Account | Debit $ | Credit $ |
|---|---|---|
| Cash at bank | 30 000 | |
| Deposits at call | 20 000 | |
| Term deposit (maturing in 9 months) | 20 000 | |
| Accounts receivable | 65 000 | |
| Allowance for doubtful debts | | 1 000 |
| Stock on hand | 12 000 | |
| Prepaid wages | 1 800 | |
| Term loan to GB Ltd (repayable in 5 years) | 200 000 | |
| Furniture and equipment | 400 000 | |
| Accumulated depreciation – furniture and equipment | | 72 000 |
| Land and buildings (directors' valuation) | 500 000 | |
| Deferred tax asset | 10 500 | |
| Investment shares in Laker Ltd (purchased for short-term gain) | 90 000 | |
| Accumulated impairment loss – shares in Laker Ltd | | 1 200 |
| Goodwill | 9 500 | |

# Reporting and disclosing liabilities

Liabilities on the statement of financial position should identify current and non-current assets. AASB101: Presentation of Financial Statements defines current liabilities and non-current liabilities as follows:

A liability shall be classified as a *current* liability when it satisfies any of the following criteria:

a    it is expected to be settled in the entity's normal operating cycle;
b    it is held primarily for the purpose of being traded;
c    it is due to be settled within 12 months after the reporting date; or
d    the entity does not have an unconditional right to defer settlement of the liability for at least 12 months
     after the reporting date.

All other liabilities shall be classified as *non-current*.

The following table lists the line items that should be included on the statement of financial position and provides examples of liabilities associated with each line item and the related accounting standard.

| | Examples | AASB |
|---|---|---|
| *Current liabilities* | | |
| Trade and other payables | Creditors, accounts payable | |
| Financial liabilities | Bank overdrafts and other short-term loans and the current portion of long-term liabilities such as mortgages | 132 & 139 |
| Current tax payable | Income tax payable, GST payable | 112 |
| Short-term provisions | Provisions for annual leave, long service leave, employee entitlements and dividends payable within 12 months | 119 & 137 |
| *Non-current liabilities* | | |
| Financial liabilities | Mortgage loans, long-term loans, debentures payable after 12 months | 132 & 139 |
| Deferred tax liabilities | Arising from differences in the calculation of income tax expense and income tax payable | 112 |
| Long-term provisions | Provisions for long service leave, employee entitlements and dividends payable later than 12 months | 119 & 137 |

## Illustration

The following is an extract of the trial balance of Challenge Ltd.

**Trial balance at 30 June**

| Account | Debit $ | Credit $ |
|---|---|---|
| Accrued wages | | 5 000 |
| Bank loan (unsecured and due in 9 months) | | 10 000 |
| Bank overdraft | | 15 000 |
| Creditors | | 8 000 |
| Dividends payable | | 30 000 |
| Mortgage loan (secured over buildings) | | 150 000 |
| Prepaid interest revenue | | 2 500 |
| Annual leave payable | | 35 000 |
| Deferred tax liability | | 3 000 |
| Income tax payable | | 55 000 |
| Long service leave payable | | 85 000 |
| GST payable | | 18 000 |
| Sundry creditors | | 1 000 |
| Term loan (unsecured and due in 5 years) | | 20 000 |

### Additional information

- It is company policy that annual leave is taken within 12 months of accrual.
- Ten per cent of the long service leave is due within the next 12 months.
- The mortgage is being paid over 10 years in equal instalments.

The statement of financial position (liabilities section) prepared from these accounts to conform to AASB101 could be presented as follows:

**Challenge Ltd**
**Statement of financial position (extract)**
**at 30 June**

| Liabilities | Note | $ | $ |
|---|---|---|---|
| **Current liabilities** | | | |
| Trade payables | 15 | 9 000 | |
| Financial liabilities | 16 | 40 000 | |
| Current tax payable | 17 | 73 000 | |
| Short-term provisions | 18 | 73 500 | |
| Other | 19 | 7 500 | |
| **Total current liabilities** | | | 203 000 |
| **Non-current liabilities** | | | |
| Financial liabilities | 20 | 155 000 | |
| Deferred tax liabilities | 21 | 3 000 | |
| Long-term provisions | 22 | 76 500 | |
| **Total non-current liabilities** | | | 234 500 |
| **Total liabilities** | | | 437 500 |

Notes to and forming part of the accounts

| Note | | $ | $ |
|---|---|---|---|
| 15 | Trade payables | | |
| | Creditors | 8 000 | |
| | Sundry creditors | 1 000 | 9 000 |
| 16 | Financial liabilities | | |
| | Bank overdraft | 15 000 | |
| | Bank loan (unsecured and due in 9 months) | 10 000 | |
| | Mortgage (secured over buildings) | 15 000 | 40 000 |
| 17 | Current tax payable | | |
| | GST payable | 18 000 | |
| | Income tax payable | 55 000 | 73 000 |
| 18 | Short-term provisions | | |
| | Dividends payable | 30 000 | |
| | Annual leave payable | 35 000 | |
| | Long service leave payable | 8 500 | 73 500 |
| 19 | Other | | |
| | Accrued wages | 5 000 | |
| | Prepaid interest revenue | 2 500 | 7 500 |
| 20 | Financial liabilities | | |
| | Mortgage loan (secured over buildings) | 135 000 | |
| | Term loan (unsecured and due in 5 years) | 20 000 | 155 000 |
| 21 | Deferred tax liabilities | | 3 000 |
| 22 | Long-term provisions | | |
| | Long service leave payable | | 76 500 |

## Reporting and disclosing shareholders' equity

AASB101 requires shareholders' equity to disclose issued capital and reserves as follows:

| Share capital | Issued capital<br>*less* calls in arrears<br>*Note:* AASB101 requires each class of share to be disclosed separately and that the number and issue price of all shares be disclosed |
|---|---|
| Reserves | Reserves include:<br>*revenue reserves: general reserve, dividend reserve*<br>*capital reserves: asset revaluation reserve* |
| Retained profits | Represented by the closing balance of retained profits |

## Illustration

The shareholders' equity accounts of Challenge Ltd at 30 June included the following:

### Trial balance at 30 June (extract)

| Account | Debit<br>$ | Credit<br>$ |
|---|---|---|
| Share capital – ordinary shares (100 000 @ $1.00 each) | | 100 000 |
| Calls in arrears – ordinary shares (5 000 @ $0.50 each) | 2 500 | |
| Share capital – preference shares | | 100 000 |
| Dividend reserve | | 15 000 |
| General reserve | | 5 000 |
| Asset revaluation reserve | | 250 000 |
| Retained profits | | 120 000 |

The statement of financial position (equity section) could be presented as follows:

### Challenge Ltd
### Statement of financial position
### at 30 June

| | Note | $ | $ |
|---|---|---|---|
| **Equity** | | | |
| Share capital | 23 | 197 500 | |
| Reserves | 24 | 270 000 | |
| Retained profits | | 120 000 | |
| Total equity | | | 587 500 |

Notes to and forming part of the accounts

| Note | | $ | $ |
|---|---|---|---|
| 23 | Share capital | | |
| | Ordinary shares issued total (100 000 @ $1.00 each) | 100 000 | |
| | Calls in arrears (5 000 ordinary shares @ $0.50 each) | (2 500) | |
| | | 97 500 | |
| | Preference shares total (50 000 @ $2.00 each) | 100 000 | 197 500 |
| 24 | Reserves | | |
| | Dividend reserve | 15 000 | |
| | General reserve | 5 000 | |
| | Asset revaluation reserve | 250 000 | 270 000 |

# Question 8.15

From the following trial balance extract of Hope Ltd you are required to prepare a statement of financial position (liabilities and equity sections) and disclosure notes that would meet the requirements of AASB101.

### Trial balance (extract) at 30 June

| Account | Debit $ | Credit $ |
|---|---|---|
| Accounts payable | | 10 000 |
| Accrued expenses | | 15 000 |
| Bank loan (due in 6 months) | | 20 000 |
| Bank overdraft | | 5 000 |
| Dividends payable | | 40 000 |
| Mortgage loan | | 130 000 |
| Prepaid interest revenue | | 3 000 |
| Annual leave payable | | 12 000 |
| Deferred tax liability | | 5 500 |
| Income tax payable | | 28 000 |
| Long service leave payable | | 80 000 |
| GST collected (payable) | | 2 500 |
| Term loan (unsecured and due in 2020) | | 25 000 |
| Share capital – ordinary shares (200 000 shares @ $1.00 each) | | 200 000 |
| Calls in arrears – ordinary shares (10 000 shares @ $0.50 each) | 5 000 | |
| Share capital – preference shares (50 000 shares @ 2.00 each) | | 100 000 |
| Dividend reserve | | 25 000 |
| General reserve | | 15 000 |
| Asset revaluation reserve | | 300 000 |
| Retained profits | | 33 000 |

### Additional information

- Total assets amount to $1 044 000.
- It is company policy that annual leave is taken within 12 months of accrual.
- Half of the long service leave is due within the next 12 months.
- The mortgage is being paid over 20 years in equal instalments.

# Question 8.16

Glen Ltd's statement of financial position for internal purposes is shown below. You are required to present the statement and disclosure notes to comply with the current Australian Accounting Standards.

**Glen Ltd**
**Statement of financial position**
**at 30 June**

| Shareholders' equity | $ | $ | $ |
|---|---|---|---|
| Share capital – 500 000 ordinary shares | | 500 000 | |
| Reserves | | | |
| Asset revaluation reserve | 385 000 | | |
| General reserve | 30 000 | | |
| Retained profits | 709 000 | 1 124 000 | 1 624 000 |
| Current assets | | | |
| Cash in hand | | 12 000 | |
| Cash at bank | | 30 000 | |
| Trade debtors | 150 000 | | |
| Less allowance for doubtful debts | 5 000 | 145 000 | |
| Stock at cost | | 380 000 | |
| Deferred tax asset | | 7 000 | 574 000 |
| Current liabilities | | | |
| Trade creditors | | 90 000 | |
| Income tax payable | | 100 000 | |
| Dividends payable | | 20 000 | |
| Deferred tax liability | | 5 000 | 215 000 |
| Working capital | | | 359 000 |
| Fixed assets | | | |
| Land and premises | | 1 000 000 | |
| Furniture and fittings – at cost | 150 000 | | |
| Less accumulated depreciation | 30 000 | 120 000 | 1 120 000 |
| Intangible assets | | | |
| Goodwill | | 70 000 | |
| Trademarks | | 50 000 | 120 000 |
| Investments | | | |
| Shares in ABC Ltd (long term) | 200 000 | | |
| Less accumulated impairment loss of shares | 150 000 | 50 000 | |
| Government bonds (due 2020) | | 250 000 | 300 000 |
| | | | 1 899 000 |
| Non-current liabilities | | | |
| Loan (due 2020) | | 260 000 | |
| Long service leave payable | | 15 000 | 275 000 |
| Net Assets | | | 1 624 000 |

## Question 8.17

From the following trial balance of Tafe Ltd, you are required to prepare a statement of financial position at 30 June which conforms to the Australian Accounting Standards.

**Tafe Ltd**
**Trial balance at 30 June**

| Account | Debit $ | Credit $ |
|---|---|---|
| Share capital – ordinary shares (@ $1.00 each) | | 500 000 |
| Calls in arrears (125 000 ordinary shares) | 25 000 | |
| Asset revaluation reserve | | 1 200 000 |
| General reserve | | 52 000 |
| Retained profits | | 296 000 |
| Bank | 969 000 | |
| Deposits at call | 160 000 | |
| Debtors | 102 000 | |
| Allowance for doubtful debts | | 12 000 |
| Stock | 185 000 | |
| Plant and equipment – at directors' valuation | 2 200 000 | |
| Accumulated depreciation – plant and equipment | | 980 000 |
| Shares in Langer Ltd | 220 000 | |
| Accumulated impairment loss – shares in Langer Ltd | | 20 000 |
| Term deposits (maturing in 5 years) | 180 000 | |
| Dividends payable | | 64 000 |
| Income tax payable | | 135 000 |
| Long service leave payable | | 230 000 |
| Deferred tax asset | 20 000 | |
| Deferred tax liability | | 45 000 |
| Creditors | | 78 000 |
| Mortgage loan | | 460 000 |
| Prepaid expenses | 16 000 | |
| Accrued expenses | | 5 000 |
| | 4 077 000 | 4 077 000 |

*Additional information*

- Shares in Langer Ltd were purchased for resale.
- Long service leave of $30 000 falls due in the next 12 months.
- The mortgage loan will be reduced by $40 000 in the forthcoming period.

# 8.6 COMPLETE SET OF FINANCIAL STATEMENTS

When an entity presents its financial statements AASB101 requires the statements to be presented as a complete set with each statement being given equal prominence in the presentation.

## Illustration

The following financial statements (including disclosure notes) for Challenge Ltd were presented throughout this chapter as separate statements. They are re-presented in this illustration as a complete set of financial statements.

**Challenge Ltd**
**Statement of profit and loss and other comprehensive income**
**for year ended 30 June**

|  | Note | $ |
|---|---|---|
| Revenue | 1 | 900 000 |
| *Less* cost of sales |  | (300 000) |
| Gross profit |  | 600 000 |
| *Add* other income | 1 | 50 000 |
| *Less* |  |  |
| Distribution costs | 2 | (263 000) |
| Administrative expenses | 2 | (102 000) |
| Finance costs |  | (20 000) |
| Other expenses | 2 & 3 | (150 000) |
| Profit (before tax) |  | 115 000 |
| *Less* income tax expense | 4 | (43 500) |
| Profit (after tax) |  | 71 500 |
| *Add* other comprehensive income | 5 | 50 000 |
| Profit and loss and other comprehensive income |  | 121 500 |

**Challenge Ltd**
**Statement of changes in equity**
**for year ended 30 June**

| Equity | Share capital $ | Reserves $ | Retained profits $ | Total equity $ |
|---|---|---|---|---|
| Balance (at start of period) | 200 000 | 200 000 | 200 000 | 600 000 |
| Share capital issued | 150 000 |  |  | 150 000 |
| Calls in arrears | (10 000) |  |  | (10 000) |
| Bonus shares issued | 100 000 | (100 000) |  | Nil |
| Asset revaluation increase |  | 50 000 |  | 50 000 |
| Profit (for the period) |  |  | 71 500 | 71 500 |
| Transfers from reserves |  | (60 000) | 60 000 | Nil |
| Transfers to reserves |  | 50 000 | (50 000) | Nil |
| Interim dividends |  |  | (100 000) | (100 000) |
| Final dividends |  |  | (150 000) | (150 000) |
| Balance (at end of period) | 440 000 | 140 000 | 31 500 | 611 500 |

**Challenge Ltd**
**Statement of financial position**
**at 30 June**

|  | Note | $ | $ |
|---|---|---|---|
| Assets | | | |
| Current assets | | | |
| Cash | 6 | 118 000 | |
| Trade receivables | 7 | 47 500 | |
| Inventories | 8 | 75 000 | |
| Other | 9 | 13 500 | |
| Total current assets | | | 254 000 |
| Non-current assets | | | |
| Available for sale investments | 10 | 54 000 | |
| Financial assets | 11 | 30 000 | |
| Deferred tax assets | 12 | 6 000 | |
| Property, plant and equipment | 13 | 380 000 | |
| Intangibles | 14 | 325 000 | |
| Total non-current assets | | | 795 000 |
| Total assets | | | 1 049 000 |
| Liabilities | | | |
| Current liabilities | | | |
| Trade payables | 15 | 9 000 | |
| Financial liabilities | 16 | 40 000 | |
| Current tax payable | 17 | 73 000 | |
| Short-term provisions | 18 | 73 500 | |
| Other | 19 | 7 500 | |
| Total current liabilities | | | 203 000 |
| Non-current liabilities | | | |
| Financial liabilities | 20 | 155 000 | |
| Deferred tax liabilities | 21 | 3 000 | |
| Long-term provisions | 22 | 76 500 | |
| Total non-current liabilities | | | 234 500 |
| Total liabilities | | | 437 500 |
| Net assets | | | 611 500 |
| Shareholder's equity | | | |
| Share capital | 23 | 440 000 | |
| Reserves | 24 | 140 000 | |
| Retained profits | | 31 500 | |
| Total equity | | | 611 500 |

Note: The total value of shareholder's equity must reconcile with the total shareholders' equity in the statement of changes in equity.

Notes to and forming part of the accounts

| Note | | | $ | $ |
|---|---|---|---|---|
| 6 | Cash | | | |
| | | Cash at bank | 15 000 | |
| | | Cash on hand | 2 000 | |
| | | Petty cash | 1 000 | |
| | | Deposits at call | 100 000 | 118 000 |
| 7 | Trade receivables | | | |
| | | Debtors | 50 000 | |
| | | Allowance for doubtful debts | (2 500) | 47 500 |
| 8 | Inventories | | | |
| | | Stock of finished goods | 35 000 | |
| | | Stock of materials | 40 000 | 75 000 |
| 9 | Other | | | |
| | | Accrued revenues | 10 000 | |
| | | Prepaid expenses | 3 500 | 13 500 |
| 10 | Available for sale investments | | | |
| | | Shares in Gold Ltd | 60 000 | |
| | | Accumulated impairment losses – shares in Gold Ltd | (6 000) | 54 000 |
| 11 | Financial assets | | | |
| | | Government bonds (due 1 December 2020) | | 30 000 |
| 12 | Deferred tax assets | | | 6 000 |
| 13 | Property, plant and equipment | | | |
| | | Equipment | 220 000 | |
| | | Accumulated depreciation – equipment | (72 000) | 148 000 |
| | | Motor vehicles | 80 000 | |
| | | Accumulated depreciation – motor vehicles | (48 000) | 32 000 |
| | | Land and buildings (independent valuation) | | 200 000 |
| | | | | 380 000 |
| 14 | Intangibles | | | |
| | | Goodwill | 25 000 | |
| | | Franchise | 200 000 | |
| | | Patents | 100 000 | 325 000 |
| 15 | Trade payables | | | |
| | | Creditors | 8 000 | |
| | | Sundry creditors | 1 000 | 9 000 |
| 16 | Financial liabilities | | | |
| | | Bank overdraft | 15 000 | |
| | | Bank loan (unsecured and due in 9 months) | 10 000 | |
| | | Mortgage loan (secured over buildings) | 15 000 | 40 000 |
| 17 | Current tax payable | | | |
| | | GST payable | 18 000 | |
| | | Income tax payable | 55 000 | 73 000 |
| 18 | Short-term provisions | | | |
| | | Dividends payable | 30 000 | |
| | | Annual leave payable | 35 000 | |
| | | Long service leave payable | 8 500 | 73 500 |
| 19 | Other | | | |
| | | Accrued wages | 5 000 | |
| | | Prepaid interest revenue | 2 500 | 7 500 |
| 20 | Financial liabilities | | | |
| | | Mortgage loan (secured over buildings) | 135 000 | |
| | | Term loan (unsecured and due in 5 years) | 20 000 | 155 000 |

▶

| Note | | $ | $ |
|---|---|---|---|
| 21 | Deferred tax liabilities | | 3 000 |
| 22 | Long-term provisions | | |
| | Long service leave payable | | 76 500 |
| 23 | Share capital | | |
| | Ordinary shares issued total (450 000 @ $1.00 each) | 450 000 | |
| | Calls in arrears (20 000 ordinary shares @ $0.50 each) | (10 000) | 440 000 |
| 24 | Reserves | | |
| | Dividend reserve | 10 000 | |
| | General reserve | 60 000 | |
| | Asset revaluation reserve | 70 000 | 140 000 |

## Question 8.18

Using the following information provided by Space Ltd for the year ended 30 June you are required to prepare a complete set of financial statements that complies with the Australian Accounting Standards.

### Space Ltd
### Trial balance at 30 June

| Account | Debit $000's | Credit $000's |
|---|---|---|
| Cash on hand | 20 | |
| Deposits – at call | 250 | |
| Trade debtors | 380 | |
| Allowance for doubtful debts | | 10 |
| Stock | 1 550 | |
| Prepaid expenses | 160 | |
| Goodwill | 155 | |
| Land and buildings (at cost) | 1 500 | |
| Land and buildings (at valuation) | 3 000 | |
| Motor vehicles | 100 | |
| Accumulated depreciation – motor vehicles | | 40 |
| Plant and machinery | 2 600 | |
| Accumulated depreciation – plant and machinery | | 1 100 |
| Shares in Galaxy Ltd | 100 | |
| Accumulated impairment loss – shares in Galaxy Ltd | | 50 |
| Trade creditors | | 331 |
| Bank overdraft | | 300 |
| Income tax payable | | 50 |
| Prepaid revenue | | 300 |
| Employee leave entitlements payable | | 80 |
| Dividends payable | | 210 |
| Debenture loan (due in 10 years) | | 100 |
| Mortgage loan | | 1 000 |
| Share capital – ordinary shares (@ $1.00 per share) | | 3 000 |
| Asset revaluation reserve | | 1 400 |
| General reserve | | 580 |
| Dividend reserve | | 300 |
| Retained profits | | 964 |
| | 9 815 | 9 815 |

**General ledger (extract) – Space Ltd**

| Date | Particulars | | Debit $000's | Credit $000's | Balance $000's |
|------|-------------|---|-------|--------|---------|
| **Profit and loss** | | | | | |
| 30 June | Sales | | | 10 500 | 10 500 Cr |
| | Cost of goods sold | | 7 807 | | 2 693 Cr |
| | Profit on sale of assets | | | 120 | 2 813 Cr |
| | Interest on deposits | | | 38 | 2 851 Cr |
| | Dividends from Galaxy Ltd | | | 8 | 2 859 Cr |
| | Depreciation expense | * | 410 | | 2 449 Cr |
| | Lease expense | * | 170 | | 2 279 Cr |
| | Maintenance | * | 90 | | 2 189 Cr |
| | Employee entitlements | * | 830 | | 1 359 Cr |
| | Selling and distribution expenses | | 60 | | 1 299 Cr |
| | Administration expenses | | 80 | | 1 219 Cr |
| | Directors' fees | | 220 | | 999 Cr |
| | Auditors' fees | | 50 | | 949 Cr |
| | Debenture interest | | 27 | | 922 Cr |
| | Interest on mortgage loan | | 36 | | 886 Cr |
| | Bad debts | | 46 | | 840 Cr |
| | Impairment loss – investments | | 70 | | 770 Cr |
| | Income tax expense | | 216 | | 554 Cr |
| | Retained profits | | 554 | | Nil |
| **Retained profits** | | | | | |
| 1 July | Balance | | | | 800 Cr |
| 30 June | Profit and loss | | | 554 | 1 354 Cr |
| | General reserve | | | 20 | 1 374 Cr |
| | Interim dividend | | 200 | | 1 174 Cr |
| | Final dividend | | 210 | | 964 Cr |

*Adjustment (to be made)*

- Land and buildings (at cost) are to be revalued at their fair value of $1 750 000 as per directors' valuation.

*Classification requirements*

- Expenses are to be reported on a functional basis.
- Expenses marked with an asterisk (*) are apportioned 60% to distribution and 40% to administration.
- Income tax is applied at 30%. Impairment losses – investments and the profit on the sale of assets are not tax deductible or tax assessable. There are no temporary differences.

- $30 000 will be paid to employees for long service leave during the following year.
- Bad debts totalling $30 000 are considered material.
- The mortgage loan is being repaid at $200 000 per year.
- Shares in Galaxy Ltd have been acquired as a long-term investment.

# Question 8.19

The following information has been provided by Smart Ltd. You are required to prepare a complete set of financial statements that complies with the Australian Accounting Standards.

### Trial balance at 30 June – Smart Ltd

| Account | Debit $000's | Credit $000's |
|---|---|---|
| Term deposit (180 days) | 20 | |
| Accounts receivable | 1 570 | |
| Allowance for doubtful debts | | 150 |
| Stock on hand | 2 000 | |
| Prepaid expenses | 86 | |
| Equipment | 1 900 | |
| Accumulated depreciation – equipment | | 560 |
| Land and buildings (at fair value) | 7 300 | |
| Shares in Wire Ltd (long-term investment) | 900 | |
| Accumulated impairment loss – shares in Wire Ltd | | 880 |
| Franchises | 3 000 | |
| Deferred tax asset | 204 | |
| Bank | | 346 |
| Trade creditors | | 1 025 |
| Employee benefits payable | | 300 |
| Dividends payable | | 424 |
| Mortgage loan (due in 6 months) | | 900 |
| Debenture loan (due in 5 years) | | 3 000 |
| Share capital – ordinary shares (@ $1.00 each) | | 2 000 |
| Calls in arrears – ordinary shares (@ $0.50 each) | 20 | |
| Share capital – preference shares (@ $10.00 each) | | 5 000 |
| Dividend reserve | | 320 |
| General reserve | | 250 |
| Asset revaluation reserve | | 1 430 |
| Retained profits | | 415 |
| | 17 000 | 17 000 |

General ledger (extract) – Smart Ltd

| Date | Details | Debit $000's | Credit $000's | Balance $000's | |
|---|---|---|---|---|---|
| **Profit and loss** | | | | | |
| 30 June | Sales | | 12 000 | 12 000 | Cr |
| | Stock on hand (1 July) | 100 | | 11 900 | Cr |
| | Purchases | 8 790 | | 3 110 | Cr |
| | Stock on hand (30 June) | | 80 | 3 190 | Cr |
| | Rent of premises | | 810 | 4 000 | Cr |
| | Profit on sale of store | | 2 000 | 6 000 | Cr |
| | Directors' fees | 230 | | 5 770 | Cr |
| | Auditors' fees | 100 | | 5 670 | Cr |
| | Interest debentures | 110 | | 5 560 | Cr |
| | Interest on mortgage loan | 600 | | 4 960 | Cr |
| | Interest on overdraft | 40 | | 4 920 | Cr |
| | Lease costs | 470 | | 4 560 | Cr |
| | Bad debts | 460 | | 3 990 | Cr |
| | Wages and employee benefits | 1 680 | | 2 310 | Cr |
| | Depreciation – vehicles | 610 | | 1 700 | Cr |
| | Loss on disposal of vehicles | 200 | | 1 500 | Cr |
| | Impairment losses on assets | 1 400 | | 100 | Cr |
| | Income tax credit | | 150 | 250 | Cr |
| | Retained profits | 250 | | Nil | |
| **Retained profits** | | | | | |
| 1 July | Balance | | 900 | 900 | Cr |
| 30 June | Profit and loss | | 250 | 1 150 | Cr |
| | Dividend reserve | | 115 | 1 265 | Cr |
| | General reserve | 150 | | 1 115 | Cr |
| | Interim dividend | 280 | | 835 | Cr |
| | Final dividend | 420 | | 415 | Cr |

### Additional information

- The profit on sale of the store and impairment losses does not form part of taxable income. The tax rate is 30%.
- During the year a call of $0.50 per share was made on 2 000 000 ordinary shares.
- The holders of 40 000 ordinary shares have failed to pay the call.
- Land and buildings were increased in value by $3 000 000 during the year.
- Preference shares were issued during the year from the asset revaluation reserve as bonus shares.

### Classification requirements

- Expenses are to be reported disclosing their nature of expense.
- Bad debts are larger than normal by $450 000.
- Employees will be paid $90 000 for long service leave during the year ended 30 June.

# Comprehensive Assessment Activity

From the following information provided by RTO Ltd you are required to prepare a complete set of financial statements in accordance with the requirements of the Australian Accounting Standards.

### General ledger (extract) – RTO Ltd

| Date | Details | Debit $ | Credit $ | Balance $ |
|---|---|---|---|---|
| **Profit and loss** | | | | |
| 30 June | Sales | | 1 400 000 | 1 400 000 Cr |
| | Service revenue | | 2 100 000 | 3 500 000 Cr |
| | Stock (at start of year) | 200 000 | | 3 300 000 Cr |
| | Stock purchased | 2 395 500 | | 904 500 Cr |
| | Stock (at end of year) | | 240 000 | 1 144 500 Cr |
| | Selling expenses | 1 750 | | 1 142 750 Cr |
| | Audit fees | 2 800 | | 1 139 950 Cr |
| | Depreciation – plant and machinery | 42 000 | | 1 097 950 Cr |
| | Directors' fees | 19 250 | | 1 078 700 Cr |
| | Doubtful debts | 3 500 | | 1 075 200 Cr |
| | Employee benefits | 10 500 | | 1 064 700 Cr |
| | Insurances | 7 000 | | 1 057 700 Cr |
| | Interest on bank overdraft | 8 750 | | 1 048 950 Cr |
| | Interest on debentures | 52 500 | | 996 450 Cr |
| | Interest on deposits | | 7 000 | 1 003 450 Cr |
| | Interest on mortgage | 26 250 | | 977 200 Cr |
| | Lease payments | 5 950 | | 971 250 Cr |
| | Loss on machinery sale | 3 500 | | 967 750 Cr |
| | Loss on sale of segment | 140 000 | | 827 750 Cr |
| | Utility expenses | 49 000 | | 778 750 Cr |
| | Wages | 166 250 | | 612 500 Cr |
| | Impairment in investments | 122 500 | | 490 000 Cr |
| | Impairment of goodwill | 2 100 | | 487 900 Cr |
| | Income tax expense | 225 750 | | 262 150 Cr |
| | Retained profits | 262 150 | | Nil |
| **Retained profits** | | | | |
| 1 July | Balance | | 143 500 | 143 500 Cr |
| 30 June | Profit and loss | | 262 150 | 405 650 Cr |
| | Interim dividend | 122 500 | | 283 150 Cr |
| | Final dividend | 145 243 | | 137 907 Cr |
| | General reserve | 35 000 | | 102 907 Cr |
| | Dividend reserve | | 52 500 | 155 407 Cr |

RTO Ltd
Trial balance
at 30th June

| Details | Debit $ | Credit $ |
|---|---|---|
| Accrued interest on deposits | 2 800 | |
| Accumulated depreciation – plant and machinery | | 115 500 |
| Accumulated impairment – investments | | 122 500 |
| Allowance for doubtful debts | | 8 750 |
| Asset revaluation reserve | | 350 000 |
| Calls in arrears (70 000 shares) | 35 000 | |
| Cash at bank | | 236 250 |
| Cash in hand | 3 500 | |
| Debenture loan (due in 5 years) | | 525 000 |
| Deferred tax asset | 10 115 | |
| Deferred tax liability | | 20 265 |
| Deposits at call | 61 250 | |
| Dividend reserve | | 297 500 |
| Dividends payable | | 143 493 |
| Employee benefits payable | | 70 000 |
| General reserve | | 35 000 |
| Goodwill | 18 900 | |
| Income tax payable | | 86 100 |
| Investments (long term) | 157 500 | |
| Land and buildings (at cost) | 2 800 000 | |
| Land and buildings (at valuation) | 1 400 000 | |
| Mortgage loan | | 262 500 |
| Ordinary shares ((@ $2.00 each) | | 2 461 500 |
| Plant and machinery | 210 000 | |
| Retained profits | | 155 407 |
| Stock on hand | 240 000 | |
| Accounts payable | | 148 800 |
| Accounts receivable | 99 500 | |
| | 5 038 565 | 5 038 565 |

## Additional information

- The loss on sale of segment and asset impairments is not tax deductible.
- A bonus dividend of one ordinary share for 10 ordinary shares held is to be declared and issued.
- Land and buildings (at cost) are to be revalued upward by 25% of their cost price.
- The mortgage loan is being paid over 20 years.
- Half of the employee benefits will fall due in 12 months.

# Assessment Checklist

Complete the following checklist to identify if you consider yourself capable of being assessed against each of the following outcomes.

| I can: | Chapter reference | Check ✓ |
|---|---|---|
| explain the financial reporting requirements of a reporting entity | 8.2 | |
| explain the financial reporting obligations of company directors | 8.2 | |
| prepare a statement of profit and loss and other comprehensive income in accordance with the Australian Accounting Standards | 8.3 | |
| prepare a statement of changes in equity in accordance with the Australian Accounting Standards | 8.4 | |
| prepare a statement of financial position in accordance with the Australian Accounting Standards | 8.5 | |
| explain the meaning of a complete set of financial statements | 8.6 | |

# CHAPTER 9

## THE STATEMENT OF
## CASH FLOWS

## WHAT YOU WILL LEARN IN THIS CHAPTER

Upon satisfactory completion of this chapter you should be able to:
- identify cash flows from operating, investing and financing activities;
- prepare a statement of cash flows from the cash journals; and
- prepare a statement of cash flows from the financial statements.

**Are you already competent at these tasks?**

If you have already accomplished these tasks as a result of your recent workplace or training experiences you may wish to proceed to the Comprehensive Assessment Activity at the end of this chapter to assess your skills in these areas.

## 9.1 INTRODUCTION

When presenting a complete set of financial statements reporting entities are required to prepare a statement of cash flows in accordance with AASB107: Statement of Cash Flows.

This statement of cash flows provides information about an entity's cash position and discloses the entity's sources and uses of cash, thereby revealing if the entity has a sound or weak funding structure.

## 9.2 STATEMENT OF CASH FLOWS

AASB107 requires the following disclosures on the statement of cash flows:
1. Cash flows received and paid resulting from:
   - **operating activities:** associated with the provision of goods and services;
   - **investing activities:** related to the purchase or disposal of non-current assets; and
   - **financing activities:** related to long-term debt and equity finance.
2. Amounts received and paid in respect of:
   - interest;
   - dividends; and
   - income tax.
3. Cash holdings which are defined as:
   - **cash:** 'cash on hand' and 'demand deposits'; that is, cash held in the bank, cash on hand, cash in registers, petty cash, bank overdraft; and
   - **cash equivalents:** short-term, highly liquid investments that are readily convertible to cash such as deposits at-call.

In addition, the standard requires a reconciliation of the amounts representing cash reported on the statement of cash flows with the amounts disclosed on the statement of financial position.

### Cash flow activities

Shown below are the three activities that derive cash flows, where the information can be found, and the transactions that comprise the activity.

| Operating activities |
| --- |
| **Source of information:** operating activities relate to transactions associated with the profit and loss account (income statement). This includes: |
| Receipts from customers (+) |
| Payments to suppliers of goods and services (−) |
| Payments to employees (−) |
| Interest received (+) |
| Interest paid (−) |
| Dividends received (+) |
| GST received (+) |
| GST paid (−) |
| Income tax paid (−) |

| Investing activities |
| --- |
| **Source of information:** investing activities relate to movements in non-current assets on the statement of financial position. This includes:<br><br>*Purchase of property, plant and equipment (−)*<br><br>*Proceeds from the sale of property, plant and equipment (+)*<br><br>*Purchase of investments (−)*<br><br>*Proceeds from sale of investments (+)*<br><br>*Loans given to others (−)*<br><br>*Loans repaid by others (+)* |

| Financing activities |
| --- |
| **Source of information:** financing activities relate to movements in non-current liabilities and shareholders' equity on the statement of financial position. This includes:<br><br>*Borrowings acquired (+)*<br><br>*Borrowing repaid (−)*<br><br>*Proceeds from share issues (+)*<br><br>*Dividends paid to shareholders (−)* |

The relationship between the three cash flow activities and the financial statements is illustrated in Figure 9.1.

**Figure 9.1** Sources of cash flows and the financial statements

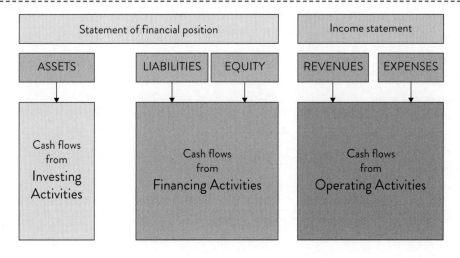

## Question 9.1

Complete the table in the Workbook by classifying each transaction as either an operating, investing or financing activity and indicating if cash has been received (+) or spent (−).

## Format of the statement of cash flows

To comply with the disclosure and reconciliation requirements of AASB107 the following format for the statement of cash flows and cash reconciliation will be used in this text.

**Statement of cash flows**
**for year ended …**

| | $ | $ |
|---|---|---|
| Cash flows related to operating activities | | |
| Receipts from customers | xx | |
| Payments to suppliers | (xx) | |
| Payments to employees | (xx) | |
| Dividends received | xx | |
| Interest received | xx | |
| Interest paid | (xx) | |
| GST received | xx | |
| GST paid | (xx) | |
| Income taxes paid | (xx) | |
| Other | xx | |
| Net operating cash flows | | xx |
| Cash flows related to investing activities | | |
| Cash paid for purchase of non-current assets | (xx) | |
| Cash proceeds from sale of non-current assets | xx | |
| Net investing cash flows | | xx |
| Cash flows related to financing activities | | |
| Cash proceeds from issues of shares | xx | |
| Borrowings acquired | xx | |
| Repayment of borrowings | (xx) | |
| Dividends paid | (xx) | |
| Net financing cash flows | | xx |
| Net increase (decrease) in cash held | | xx |
| Cash at beginning of year | | xx |
| Cash at end of year | | xx |

## 9.3    COMPLETING A STATEMENT CASH FLOW FROM THE CASH RECORDS

A statement of cash flows can be prepared by using an entity's cash records; that is, the cash journals or the cash at bank account.

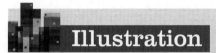

## Illustration

For the month ended 30 June Mash Ltd reported the following cash amounts and cash journals.

| Cash or cash equivalents | 1 June | 30 June |
|---|---|---|
| Cash at bank (overdraft) | ($50 000) | ($32 050) |

The cash at bank account for June included the following receipts and payments:

### Cash at bank account

| Date | Details | Debit $ | Credit $ | Balance $ | |
|---|---|---|---|---|---|
| 1 June | Balance | | | 50 000 | Cr |
| 30 June | Debtors | 8 000 | | 42 000 | Cr |
| | Sales | 12 000 | | 30 000 | Cr |
| | Interest received | 500 | | 29 500 | Cr |
| | GST collected | 3 750 | | 25 750 | Cr |
| | Proceeds from sale of assets | 25 500 | | 2 250 | Cr |
| | Bank trust (ordinary shares) | 20 000 | | 17 750 | Dr |
| | Loan from ABC Bank | 50 000 | | 67 750 | Dr |
| | Creditors | | 11 000 | 58 750 | Dr |
| | Purchases | | 18 000 | 40 750 | Dr |
| | Rent | | 5 000 | 35 750 | Dr |
| | Wages | | 4 000 | 31 750 | Dr |
| | GST paid | | 10 800 | 20 950 | Dr |
| | Interest expense | | 1 000 | 19 950 | Dr |
| | Income tax paid | | 10 000 | 9 950 | Dr |
| | Vehicle purchase | | 35 000 | 25 050 | Cr |
| | Dividends paid | | 4 000 | 29 050 | Cr |
| | Loan from ABC Bank | | 3 000 | 32 050 | Cr |

An analysis of these amounts shows the following cash flow classifications:

### Cash at bank account

| Date | Details | O | I | F | Debit $ | Credit $ | Balance $ |
|---|---|---|---|---|---|---|---|
| 1 June | Balance | | | | | | 50 000  Cr |
| 30 June | Debtors | + | | | 8 000 | | 42 000  Cr |
| | Sales | + | | | 12 000 | | 30 000  Cr |
| | Interest received | + | | | 500 | | 29 500  Cr |
| | GST collected | + | | | 3 750 | | 25 750  Cr |
| | Proceeds from sale of assets | | + | | 25 500 | | 2 250  Cr |
| | Bank trust (ordinary shares) | | | + | 20 000 | | 17 750  Dr |
| | Loan from ABC Bank | | | + | 50 000 | | 67 750  Dr |
| | Creditors | – | | | | 11 000 | 58 750  Dr |
| | Purchases | – | | | | 18 000 | 40 750  Dr |
| | Rent | – | | | | 5 000 | 35 750  Dr |
| | Wages | – | | | | 4 000 | 31 750  Dr |
| | GST paid | – | | | | 10 800 | 20 950  Dr |
| | Interest expense | – | | | | 1 000 | 19 950  Dr |
| | Income tax paid | – | | | | 10 000 | 9 950  Dr |
| | Vehicle purchase | | – | | | 35 000 | 25 050  Cr |
| | Dividends paid | | | – | | 4 000 | 29 050  Cr |
| | Loan from ABC Bank | | | – | | 3 000 | 32 050  Cr |

From this information the cash flows would be classified as follows:

| Cash received | $ | $ |
|---|---|---|
| **Operating activities** | | |
| Receipts from customers: | | |
|   Debtors | 8 000 | |
|   Sales | 12 000 | 20 000 |
| Interest received | | 500 |
| GST received | | 3 750 |
| **Investing activities** | | |
| Sale of assets | | 25 500 |
| **Financing activities** | | |
| Shares issued | 20 000 | |
| Loan from ABC Bank | 50 000 | 70 000 |
| **Total cash inflows** | | 119 750 |

| Cash paid | $ | $ |
|---|---|---|
| **Operating activities** | | |
| Payments to suppliers: | | |
|   Creditors | (11 000) | |
|   Purchases | (18 000) | |
|   Rent | (5 000) | (34 000) |
| Payments to employees | | (4 000) |
| GST paid | | (10 800) |
| Interest expense | | (1 000) |
| Income tax paid | | (10 000) |
| **Investing activities** | | |
| Purchase of vehicle | | (35 000) |
| **Financing activities** | | |
| Dividends paid | (4 000) | |
| Loan from ABC Bank | (3 000) | (7 000) |
| **Total cash outflows** | | (101 800) |

The statement of cash flows and reconciliation of cash resulting from these classifications would be as follows:

**Mash Trading Ltd**
**Cash flow statement for month ended 31 July**

| Cash flows related to operating activities | $ | $ |
|---|---|---|
| Receipts from customers | 20 000 | |
| Payments to suppliers | (34 000) | |
| Payments to employees | (4 000) | |
| Interest received | 500 | |
| Interest paid | (1 000) | |
| GST received | 3 750 | |
| GST paid | (10 800) | |
| Income tax paid | (10 000) | |
| Net operating cash flows | | (35 550) |
| Cash flows related to investing activities | | |
| Cash paid for purchases of assets | (35 000) | |
| Cash proceeds from sale of assets | 25 500 | |
| Net investing cash flows | | (9 500) |
| Cash flows related to financing activities | | |
| Cash proceeds from the issue of shares | 20 000 | |
| Borrowings acquired | 50 000 | |
| Repayment of borrowings | (3 000) | |
| Dividends paid | (4 000) | |
| Net financing cash flows | | 63 000 |
| Net increase (decrease) in cash held | | 17 950 |
| Cash at beginning of year | | (50 000) |
| Cash at end of year | | (32 050) |

**Reconciliation of cash at 30 June**

| | 1 June | 30 June |
|---|---|---|
| | $ | $ |
| Cash at bank | (50 000) | (32 050) |
| Total cash available | (50 000) | (32 050) |

This statement and reconciliation reveals that the business:
1 made a cash loss on operating activities of ($35 550);
2 spent a net figure of $9500 on acquiring assets; and
3 raised $63 000 from financing activities;
which resulted in:
1 a net change (increase) in the cash position of $17 950; and
2 improved cash holdings from ($50 000) to ($32 050).

## Question 9.2

Olly Ltd has provided you with its cash at bank account for June from which you are required to prepare a statement of cash flows that complies with Accounting Standard AASB107.

### Cash at bank account

| Date | Details | Debit $ | Credit $ | Balance $ |
|---|---|---|---|---|
| 1 July | Opening balance | | | 20 000  Dr |
| 30 July | Sales income | 150 000 | | 170 000  Dr |
| | Accounts receivable | 50 000 | | 220 000  Dr |
| | Wages | | 20 000 | 200 000  Dr |
| | Leave payable | | 5 000 | 195 000  Dr |
| | Supplies | | 5 000 | 190 000  Dr |
| | Accounts payable | | 125 000 | 65 000  Dr |
| | Equipment (purchase) | | 100 000 | 35 000  Cr |
| | Share applications | 80 000 | | 45 000  Dr |
| | Dividends payable | | 40 000 | 5 000  Dr |
| | Equipment (sale) | 10 000 | | 15 000  Dr |
| | Interest received | 2 000 | | 17 000  Dr |
| | GST received | 15 000 | | 32 000  Dr |
| | GST paid | | 20 000 | 12 000  Dr |
| | Income tax paid | | 15 000 | 3 000  Cr |
| | Bank loan (paid) | | 15 000 | 18 000  Cr |

## Question 9.3

The following information has been provided by Chang Ltd. You are required to prepare a statement of cash flows for the month of October.

| Cash or cash equivalents | Start of month $ | End of month $ |
|---|---|---|
| Cash at bank | (10 000) | 31 700 |
| Deposits at call | 30 000 | 30 000 |

### Cash receipts journal

| Date October | Details | Bank $ | Debtors $ | Sales $ | Other $ | GST collected $ |
|---|---|---|---|---|---|---|
| 3 | Sales | 22 000 | | 20 000 | | 2 000 |
| 8 | Account – BP Ltd | 50 000 | 50 000 | | | |
| 9 | Sales | 110 000 | | 100 000 | | 10 000 |
| 10 | Share capital (applications) | 50 000 | | | 50 000 | |
| 13 | Interest received | 2 000 | | | 2 000 | |
| 21 | Proceeds from equipment | 27 500 | | | 25 000 | 2 500 |
| 25 | Loan acquired – BB Bank | 50 000 | | | 50 000 | |
| 31 | Account – K. Lawson | 30 000 | 30 000 | | | |
| | | 341 500 | 80 000 | 120 000 | 127 000 | 14 500 |

Cash payments journal

| Date October | Details | Bank $ | Creditors $ | Purchases $ | Wages $ | Other $ | GST paid $ |
|---|---|---|---|---|---|---|---|
| 2 | Purchases | 16 500 | | 15 000 | | | 1 500 |
| 8 | Account – J. West | 4 000 | 4 000 | | | | |
| 9 | Wages | 5 000 | | | 5 000 | | |
| 10 | Purchases | 19 800 | | 18 000 | | | 1 800 |
| 14 | Dividends paid | 110 000 | | | | 110 000 | |
| 15 | Interest expense | 10 000 | | | | 10 000 | |
| 19 | Purchase of equipment | 55 000 | | | | 50 000 | 5 000 |
| 21 | Wages | 5 000 | | | 5 000 | | |
| 33 | Rent expense | 16 500 | | | | 15 000 | 1 500 |
| 25 | Loan payment | 10 000 | | | | 10 000 | |
| 28 | ATO (GST) | 12 000 | | | | | 12 000 |
| | ATO (income tax) | 20 000 | | | | 20 000 | |
| 30 | Account – J. West | 16 000 | 16 000 | | | | |
| | | 299 800 | 20 000 | 33 000 | 10 000 | 215 000 | 21 800 |

## 9.4 COMPLETING A CASH FLOW STATEMENT FROM THE FINANCIAL REPORTS

A statement of cash flows can also be prepared from the financial reports: the income statement and statement of financial position.

When preparing the statement of cash flows from the financial reports AASB107 requires cash flows from operating activities to be reported using either:

a   the **direct method** which discloses individual amounts for cash received and cash paid; or

b   the **indirect method** which reports profit or loss and discloses the effect on this operating result for non-cash transactions, prepayments and accruals.

AASB107 indicates a preference for reporting cash flows from operating activities using the direct method.

When preparing the statement of cash flows using either method, adjustments will need to made to the amounts reported on the profit and loss statement and the statement of financial position as these statements will have been prepared using **accrual** accounting concepts, whereas the statement of cash flows must be reported using **cash** accounting concepts.

Hence adjustments will need to be made to remove the effects of transactions that:

a   did not involve a cash flow; and

b   involved accrual accounting adjustments.

This will result when:

• sales made on invoice to debtors are included in the income statement as credit sales;

• purchases of stock on credit are included in the calculation of the cost of sales in the income statement;

• revenue and expense accounts have been adjusted due to accruals;

• annual leave, long service leave and other employee entitlements appear in the income statement;

• non-cash transactions are included in the calculation of profit; and

• income tax expense remains unpaid.

Where the statement of financial position includes current asset or current liability accounts this usually indicates that accrual adjustments have been made to amounts appearing in the profit and loss statement.

Current asset accounts indicating that accrual amounts rather than cash amounts appear on the income statement include:

• debtors (accounts receivable), which result from credit sales being reported on the income statement;

• stock (inventory) which affects cost of goods sold and purchases; and

• prepaid expenses and accrued revenues which arise as a result of revenues and expenses being adjusted on the profit and loss statement.

Current liability accounts indicating that accrual amounts appear on the income statement and not cash amounts include:

- creditors (accounts payable), which are only brought to account when the profit includes credit purchases;
- prepaid revenues and accrued expenses resulting from revenues and expenses adjustments made on the income statement;
- annual leave payable, long service leave payable and employee entitlements payable arising from leave expenses reported in the calculation of profit; and
- income tax payable, which results when income tax remains unpaid.

Where the financial position includes current assets or current liabilities that have resulted from accrual entries in the calculation of profit or loss, account reconstructions will need to be made to determine the cash flow associated with the asset or liability.

# 9.5 REPORTING CASH FLOWS FROM OPERATING ACTIVITIES USING THE DIRECT METHOD

The direct method of reporting cash flows from operating activities is the recommended method in AASB107. This method requires the separate reporting of individual operating cash flows resulting from the calculation of profit or loss.

The following format can be used to disclose operating cash flows under the direct method.

**Statement of cash flows**
**for the year ended ...**

|  | $ | $ |
|---|---|---|
| Cash flows related to operating activities | | |
| Receipts from customers | XX | |
| Payments to suppliers | (XX) | |
| Payments to employees | (XX) | |
| Dividends received | XX | |
| Interest received | XX | |
| Interest paid | (XX) | |
| GST received | XX | |
| GST paid | (XX) | |
| Income taxes paid | (XX) | |
| Other | XX | |
| Net operating cash flows | | XX |
| Net increase (decrease) in cash held | | XX |
| Cash at beginning of year | | XX |
| Cash at end of year | | XX |

The amounts for each of the operating cash flows shown on the statement can be derived from the amounts reported on the income statement and the statement of financial position.

The following illustrations will show how to calculate each of the significant operating cash flows using information presented in the financial statements.

## Calculating and reporting GST

Revenues and expenses disclosed in the profit and loss statement do not include GST; however, amounts shown as assets and liabilities may include GST. GST must be included in account reconstruction to determine the true cash flow related.

The GST account includes GST on cash and credit transactions and it includes payments made to the ATO. Due to the complexities associated with the GST account all illustrations and questions will state the GST received in cash and paid in cash for inclusion on the statement of cash flows.

## Receipts from customers

An entity may conduct business with customers on a cash and credit basis. Where customers are provided with credit the entity may offer discount and incur bad debts. Credit sales, discount and bad debts attract GST, hence the accounts receivable account will need to be reconstructed to calculate cash received from account customers.

In addition, an entity may provide for doubtful debts. This is not a cash transaction and will not impact on the calculation of cash received from customers.

 **Illustration**

Rusty Ltd has provided the following accrual information for the year ended 30 June.

| Income statement for year ended 30 June | | Statement of financial position | | |
|---|---|---|---|---|
| | **$** | | **1 July** | **30 June** |
| Cash services | 50 000 | | **$** | **$** |
| Credit services | 250 000 | **Current assets** | | |
| | 300 000 | Cash at bank | 30 000 | 317 000 |
| Less expenses | | Accounts receivable | 100 000 | 90 000 |
| Doubtful debts | 10 000 | Less allowance for doubtful debts | | (10 000) |
| Bad debts | 25 000 | | 130 000 | 397 000 |
| Discount expense | 5 000 | **Current liabilities** | | |
| Profit | 260 000 | GST payable | | 7 000 |
| | | **Shareholders' equity** | | |
| **GST information:** | | Share capital | 130 000 | 130 000 |
| GST received in cash | 5 000 | Retained profits | 0 | 260 000 |
| GST paid to the ATO | 20 000 | | 130 000 | 397 000 |

Analysis of the financial statements reveals the following:

**Income statement**
- cash services of $50 000 have been received; and
- services have been provided on credit for $250 000 with related expenses of doubtful debts, bad debts and discount expense.

**Statement of financial position**
- accounts receivable has decreased from $100 000 at the start of the year to $90 000 at 30 June;
- an allowance for doubtful debts of $10 000 has been brought to account; and
- the bank account has increased by $287 000 from $30 000 at the start of the year to $317 000 at 30 June.

Consequently the accounts receivable account needs to be reconstructed to determine the cash received from credit customers. The reconstruction of accounts receivable must include transactions that influence the amount that customers would owe; that is, account balances, sales, expenses and GST. Doubtful debts expense must be excluded as it is not a transaction that results in a cash flow.

The cash received from accounts receivable can be calculated using one of the following methods:

**Accounts receivable (narrative format)**

|  |  | $ |
|---|---|---|
| Opening balance |  | 100 000 |
| Add credit services (plus GST) | ($250 000 X 1.1) | 275 000 |
|  |  | 375 000 |
| Less |  |  |
| Bad debts (plus GST) | ($25 000 X 1.1) | 27 500 |
| Discount expense (plus GST) | ($5 000 X 1.1) | 5 500 |
| Closing balance |  | 90 000 |
| Cash received |  | 252 000 |

Or

**Accounts receivable (account format)**

| Date | Details | Dr $ | Cr $ | Balance $ |
|---|---|---|---|---|
| 1 July | Opening balance | 100 000 |  | 100 000  Dr |
| 30 June | Sales (+ GST) | 275 000 |  | 375 000  Dr |
|  | Bad debts (+ GST) |  | 27 500 | 347 500  Dr |
|  | Discount (+ GST) |  | 5 500 | 342 000  Dr |
|  | Bank (missing figure) |  | 252 000 | 90 000  Dr |

Hence the cash flows received from customers include:

| Cash received from cash sales | $50 000 |
|---|---|
| Cash received from account customers | $252 000 |
| Total cash received from customers | $302 000 |

The statement of cash flows and reconciliation arising from the financial statements would be as follows:

**Rusty Ltd**
**Statement of cash flows**
**for the year ended 30 June**

|  | $ | $ |
|---|---|---|
| Cash flows related to operating activities |  |  |
| Receipts from customers | 302 000 |  |
| GST received | 5 000 |  |
| GST paid | (20 000) |  |
| Net operating cash flows |  | 287 000 |
| Net increase (decrease) in cash held |  | 287 000 |
| Cash at beginning of year |  | 30 000 |
| Cash at end of year |  | 317 000 |

**Reconciliation of cash at 30 June**

|  | 1 June | 30 June |
|---|---|---|
|  | $ | $ |
| Cash at bank | 30 000 | 317 000 |

## Question 9.4

Using the following information provided by Fox Ltd you are required to prepare a statement of cash flows and reconciliation of cash for the year ended 30 June.

### Income statement for year ended 30 June

| | $ |
|---|---|
| Cash services | 30 000 |
| Credit services | 200 000 |
| | 230 000 |
| Less expenses | |
| Doubtful debts | 5 000 |
| Bad debts | 10 000 |
| Discount expense | 2 000 |
| Profit | 213 000 |
| | |
| **GST information:** | |
| GST received in cash | 3 000 |
| GST paid to the ATO | 18 000 |

### Statement of financial position

| | 1 July | 30 June |
|---|---|---|
| | $ | $ |
| **Current assets** | | |
| Cash at bank | 101 800 | 313 600 |
| Accounts receivable | 50 000 | 60 000 |
| Less allowance for doubtful debts | – | (5 000) |
| | 151 800 | 368 600 |
| **Current liabilities** | | |
| GST payable | 1 800 | 5 600 |
| **Shareholders' equity** | | |
| Share capital | 130 000 | 130 000 |
| Retained profits | 20 000 | 233 000 |
| | 151 800 | 368 600 |

## Payments to suppliers

Where an entity purchases inventory on credit from suppliers the accounts payable account will need to be reconstructed to determine the amount paid to suppliers. In addition, the stock on hand account will also need to be reconstructed to include the cost of goods sold to determine the amount of goods purchased from suppliers with GST added.

## Illustration

Banjo Ltd has provided the following accrual information for the year ended 30 June.

### Income statement for year ended 30 June

| | $ |
|---|---|
| Cash sales | 400 000 |
| Less cost of goods sold | 250 000 |
| | 150 000 |
| Add discount received | 10 000 |
| Profit | 160 000 |
| | |
| **GST information:** | |
| GST received in cash | 65 000 |
| GST paid to the ATO | 40 000 |

### Statement of financial position

| | 1 July | 30 June |
|---|---|---|
| | $ | $ |
| **Current assets** | | |
| Cash at bank | 30 000 | 175 000 |
| Stock on hand | 50 000 | 60 000 |
| | 80 000 | 235 000 |
| **Current liabilities** | | |
| Accounts payable | 30 000 | 25 000 |
| **Shareholders' equity** | | |
| Share capital | 50 000 | 50 000 |
| Retained profits | 0 | 160 000 |
| | 80 000 | 235 000 |

Analysis of the financial statements reveals the following:

**Income statement**
- cash sales of $400 000 has been received;
- cost of goods sold total $250 000; and
- discount of $10 000 has been received from suppliers.

**Statement of financial position**
- stock on hand has increased from $50 000 to $60 000;
- accounts payable has fallen from $30 000 to $25 000; and
- the bank account has increased by $145 000 from $30 000 at the start of the year to $175 000 at 30 June.

Consequently the stock on hand account must to be reconstructed to determine the value of goods purchased from suppliers (plus GST) and the accounts payable account will need to be reconstructed to calculate the amount paid to suppliers.

The account reconstructions may be performed using one of the following methods:

**Stock on hand (narrative format)**

|  | $ |
|---|---|
| Cost of goods sold | 250 000 |
| Add stock (end of year) | 60 000 |
|  | 310 000 |
| Less stock (start of year) | (50 000) |
| Purchases | 260 000 |
| Add GST | 26 000 |
| Purchases (including GST) | 286 000 |

**Accounts payable (narrative format)**

|  | $ |
|---|---|
| Opening balance | 30 000 |
| Add purchases (including GST) | 286 000 |
|  | 316 000 |
| Less |  |
| Discount (+ GST) | (11 000) |
| Closing balance | (25 000) |
| Cash paid to suppliers | 280 000 |

Or

| Date | Details | Dr $ | Cr $ | Balance $ |
|---|---|---|---|---|
| **Stock on hand (account format)** | | | | |
| 1 July | Opening balance | 50 000 |  | 50 000  Dr |
| 30 June | Cost of goods sold |  | 250 000 | 200 000  Cr |
|  | Purchases (missing figure) | 260 000 |  | 60 000  Dr |
| **Accounts payable (account format)** | | | | |
| 1 July | Opening balance |  | 30 000 | 30 000  Cr |
| 30 June | Purchases (+ GST) |  | 286 000 | 316 000  Cr |
|  | Discount (+ GST) | 11 000 |  | 305 000  Cr |
|  | Bank (missing figure) | 280 000 |  | 25 000  Cr |

The statement of cash flows and reconciliation of cash arising from the financial statements would be as follows:

**Banjo Ltd**
**Statement of cash flows**
**for the year ended 30 June**

| | $ | $ |
|---|---|---|
| Cash flows related to operating activities | | |
| Receipts from customers | 400 000 | |
| Payments to suppliers | (280 000) | |
| GST received | 65 000 | |
| GST paid | (40 000) | |
| Net operating cash flows | | 145 000 |
| Net increase (decrease) in cash held | | 145 000 |
| Cash at beginning of year | | 30 000 |
| Cash at end of year | | 175 000 |

**Reconciliation of cash at 30 June**

| | 1 June | 30 June |
|---|---|---|
| | $ | $ |
| Cash at bank | 30 000 | 175 000 |

## Question 9.5

Using the following information provided by Craze Ltd, you are required to prepare a statement of cash flows.

**Income statement for year ended 30 June**

| | $ |
|---|---|
| Cash sales | 550 000 |
| Less cost of goods sold | 500 000 |
| | 50 000 |
| Add discount received | 5 000 |
| Profit | 55 000 |
| | |
| GST information: | |
| GST received in cash | 104 000 |
| GST paid to ATO | 55 000 |

**Statement of financial position**

| | 1 July | 30 June |
|---|---|---|
| | $ | $ |
| Current assets | | |
| Cash at bank | 45 000 | 95 000 |
| Stock on hand | 20 000 | 15 000 |
| | 65 000 | 110 000 |
| Current liabilities | | |
| Accounts payable | 40 000 | 30 000 |
| Shareholders' equity | | |
| Share capital | 20 000 | 20 000 |
| Retained profits | 5 000 | 60 000 |
| | 65 000 | 110 000 |

## Question 9.6

From the following information provided by Oslo Ltd, you are required to prepare a statement of cash flows and cash reconciliation report.

### Income statement for year ended 30 June

|  | $ |
|---|---|
| Cash services | 200 000 |
| Credit sales | 500 000 |
|  | 700 000 |
| Less cost of goods sold | 600 000 |
| Gross profit | 100 000 |
| Add discount received | 10 000 |
|  | 110 000 |
| Less expenses |  |
| Doubtful debts | 5 000 |
| Bad debts | 20 000 |
| Discount expense | 4 000 |
| Profit | 81 000 |
| GST information: |  |
| GST received in cash | 80 000 |
| GST paid to the ATO | 65 000 |

### Statement of financial position

|  | 1 July | 30 June |
|---|---|---|
|  | $ | $ |
| Current assets |  |  |
| Cash at bank | 55 000 | 123 600 |
| Accounts receivable | 30 000 | 50 000 |
| Less allowance for doubtful debts |  | (5 000) |
| Inventory | 20 000 | 30 000 |
|  | 105 000 | 198 600 |
| Current liabilities |  |  |
| Accounts payable | 40 000 | 50 000 |
| GST payable | 5 000 | 7 600 |
| Shareholders' equity |  |  |
| Share capital | 50 000 | 50 000 |
| Retained profits | 10 000 | 91 000 |
|  | 105 000 | 198 600 |

## Question 9.7

From the following information provided by Karma Ltd, you are required to prepare a statement of cash flows and cash reconciliation report.

### Income statement for year ended 30 June

|  | $ |
|---|---|
| Credit sales | 900 000 |
| Less cost of goods sold | 800 000 |
| Gross profit | 100 000 |
| Add discount received | 5 000 |
|  | 105 000 |
| Less expenses |  |
| Doubtful debts | 10 000 |
| Bad debts | 30 000 |
| Discount expense | 5 000 |
| Profit | 60 000 |
| GST information: |  |
| GST received in cash | 80 500 |
| GST paid to the ATO | 45 000 |

### Statement of financial position

|  | 1 July | 30 June |
|---|---|---|
|  | $ | $ |
| Current assets |  |  |
| Cash at bank | (50 000) | 61 500 |
| Debtors | 80 000 | 85 000 |
| Less allowance for doubtful debts |  | (10 000) |
| Stock | 50 000 | 60 000 |
|  | 80 000 | 196 500 |
| Current liabilities |  |  |
| Creditors | 35 000 | 50 000 |
| GST payable | 5 000 | 46 500 |
| Shareholders' equity |  |  |
| Share capital | 20 000 | 20 000 |
| Retained profits | 20 000 | 80 000 |
|  | 80 000 | 196 500 |

## Payments to employees

Expenses relating to employees include wages and salaries, sales commission, annual leave, long service leave and other employee entitlements.

These amounts appear on the income statement but will not represent the actual cash paid if the statement of financial position includes accrued wages or leave liability amounts. Account reconstructions may be required to determine the cash flow amount related to payments to employees.

## Illustration

Finito Ltd has provided the following financial information for the year ended 30 June.

### Income statement for year ended 30 June

| | $ |
|---|---|
| Cash services | 180 000 |
| Less expenses | |
| Wages and salaries | 120 000 |
| Annual leave expense | 30 000 |
| Profit | 30 000 |
| | |
| GST information: | |
| GST received in cash | 18 000 |
| GST paid to the ATO | 19 000 |

### Statement of financial position

| | 1 July | 30 June |
|---|---|---|
| | $ | $ |
| **Current assets** | | |
| Cash at bank | 48 000 | 78 000 |
| **Current liabilities** | | |
| Accrued wages | 6 000 | 10 000 |
| Leave payable | 15 000 | 12 000 |
| GST payable | 2 000 | 1 000 |
| **Shareholders' equity** | | |
| Share capital | 20 000 | 20 000 |
| Retained profits | 5 000 | 35 000 |
| | 48 000 | 78 000 |

Analysis of the financial statements reveals the following:

**Income statement**
- wages and salaries expense of $120 000; and
- annual leave expense of $30 000.

**Statement of financial position**
- accrued wages at the start and end of the year; and
- leave payable owing at the start and end of the year.

Consequently the wages expense account and leave payable accounts will need reconstructing to determine the cash paid for wages and leave during the year.

The account reconstructions may be performed using one of the following methods:

### Wage expense (narrative format)

| | $ |
|---|---|
| Wages expensed | 120 000 |
| Add accrued wages (start of year) | 6 000 |
| | 126 000 |
| Less accrued wages (end of year) | (10 000) |
| **Wages paid** | **116 000** |

### Leave payable (narrative format)

| | $ |
|---|---|
| Opening balance | 15 000 |
| Leave expensed | 30 000 |
| | 45 000 |
| Less closing balance | (12 000) |
| **Leave paid** | **33 000** |

Or

| Date | Details | Dr $ | Cr $ | Balance $ |
|---|---|---|---|---|
| **Wages expense (account format)** | | | | |
| 1 July | Accrued wages (at start) | | | 6 000 Cr |
| 30 June | Profit and loss | | 120 000 | 126 000 Cr |
| | Accrued wages (at end) | 10 000 | | 116 000 Cr |
| | Bank (missing figure) | 116 000 | | Nil Cr |
| **Leave payable (account format)** | | | | |
| 1 July | Opening balance | | | 15 000 Cr |
| 30 June | Leave expense | | 30 000 | 45 000 Cr |
| | Bank (missing figure) | 33 000 | | 12 000 Cr |

Hence the cash flows for payments to employees include:

| Wages paid | $116 000 |
|---|---|
| Leave paid | $33 000 |
| Total payments to employees | $149 000 |

The statement of cash flows arising from the financial statements would be as follows:

**Finito Ltd**
**Statement of cash flows**
**for year ended 30 June**

| | $ | $ |
|---|---|---|
| Cash flows related to operating activities | | |
| Receipts from customers | 180 000 | |
| Payments to employees | (149 000) | |
| GST received | 18 000 | |
| GST paid | (19 000) | |
| Net operating cash flows | | 30 000 |
| Net increase (decrease) in cash held | | 30 000 |
| Cash at beginning of year | | 48 000 |
| Cash at end of year | | 78 000 |

## Question 9.8

Using the following extracts of financial statements calculate the amount paid to employees.

**Financial statements (extracts)**

| Income statement for year ended 30 June | $ |
|---|---|
| Expenses | |
| Wages and salaries | 600 000 |
| Leave expense | 50 000 |

| Statement of financial position | 1 July $ | 30 June $ |
|---|---|---|
| Current liabilities | | |
| Accrued wages | 15 000 | 20 000 |
| Leave payable | 4 000 | 6 000 |

## Income tax paid and other expenses

All expenses shown on the income statement must be analysed to determine if they will be reported on the statement of cash flows, and if so, under which operating category.

Some expenses do not relate to a cash flow and will not be included in the statement of cash flows. These transactions include doubtful debts, depreciation expenses, impairment of assets and profit or losses on asset disposals.

When income tax expense is included in the calculation of profit the amount of income tax paid will need to be determined by reconstructing the income tax payable account and reported on the statement of cash flows as *income tax paid*.

All other expenses can be categorised as *payments to suppliers*. This includes expenses incurred for the provision of services such as advertising, rent, vehicle expenses, stationery, cleaning, utility costs and so on.

When analysing expenses to identify their impact on the entity's cash position it is also necessary to analyse the statement of financial position for the existence of current assets or liabilities arising from accrual adjustments relating to expenses or revenues.

## Illustration

Asheeba Ltd has provided the following financial information for the year ended 30 June.

<table>
<tr><th colspan="3">Profit statement for year ended 30 June</th></tr>
<tr><th></th><th>$</th><th>$</th></tr>
<tr><td>Cash services</td><td></td><td>500 000</td></tr>
<tr><td>Less expenses</td><td></td><td></td></tr>
<tr><td>Depreciation expense</td><td>20 000</td><td></td></tr>
<tr><td>Loss – disposal of machinery</td><td>5 000</td><td></td></tr>
<tr><td>Impairment loss – goodwill</td><td>30 000</td><td></td></tr>
<tr><td>Supplies</td><td>250 000</td><td></td></tr>
<tr><td>Advertising expense</td><td>20 000</td><td></td></tr>
<tr><td>Rent expense</td><td>40 000</td><td></td></tr>
<tr><td>Wages</td><td>100 000</td><td>465 000</td></tr>
<tr><td>Profit (before tax)</td><td></td><td>35 000</td></tr>
<tr><td>Less income tax expense</td><td></td><td>19 500</td></tr>
<tr><td>Profit (after tax)</td><td></td><td>15 500</td></tr>
<tr><td></td><td></td><td></td></tr>
<tr><td>GST information:</td><td></td><td></td></tr>
<tr><td>   GST received in cash</td><td></td><td>50 000</td></tr>
<tr><td>   GST paid to ATO</td><td></td><td>51 000</td></tr>
</table>

<table>
<tr><th colspan="3">Statement of financial position</th></tr>
<tr><th></th><th>1 July</th><th>30 June</th></tr>
<tr><th></th><th>$</th><th>$</th></tr>
<tr><td>Current assets</td><td></td><td></td></tr>
<tr><td>Cash at bank</td><td>(23 000)</td><td>46 500</td></tr>
<tr><td>Prepaid rent</td><td>5 000</td><td>6 000</td></tr>
<tr><td>Non-current assets</td><td></td><td></td></tr>
<tr><td>Plant and machinery</td><td>80 000</td><td>75 000</td></tr>
<tr><td>Accumulated depreciation</td><td>(10 000)</td><td>(30 000)</td></tr>
<tr><td>Goodwill</td><td>30 000</td><td>0</td></tr>
<tr><td></td><td>82 000</td><td>97 500</td></tr>
<tr><td>Current liabilities</td><td></td><td></td></tr>
<tr><td>GST payable</td><td>10 000</td><td>9 000</td></tr>
<tr><td>Income tax payable</td><td>2 000</td><td>3 000</td></tr>
<tr><td>Shareholders' equity</td><td></td><td></td></tr>
<tr><td>Share capital</td><td>50 000</td><td>50 000</td></tr>
<tr><td>Retained profits</td><td>20 000</td><td>35 500</td></tr>
<tr><td></td><td>82 000</td><td>97 500</td></tr>
</table>

Analysis of the financial statements reveals the following:

**Income statement**
- non-cash transactions include doubtful debts expense, depreciation expense, loss on disposal of machinery and impairment losses of assets;
- payments to suppliers include supplies expense, advertising and rent;
- employees were paid; and
- income tax has been expensed.

**Statement of financial position**
- accrued adjustments have been made for prepaid rent and income tax payable; and
- movements in plant and machinery, accumulated depreciation and goodwill have been caused by non-cash transactions.

Consequently the rent expense account and income tax payable accounts will need reconstructing to determine the cash paid for rent and income tax during the year.

The account reconstructions may be performed using one of the following methods:

<table>
<tr><th colspan="2">Rent expense (narrative format)</th></tr>
<tr><th></th><th>$</th></tr>
<tr><td>Rent expensed</td><td>40 000</td></tr>
<tr><td>Less prepaid rent (start of year)</td><td>(5 000)</td></tr>
<tr><td></td><td>35 000</td></tr>
<tr><td>Add prepaid rent (end of year)</td><td>6 000</td></tr>
<tr><td>Rent paid</td><td>41 000</td></tr>
</table>

<table>
<tr><th colspan="2">Income tax payable (narrative format)</th></tr>
<tr><th></th><th>$</th></tr>
<tr><td>Opening balance</td><td>2 000</td></tr>
<tr><td>Income tax expensed</td><td>19 500</td></tr>
<tr><td></td><td>21 500</td></tr>
<tr><td>Less closing balance</td><td>(3 000)</td></tr>
<tr><td>Income tax paid</td><td>18 500</td></tr>
</table>

Or

| Date | Details | Dr $ | Cr $ | Balance $ |
|---|---|---|---|---|
| **Rent expense (account format)** | | | | |
| 1 July | Prepaid rent (at start) | 5 000 | | 5 000 Dr |
| 30 June | Profit and loss | | 40 000 | 35 000 Cr |
| | Prepaid rent (at end) | | 6 000 | 41 000 Cr |
| | Bank (missing figure) | 41 000 | | Nil |
| **Income tax payable (account format)** | | | | |
| 1 July | Opening balance | | 2 000 | 2 000 Cr |
| 30 June | Leave expense | | 19 500 | 21 500 Cr |
| | Bank (missing figure) | 18 500 | | 5 000 Cr |

Hence the cash flows for payments to suppliers include:

| | |
|---|---|
| Rent paid | $41 000 |
| Supplies paid | $250 000 |
| Advertising paid | $20 000 |
| Total payments to suppliers | $311 000 |

The statement of cash flows arising from the financial statements would be as follows:

**Asheeba Ltd**
**Statement of cash flows**
**for year ended 30 June**

| | $ | $ |
|---|---|---|
| **Cash flows related to operating activities** | | |
| Receipts from customers | 500 000 | |
| Payments to suppliers | (311 000) | |
| Payments to employees | (100 000) | |
| Income tax paid | (18 500) | |
| GST received | 50 000 | |
| GST paid | (51 000) | |
| Net operating cash flows | | 69 500 |
| Net increase (decrease) in cash held | | 69 500 |
| Cash at beginning of year | | (23 000) |
| Cash at end of year | | 46 500 |

# Question 9.9

Using the following extract of financial statements, make a list of non-cash transactions and calculate amounts paid to suppliers and income tax.

**Financial statements (extracts)**

| Income statement for year ended 30 June | |
|---|---|
| | **$** |
| **Expenses** | |
| Depreciation expense | 50 000 |
| Impairment loss – goodwill | 10 000 |
| Advertising | 60 000 |
| Rent | 80 000 |
| Purchases | 400 000 |
| Income tax expense | 40 000 |

| Statement of financial position | | |
|---|---|---|
| | **1 July** | **30 June** |
| | **$** | **$** |
| Current assets | | |
| Prepaid advertising | 10 000 | 8 000 |
| Current liabilities | | |
| Accrued rent | 5 000 | 3 000 |
| Income tax payable | 25 000 | 20 000 |

# Question 9.10

From the following financial statements of Yabba Ltd for the year ended 30 June, you are required to prepare a statement of cash flows and reconciliation of cash.

| Income statement for year ended 30 June | | |
|---|---|---|
| | **$** | **$** |
| Cash services | | 900 000 |
| Less expenses | | |
| Purchases | 600 000 | |
| Wages | 130 000 | |
| Leave expense | 20 000 | |
| Advertising expense | 30 000 | |
| Rent expense | 20 000 | |
| Depreciation expense | 20 000 | |
| Impairment loss – goodwill | 15 000 | 835 000 |
| Profit (before tax) | | 65 000 |
| Less Income tax expense | | 24 000 |
| Profit (after tax) | | 41 000 |
| GST information: | | |
| GST received in cash | | 90 000 |
| GST paid to ATO | | (85 000) |

| Statement of financial position | | |
|---|---|---|
| | **1 July** | **30 June** |
| | **$** | **$** |
| Current assets | | |
| Cash at bank | (5 000) | 79 000 |
| Prepaid rent | 8 000 | 10 000 |
| Non-current assets | | |
| Vehicles | 80 000 | 80 000 |
| Accumulated depreciation | (10 000) | (30 000) |
| Goodwill | 40 000 | 25 000 |
| | 113 000 | 164 000 |
| Current liabilities | | |
| Accrued wages | 8 000 | 5 000 |
| Leave liability | 5 000 | 8 000 |
| GST payable | 20 000 | 25 000 |
| Income tax payable | 10 000 | 15 000 |
| Shareholders' equity | | |
| Share capital | 50 000 | 50 000 |
| Retained profits | 20 000 | 61 000 |
| | 113 000 | 164 000 |

## Question 9.11

Using the following financial statements of Broome Ltd for the year ended 30 June, you are required to prepare a statement of cash flows and reconciliation of cash.

### Income statement for year ended 30 June

| | $ | $ |
|---|---|---|
| Cash services | 150 000 | |
| Credit sales | 650 000 | 800 000 |
| Cost of goods sold | | 500 000 |
| Gross profit | | 300 000 |
| Less expenses | | |
| Wages | 120 000 | |
| Interest expense | 10 000 | |
| Bad debts | 5 000 | |
| Rent expense | 40 000 | |
| Depreciation expense | 30 000 | 205 000 |
| Profit (before tax) | | 95 000 |
| Less income tax expense | | 28 500 |
| Profit (after tax) | | 66 500 |
| | | |
| GST information: | | |
| GST received in cash | | 15 000 |
| GST paid to the ATO | | (34 000) |

### Statement of financial position

| | 1 July | 30 June |
|---|---|---|
| | $ | $ |
| **Current assets** | | |
| Cash at bank | (9 000) | 84 200 |
| Debtors | 30 000 | 35 000 |
| Stock | 20 000 | 18 000 |
| Prepaid rent | 4 000 | 6 000 |
| **Non-current assets** | | |
| Vehicles | 50 000 | 50 000 |
| Accumulated depreciation | (10 000) | (40 000) |
| | 85 000 | 153 200 |
| **Current liabilities** | | |
| Accrued wages | 10 000 | 12 000 |
| Creditors | 15 000 | 14 000 |
| GST payable | 10 000 | 5 700 |
| Income tax payable | 10 000 | 15 000 |
| **Shareholders' equity** | | |
| Share capital | 20 000 | 20 000 |
| Retained profits | 20 000 | 86 500 |
| | 85 000 | 153 200 |

# 9.6 REPORTING CASH FLOWS FROM OPERATING ACTIVITIES USING THE INDIRECT METHOD

To report cash flows from operating activities using the indirect method, AASB107 requires the reporting of profit (or loss) showing how the amount has been impacted by:
- non-cash transactions; and
- the effect of changes in prepayments or accruals.

Non-cash transactions include doubtful debts expense, depreciation expense, profit or loss on disposal of assets and impairment losses of assets. Non-cash expenses reduce profit and will need to be added back to the profit to derive cash profit, whilst non-cash revenues will be deducted from the reported profit.

Prepayments and accrual adjustments included in the calculation of profit will show on the statement of financial position as current assets and current liabilities. Movements in these assets and liabilities indicate that cash has been used or delayed in a transaction on the income statement.

Current assets that derive their existence due to accrual adjustments in the calculation of profit include the following:
- debtors as a result of the reporting of credit sales;
- stock (inventory) as a result of stock not being sold;
- prepaid expenses as a result of expenses being paid in advance; and
- accrued revenues as a result of reporting income that has yet to be received in cash.

Current liabilities will be brought to account when the following adjustments are made in the calculation of profit:
- creditors as a result of the reporting of purchases made on credit;
- accrued expenses as a result of expenses reported before being paid;
- prepaid revenues where income is reduced when cash is received in advance;
- leave liabilities brought to account when expenses are accrued before being paid; and
- GST and income tax liabilities incurred under accrual accounting obligations before payment is made.
  The table in Figure 9.2 summarises the impact on cash when profit includes accrued or prepaid adjustments.

**Figure 9.2** Changes in cash flows arising from prepayment and accrual adjustments

| | Debit | Credit |
|---|---|---|
| Current assets | ⬆ | ⬇ |
| Current liabilities | ⬇ | ⬆ |
| Change in cash position | Decrease | Increase |

## Illustration

The following financial statements of Garman Ltd include entries using accrual accounting:

**Income statement for year ended 30 June**

| | $ |
|---|---|
| Credit sales | 600 000 |
| Cost of goods sold | (400 000) |
| Gross profit | 200 000 |
| Interest received | 20 000 |
| Wages | (80 000) |
| Leave expense | (10 000) |
| Advertising | (40 000) |
| Other expenses | (46 000) |
| Impairment loss – goodwill | (10 000) |
| Doubtful debts | (4 000) |
| Depreciation on vehicles | (10 000) |
| Profit (before tax) | 20 000 |
| Less income tax expense | (9 000) |
| Profit (after tax) | 11 000 |
| | |
| GST paid in cash | (19 000) |

**Statement of financial position (extract)**

| | 1 July | 30 June |
|---|---|---|
| | $ | $ |
| **Current assets** | | |
| Cash at bank | 68 000 | 117 000 |
| Debtors | 25 000 | 30 000 |
| Allowance for doubtful debts | (2 000)* | (6 000) |
| Stock on hand | 40 000 | 30 000 |
| Prepaid advertising | 5 000 | 3 000 |
| **Non-current assets** | | |
| Vehicles | 110 000 | 100 000 |
| Goodwill | 10 000 | 0 |
| | 256 000 | 274 000 |
| **Current liabilities** | | |
| Creditors | 30 000 | 40 000 |
| Accrued wages | 5 000 | 4 000 |
| GST payable | 4 000 | 6 000 |
| Income tax payable | 15 000 | 10 000 |
| Leave payable | 2 000 | 3 000 |
| **Shareholders' equity** | | |
| Shares | 200 000 | 200 000 |
| Retained profits | 0 | 11 000 |
| | 256 000 | 274 000 |

Analysis of the income statement reveals the following non-cash transactions:

**Profit statement for year ended 30 June**

|  | $ |
|---|---|
| Impairment loss – goodwill | (10 000) |
| Doubtful debts | (4 000) |
| Depreciation on vehicles | (10 000) |

Analysis of the statement of financial position reveals the following movements in current assets and liabilities and their impact on the cash position:

|  | 1 July $ | 30 June $ | Movement $ | | Effect on cash |
|---|---|---|---|---|---|
| **Current assets** | | | | | |
| Debtors | 25 000 | 30 000 | 5 000 | Dr | Decrease |
| Stock on hand | 40 000 | 30 000 | (10 000) | Cr | Increase |
| Prepaid advertising | 5 000 | 3 000 | (2 000) | Cr | Increase |
| **Current liabilities** | | | | | |
| Creditors | 30 000 | 40 000 | 10 000 | Cr | Increase |
| Accrued wages | 5 000 | 4 000 | (1 000) | Dr | Decrease |
| GST payable | 4 000 | 6 000 | 2 000 | Cr | Increase |
| Income tax payable | 15 000 | 10 000 | (5 000) | Dr | Decrease |
| Leave payable | 2 000 | 3 000 | 1 000 | Cr | Increase |

The cash flows from operating activities resulting from this information would be as follows:

**Garman Ltd**
**Statement of cash flows**
**for year ended 30 June**

|  | $ | $ |
|---|---|---|
| **Cash flows related to operating activities** | | |
| Profit (after income tax) | | 11 000 |
| Adjusted for non-cash transactions: | | |
| Impairment loss – goodwill | 10 000 | |
| Doubtful debts | 4 000 | |
| Depreciation on vehicles | 10 000 | 24 000 |
| | | 35 000 |
| Adjusted for: | | |
| Increase in debtors | (5 000) | |
| Decrease in stock on hand | 10 000 | |
| Decreases in prepaid advertising | 2 000 | |
| Increase in creditors | 10 000 | |
| Decrease in accrued wages | (1 000) | |
| Increase in GST payable | 2 000 | |
| Decrease in income tax payable | (5 000) | |
| Increase in leave payable | 1 000 | 14 000 |
| **Net operating cash flows** | | 49 000 |
| Cash at beginning of year | | 68 000 |
| **Cash at end of year** | | **117 000** |

For comparison purposes the statement of cash flows prepared using the direct method of reporting would appear as follows:

**Garman Ltd**
**Cash flow statement**
**for year ended 30 June**

| Cash flows related to operating activities | $ | $ |
|---|---|---|
| Receipts from customers | 655 000 | |
| Payments to suppliers | (503 000) | |
| Payment to employees | (90 000) | |
| Interest received | 20 000 | |
| GST paid | (19 000) | |
| Income tax paid | (14 000) | |
| Net operating cash flows | | 49 000 |
| Cash at beginning of year | | 68 000 |
| Cash at end of year | | 117 000 |

**Reconciliation of cash at 30 June**

| | 1 June | 30 June |
|---|---|---|
| | $ | $ |
| Cash at bank | 68 000 | 117 000 |

# Question 9.12

The following information for Yabba Ltd was used in question 9.10 to prepare the statement of cash flows using the direct method of reporting cash flows from operating activities. You are now required to prepare the statement of cash flows using the indirect method of reporting operating cash flows.

**Income statement for year ended 30 June**

| | $ | $ |
|---|---|---|
| Cash services | | 900 000 |
| Less expenses | | |
| Purchases | 600 000 | |
| Wages | 130 000 | |
| Leave expense | 20 000 | |
| Advertising expense | 30 000 | |
| Rent expense | 20 000 | |
| Depreciation expense | 20 000 | |
| Impairment loss – goodwill | 15 000 | 835 000 |
| Profit (before tax) | | 65 000 |
| Less income tax expense | | 24 000 |
| Profit (after tax) | | 41 000 |
| GST information: | | |
| GST received in cash | | 90 000 |
| GST paid to the ATO | | (85 000) |

**Statement of financial position**

| | 1 July | 30 June |
|---|---|---|
| | $ | $ |
| Current assets | | |
| Cash at bank | (5 000) | 79 000 |
| Prepaid rent | 8 000 | 10 000 |
| Non-current assets | | |
| Vehicles | 80 000 | 80 000 |
| Accumulated depreciation | (10 000) | (30 000) |
| Goodwill | 40 000 | 25 000 |
| | 113 000 | 164 000 |
| Current liabilities | | |
| Accrued wages | 8 000 | 5 000 |
| Leave liability | 5 000 | 8 000 |
| GST payable | 20 000 | 25 000 |
| Income tax payable | 10 000 | 15 000 |
| Shareholders' equity | | |
| Share capital | 50 000 | 50 000 |
| Retained profits | 20 000 | 61 000 |
| | 113 000 | 164 000 |

## Question 9.13

Using the following information for Broome Ltd taken from question 9.11, you are required to prepare the statement of cash flows using the indirect method of reporting operating cash flows.

### Income statement for year ended 30 June

| | $ | $ |
|---|---|---|
| Cash services | 150 000 | |
| Credit sales | 650 000 | 800 000 |
| Cost of goods sold | | 500 000 |
| Gross profit | | 300 000 |
| Less expenses | | |
| Wages | 120 000 | |
| Interest expense | 10 000 | |
| Bad debts | 5 000 | |
| Rent expense | 40 000 | |
| Depreciation expense | 30 000 | 205 000 |
| Profit (before tax) | | 95 000 |
| Less income tax expense | | 28 500 |
| Profit (after tax) | | 66 500 |
| | | |
| GST information: | | |
| GST received in cash | | 15 000 |
| GST paid to ATO | | (34 000) |

### Statement of financial position

| | 1 July | 30 June |
|---|---|---|
| | $ | $ |
| **Current assets** | | |
| Cash at bank | (9 000) | 84 200 |
| Debtors | 30 000 | 35 000 |
| Stock | 20 000 | 18 000 |
| Prepaid rent | 4 000 | 6 000 |
| Non-current assets | | |
| Vehicles | 50 000 | 50 000 |
| Accumulated depreciation | (10 000) | (40 000) |
| | 85 000 | 153 200 |
| **Current liabilities** | | |
| Accrued wages | 10 000 | 12 000 |
| Creditors | 15 000 | 14 000 |
| GST payable | 10 000 | 5 700 |
| Income tax payable | 10 000 | 15 000 |
| **Shareholders' equity** | | |
| Share capital | 20 000 | 20 000 |
| Retained profits | 20 000 | 86 500 |
| | 85 000 | 153 200 |

## 9.7 CASH FLOWS FROM INVESTING ACTIVITIES

Cash flows from investing activities relate to the sale and purchase of non-current assets such as property, plant and equipment and investment assets.

Comparisons between non-current assets from year to year on the statement of financial position may show increases or decreases in the value of assets, indicating that assets have been bought and sold. An increase in the value of an asset may indicate a purchase of an asset and a reduction in cash flows, whereas a decrease in value may signify the sale of an asset and an inflow of cash.

Where non-current assets have been bought or sold, the amount paid for the asset or the proceeds from the sale (disposal) must be included in the cash flow statement under the heading 'Cash flows from investing activities'.

### Illustration

Tilby Ltd's statements of financial position revealed the following changes in non-current assets:

#### Statement of financial position (extracts)

| Non-current assets | 1 July | 30 June |
|---|---|---|
| | $ | $ |
| Machinery | 100 000 | 150 000 |
| Equipment | 250 000 | 100 000 |
| Buildings | 800 000 | 800 000 |
| Investments | 180 000 | 240 000 |
| | 1 330 000 | 1 290 000 |

Analysis of the changes in asset values over the year reveals the following movements:

**Asset analysis**

|  | 1 July | 30 June | Purchase | Sale |
|---|---|---|---|---|
|  | $ | $ | $ | $ |
| Machinery | 100 000 | 150 000 | (50 000) |  |
| Equipment | 250 000 | 100 000 |  | 150 000 |
| Buildings | 800 000 | 800 000 | 0 | 0 |
| Investments | 180 000 | 240 000 | (60 000) |  |
|  |  |  | (110 000) | 150 000 |

These purchases and sales amounts would be recorded in the cash flow statement as follows:

**Tilby Ltd**
**Cash flow statement for year ended 31 July**

|  | $ | $ |
|---|---|---|
| Cash flows related to investing activities |  |  |
|     Cash paid for purchases of assets | (110 000) |  |
|     Cash proceeds from sale of assets | 150 000 |  |
| Net investing cash flows |  | 60 000 |

## Asset revaluations

Where assets are revalued upwards or impaired in value, the transactions do not involve a cash flow and must be excluded from the statement of cash flows.

## Illustration

Putu Ltd financial statements for the year ended 30 June revealed the following:

**Income statement for year ended 30 June**

|  | $ |
|---|---|
| Cash sales | 100 000 |
| Less impairment loss | (20 000) |
| Profit (before tax) | 80 000 |
| Less income tax expense | 30 000 |
| Profit (after tax) | 50 000 |
|  |  |
| GST information: |  |
|     GST received in cash | 10 000 |
|     GST paid in cash | (10 000) |

**Statement of financial position**

|  | 1 July | 30 June |
|---|---|---|
|  | $ | $ |
| Current assets |  |  |
| Cash at bank | 10 000 | 30 000 |
| Non-current assets |  |  |
| Land | 200 000 | 300 000 |
| Vehicles | 100 000 | 150 000 |
| Investments | 80 000 | 80 000 |
| Less accumulated impairments |  | (20 000) |
|  | 390 000 | 540 000 |
|  |  |  |
| Shareholders' equity |  |  |
| Share capital | 300 000 | 300 000 |
| Retained profits | 90 000 | 140 000 |
| Asset revaluation reserve |  | 100 000 |
|  | 390 000 | 540 000 |

**Additional information**
- During the year vehicles were purchased at a cost of $50 000.
- Land was revalued upwards by $100 000.
- Investments were impaired by $20 000.

The following table summarises the cash flows associated with movements in non-current assets:

**Asset analysis**

|  | 1 July | 30 June | Movement | Transaction |
|---|---|---|---|---|
|  | $ | $ | $ | $ |
| Land | 200 000 | 300 000 | (100 000) | Revaluation |
| Vehicles | 100 000 | 150 000 | (50 000) | Purchase |
| Investments | 80 000 | 80 000 | 0 |  |
| Accumulated impairment | 0 | (20 000) | 20 000 | Non-cash |

The statement of cash flows including these movements in non-current assets would be as follows:

**Putu Ltd**
**Cash flow statement for year ended 30 June**

| Cash flows related to operating activities | $ | $ |
|---|---|---|
| Receipts from customers | 100 000 |  |
| GST received | 10 000 |  |
| GST paid | (10 000) |  |
| Income tax paid | (30 000) |  |
| Net operating cash flows |  | 70 000 |
| Cash flows related to investing activities |  |  |
| Cash paid for purchases of assets | (50 000) |  |
| Cash proceeds from sale of assets | 0 |  |
| Net investing cash flows |  | (50 000) |
| Net increase (decrease) in cash held |  | 20 000 |
| Cash at beginning of year |  | 10 000 |
| Cash at end of year |  | 30 000 |

# Question 9.14

You are required to prepare a statement of cash flows from the following information provided by Lara Ltd using the direct method of reporting cash flows from operating activities.

### Income statement for year ended 30 June

|  | $ |
|---|---|
| Credit sales | 800 000 |
| Less purchases | 500 000 |
| Gross profit | 300 000 |
| Wages | 200 000 |
| Profit (before tax) | 100 000 |
| Less income tax expense | 30 000 |
| Profit (after tax) | 70 000 |
|  |  |
| GST information: |  |
| GST paid in cash | (78 000) |

### Statement of financial position

|  | 1 July $ | 30 June $ |
|---|---|---|
| **Current assets** |  |  |
| Cash at bank | 40 000 | 2 000 |
| Debtors | 20 000 | 30 000 |
| Non-current assets |  |  |
| Buildings | 500 000 | 750 000 |
| Equipment | 200 000 | 300 000 |
|  | 760 000 | 1 082 000 |
| **Current liabilities** |  |  |
| GST payable | 10 000 | 12 000 |
| Income tax payable | 2 000 | 2 000 |
|  | 12 000 | 14 000 |
| **Shareholders' equity** |  |  |
| Share capital | 700 000 | 700 000 |
| Retained profits | 48 000 | 118 000 |
| Asset revaluation reserve |  | 250 000 |
|  | 748 000 | 1 068 000 |

*Additional information*
- Buildings were revalued upwards by $250 000.
- During the year equipment was purchased.

# Asset disposals

When a non-current asset is sold or disposed, the transaction may result in a profit (or loss) on disposal which will be reported in the income statement as revenue or expense.

The amount appearing in the income statement does not represent the cash flow from the disposal of the asset. The cash flow amount can be determined by analysing amounts relating to the asset appearing on the statement of financial position.

## Illustration

Peel Ltd has provided the following financial reports for the year ended 30 June.

### Income statement for year ended 30 June

| | $ |
|---|---|
| Service fees income | 250 000 |
| Profit on sale of truck | 10 000 |
| | 260 000 |
| Wages | (96 000) |
| Depreciation – truck | (28 000) |
| Depreciation – furniture | (10 000) |
| Loss on sale of furniture | (6 000) |
| Profit (before tax) | 120 000 |
| Less income tax expense | (36 000) |
| Profit (after tax) | 84 000 |
| | |
| GST information: | |
| GST received in cash | 30 100 |
| GST paid in cash | (35 100) |

### Statement of financial position

| | 1 July $ | 30 June $ |
|---|---|---|
| **Current assets** | | |
| Cash at bank | 36 000 | 100 000 |
| Non-current assets | | |
| Truck | 150 000 | 100 000 |
| Less accumulated depreciation | (25 000) | (10 000) |
| Furniture | 120 000 | 160 000 |
| Less accumulated depreciation | (40 000) | (30 000) |
| | 241 000 | 320 000 |
| **Current liabilities** | | |
| GST payable | 20 000 | 15 000 |
| Income tax payable | 5 000 | 5 000 |
| | 25 000 | 20 000 |
| **Shareholders' equity** | | |
| Share capital | 200 000 | 200 000 |
| Retained profits | 16 000 | 100 000 |
| | 216 000 | 300 000 |

### Additional information
- A truck was sold during the year.
- Furniture was traded-in on new furniture costing $100 000 during the year.

Analysis of the income statement reveals a profit on truck sale and loss on furniture sale, indicating that the assets on the statement of financial position will need to be analysed to determine the cash flows associated with the movements in the truck and furniture.

When analysing movements in assets to determine the proceeds from the disposal of an asset the following steps are recommended:

**Step 1** Analyse the asset account to determine purchases and disposal amounts,
**Step 2** Analyse the accumulated depreciation account to determine depreciation on disposed asset,
**Step 3** Determine the proceeds from the disposal of the asset.

Using the amounts disclosed in the statement of financial position and additional information the analysis can be made as follows:

**Disposal of truck:**

**Step 1** Analyse the asset account to determine purchases and disposal amounts.

| Date | Details | Dr $ | Cr $ | Balance $ |
|---|---|---|---|---|
| **Truck (account format)** | | | | |
| 1 July | Balance (at start) | 150 000 | | 150 000 Dr |
| 30 June | Disposal (missing figure) | | 50 000 | 100 000 Dr |

**Step 2** Analyse the accumulated depreciation account to determine depreciation on disposed asset.

| Date | Details | Dr $ | Cr $ | Balance $ |
|------|---------|------|------|-----------|
| **Accumulated depreciation – truck (account format)** | | | | |
| 1 July | Balance (at start) | | 25 000 | 25 000  Cr |
| 30 June | Depreciation expense | | 28 000 | 53 000  Cr |
| | Disposal (missing figure) | 43 000 | | 10 000  Cr |

**Step 3**   Determine the proceeds from the disposal of the asset.

| Date | Details | Dr $ | Cr $ | Balance $ |
|------|---------|------|------|-----------|
| **Disposal of truck (account format)** | | | | |
| 30 June | Truck | 50 000 | | 50 000  Dr |
| | Accumulated depreciation | | 43 000 | 7 000  Dr |
| | Profit on sale of truck | 10 000 | | 17 000  Dr |
| | Bank (missing figure) | | 17 000 | Nil |

The analysis shows that a truck with a cost price of $50 000 and written down by $43 000 to a carrying amount of $7000, was sold for a profit of $10 000. Hence the truck was sold for $17 000.

**Disposal of furniture:**

**Step 1**   Analyse the asset account to determine purchases and disposal amounts.

| Date | Details | Dr $ | Cr $ | Balance $ |
|------|---------|------|------|-----------|
| **Furniture (account format)** | | | | |
| 1 July | Balance (at start) | 120 000 | | 120 000  Dr |
| 30 June | (Purchases – bank) | 100 000 | | 220 000  Dr |
| | Disposal (missing figure) | | 60 000 | 160 000  Dr |

**Step 2**   Analyse the accumulated depreciation account to determine depreciation on disposed asset.

| Date | Details | Dr $ | Cr $ | Balance $ |
|------|---------|------|------|-----------|
| **Accumulated depreciation – furniture (account format)** | | | | |
| 1 July | Balance (at start) | | 40 000 | 40 000  Cr |
| 30 June | Depreciation expense | | 10 000 | 50 000  Cr |
| | Disposal (missing figure) | 20 000 | | 30 000  Cr |

**Step 3**   Determine the proceeds from the disposal of the asset.

| Date | Details | Dr $ | Cr $ | Balance $ |
|------|---------|------|------|-----------|
| **Disposal of furniture (account format)** | | | | |
| 30 June | Furniture | 60 000 | | 60 000  Dr |
| | Accumulated depreciation | | 20 000 | 40 000  Dr |
| | Loss on sale of furniture | | 6 000 | 34 000  Dr |
| | Bank (missing figure) | | 34 000 | Nil |

The analysis shows that furniture with a cost price of $60 000 and written down by $20 000 to a carrying amount of $40 000 was sold for a loss of $6000. Hence the furniture was sold for $34 000.

A summary of the cash flows from the asset reconstructions follows:

| | $ | $ |
|---|---|---|
| Cash paid for purchases of assets | | |
| Purchase of furniture | | (100 000) |
| Cash proceeds from sale of assets | | |
| Proceeds from disposal of truck | 17 000 | |
| Proceeds from disposal of furniture | 34 000 | 51 000 |

The statement of cash flows for Peel Ltd would be presented as follows:

**Peel Ltd**
**Cash flow statement for year ended 30 June**

| | $ | $ |
|---|---|---|
| Cash flows related to operating activities | | |
| Receipts from customers | 250 000 | |
| Payment to employees | (96 000) | |
| GST received | 30 100 | |
| GST paid | (35 100) | |
| Income tax paid | (36 000) | |
| Net operating cash flows | | 113 000 |
| Cash flows related to investing activities | | |
| Cash paid for purchases of assets | (100 000) | |
| Cash proceeds from sale of assets | 51 000 | |
| Net investing cash flows | | (49 000) |
| Net increase (decrease) in cash held | | 64 000 |
| Cash at beginning of year | | 36 000 |
| Cash at end of year | | 100 000 |

## Question 9.15

Using the following extracts from financial statements, you are required to calculate the proceeds from the sale of equipment and the motor vehicle.

**Income statement for year ended 30 June**
**(extract)**

| | $ |
|---|---|
| Profit on sale of equipment | 5 000 |
| Loss on sale of vehicle | (5 000) |
| Depreciation – vehicle | (35 000) |
| Depreciation – equipment | (15 000) |

**Statement of financial position**
**(extract)**

| | 1 July | 30 June |
|---|---|---|
| | $ | $ |
| Equipment | 140 000 | 100 000 |
| Less accumulated depreciation | (60 000) | (40 000) |
| Vehicles | 150 000 | 120 000 |
| Less accumulated depreciation | (30 000) | (45 000) |

## Question 9.16

From the following information provided by Carter Ltd, you are required to prepare a statement of cash flows using the direct method of reporting cash flows from operating activities.

**Income statement for year ended 30 June**

| | $ |
|---|---|
| Service fees income | 750 000 |
| Profit on sale of equipment | 20 000 |
| | 770 000 |
| Wages | (220 000) |
| Depreciation – equipment | (30 000) |
| Depreciation – plant | (20 000) |
| Loss on sale of plant | (50 000) |
| Profit (before tax) | 450 000 |
| Less income tax expense | (135 000) |
| Profit (after tax) | 315 000 |
| | |
| GST information: | |
| GST received in cash | 93 000 |
| GST paid in cash | (92 000) |

**Statement of financial position**

| | 1 July | 30 June |
|---|---|---|
| | $ | $ |
| Current assets | | |
| Cash at bank | 8 000 | (68 000) |
| Non-current assets | | |
| Equipment | 400 000 | 300 000 |
| Less accumulated depreciation | (350 000) | (40 000) |
| Plant | 500 000 | 600 000 |
| Less accumulated depreciation | (310 000) | (230 000) |
| | 248 000 | 562 000 |
| Current liabilities | | |
| GST payable | 8 000 | 9 000 |
| Income tax payable | 10 000 | 8 000 |
| | 18 000 | 17 000 |
| Shareholders' equity | | |
| Share capital | 200 000 | 200 000 |
| Retained profits | 30 000 | 345 000 |
| | 230 000 | 545 000 |

*Additional information*
- Damaged plant costing $300 000 was sold during the year and replaced with new plant.
- Equipment costing $250 000 was purchased during the year and obsolete equipment sold.

## Question 9.17

From the following financial statements of Ross Ltd, you are required to prepare a statement of cash flows using the direct method of reporting cash flows from operating activities.

**Income statement for year ended 30 June**

| | $ |
|---|---|
| Fees received | 350 000 |
| Depreciation – plant | (20 000) |
| Impairment loss – investments | (40 000) |
| Interest expense | (7 000) |
| Wages | (180 000) |
| Rent | (15 000) |
| Depreciation – equipment | (20 000) |
| Loss on sale of plant | (48 000) |
| Profit (before tax) | 40 000 |
| Less income tax expense | (12 000) |
| Profit (after tax) | 28 000 |
| | |
| GST information: | |
| GST received in cash | 36 700 |
| GST paid in cash | (38 700) |

**Statement of financial position**

| | 1 July | 30 June |
|---|---|---|
| | $ | $ |
| Current assets | | |
| Cash at bank | 10 000 | (7 000) |
| Non-current assets | | |
| Buildings | 200 000 | 300 000 |
| Plant | 150 000 | 200 000 |
| Less accumulated depreciation | (100 000) | (75 000) |
| Investments | 540 000 | 550 000 |
| Less accumulated impairments | (10 000) | (50 000) |
| | 790 000 | 918 000 |
| Current liabilities | | |
| GST payable | 10 000 | 8 000 |
| Income tax payable | 3 000 | 5 000 |
| | 13 000 | 13 000 |
| Shareholders' equity | | |
| Share capital | 760 000 | 760 000 |
| Retained profits | 17 000 | 45 000 |
| Asset revaluation reserve | 0 | 100 000 |
| | 777 000 | 905 000 |

*Additional information*

- During the year buildings were revalued upwards by $100 000.
- Additional plant with a cost price of $160 000 was purchased during the year.

# 9.8   CASH FLOWS FROM FINANCING ACTIVITIES

A company can obtain finance by using debt finance such as bank loans and debentures or by using equity finance through a share issue.

Movements in debt or equity finance are reported on the statement of cash flows as financing activities.

## Debt finance

Debt finance is disclosed as liabilities on a company's statement of financial position and is normally associated with long-term liabilities. Increases in non-current liabilities indicate a positive cash flow as the entity has acquired funds whilst a decrease indicates a repayment of debt and a negative cash flow.

## Illustration

Tilby Ltd's statements of financial position revealed the following changes in its non-current liabilities:

**Statement of financial position (extracts)**

| Non-current liabilities | 1 July | 30 June |
|---|---|---|
| | $ | $ |
| Bank loan | 150 000 | 250 000 |
| Debenture loan | 500 000 | 450 000 |
| | 650 000 | 700 000 |

Analysis of the changes in liability values over the year reveals the following movements:

**Liability analysis**

| | 1 July | 30 June | Borrowings acquired | Borrowings repaid |
|---|---|---|---|---|
| | $ | $ | $ | $ |
| Bank loan | 150 000 | 250 000 | 100 000 | |
| Debenture loan | 500 000 | 425 000 | | (75 000) |

The movements in debt finance would be recorded in the cash flow statement as follows:

**Tilby Ltd**
**Cash flow statement for year ended 30 June**

| | $ | $ |
|---|---|---|
| Cash flows related to financing activities | | |
| Borrowings acquired | 100 000 | |
| Borrowings repaid | (75 000) | |
| Net financing cash flows | | 25 000 |

# Question 9.18

From the following information provided by Sharky Ltd you are required to prepare a statement of cash flows.

### Income statement for year ended 30 June

| | $ |
|---|---|
| Fees income | 500 000 |
| Operating expenses | (300 000) |
| Wages | (50 000) |
| Profit (before tax) | 150 000 |
| Less income tax expense | (45 000) |
| Profit (after tax) | 105 000 |
| | |
| GST information: | |
| GST received in cash | 50 000 |
| GST paid in cash | (45 000) |

### Statement of financial position

| | 1 July | 30 June |
|---|---|---|
| | $ | $ |
| **Current assets** | | |
| Cash at bank | 100 000 | 108 000 |
| Non-current assets | | |
| Land and buildings | 800 000 | 1 000 000 |
| Investments | 200 000 | 150 000 |
| | 1 100 000 | 1 258 000 |
| **Current Liabilities** | | |
| GST payable | 15 000 | 20 000 |
| Income tax payable | 20 000 | 18 000 |
| Non-current liabilities | | |
| Term loan | 500 000 | 600 000 |
| Debenture loan | 400 000 | 350 000 |
| | 935 000 | 988 000 |
| **Shareholders' equity** | | |
| Share capital | 160 000 | 160 000 |
| Retained profits | 5 000 | 110 000 |
| | 165 000 | 270 000 |

## Equity finance

Equity finance relates to transactions with the business owners; that is, shareholders. Cash flows involved with shareholders include cash received from a share issue and the payment of dividends.

### Cash received from share issues

When a company issues shares, share capital on the statement of financial position will increase in value.

The movement in share capital may need analysis to determine the amount of cash associated with the increase as the movement may involve a bonus share issue which does not involve a cash flow.

In addition, if share capital includes calls in arrears, an adjustment must be made to the cash flow from the share issue as not all the cash was received.

## Illustration

Tilby Ltd's statements of financial position revealed the following changes in its shareholders' equity:

### Statement of financial position (extracts)

| | 1 July | 30 June |
|---|---|---|
| | $ | $ |
| **Shareholders' equity** | | |
| Share capital | | |
| Ordinary shares ($1.00 each) | 500 000 | 1 000 000 |
| Calls in arrears ($0.50 each) | | (20 000) |
| Preference shares ($5.00 each) | 100 000 | 250 000 |
| | 600 000 | 830 000 |

**Additional information**

- On 1 March a call was made on ordinary shares of $0.50 per share.
- On 1 April a bonus share issue was made on preference shares of one share for every four shares held.
- On 1 May 100 000 preference shares were issued at $5.00 each.

Analysis of the changes in equity values over the year reveals the following movements:

**Statement of financial position (extracts)**

| Share capital | 1 July | 30 June | Change | Bonus shares | Cash movement |
|---|---|---|---|---|---|
| | $ | $ | $ | $ | $ |
| Ordinary shares | 500 000 | 1 000 000 | 500 000 | | 500 000 |
| Calls in arrears | | (20 000) | (20 000) | | (20 000) |
| Preference shares | 100 000 | 250 000 | 150 000 | (25 000) | 125 000 |
| Proceeds from share issues | | | | | 605 000 |

The movements in equity finance would be recorded in the cash flow statement as follows:

**Tilby Ltd**
**Cash flow statement for year ended 30 June**

| | $ |
|---|---|
| Cash flows related to financing activities | |
| Cash proceeds from shares issued | 605 000 |

# Question 9.19

From the following information provided by Barkly Ltd, you are required to calculate the cash received from issuing shares.

**Statement of financial position (extracts)**

| | 1 July | 30 June |
|---|---|---|
| | $ | $ |
| **Shareholders' equity** | | |
| Share capital | | |
| Ordinary shares $2.00 each | 100 000 | 1 100 000 |
| Calls in arrears $1.00 each | | (50 000) |
| Preference shares $10.00 each | 100 000 | 750 000 |
| | 200 000 | 1 800 000 |

**Additional information**

During the year:

- on 1 July 500 000 ordinary shares were issued at $1.00;
- on 1 August a $1.00 call per share was made on the ordinary shares;
- on 1 October a bonus share issue at one preference share for every one share held was made; and
- on 1 May preference shares were issued via a prospectus.

## Dividend payments from retained profits

The appropriation of profits via the retained profits account involves the transfer of profits to and from revenue reserves and the distribution of dividends to shareholders.

The transfer of profits to or from reserves (such as a general reserve or dividend reserve) does not involve a cash flow and is therefore not reported in a statement of cash flows.

Dividends declared, however, do involve a cash flow and are reported on the cash flows statement. Dividends paid within a year include final dividends declared in the previous year plus interim dividends paid in the current year. Final dividends declared in the current year will not become a cash flow until the next year once they have been ratified at the annual general meeting.

Analysis of the dividends payable account can assist in calculating the dividends paid during the year.

## Illustration

Harrap Ltd's financial statements for the year ended 30 June included the following information:

**Statement of changes in equity (extract)**

|  | $ |
|---|---|
| Retained profits at 1 July | 20 000 |
| Profit (after tax) | 180 000 |
| Interim dividends | (80 000) |
| Final dividends | (120 000) |
| Transfer from dividend reserve | 50 000 |
| Transfer to general reserve | (20 000) |
| Retained profits at 30 June | 30 000 |

**Statement of financial position (extract)**

|  | 1 July | 30 June |
|---|---|---|
|  | $ | $ |
| **Current liabilities** | | |
| Dividends payable | 110 000 | 120 000 |
| **Shareholders' equity** | | |
| Share capital | 500 000 | 600 000 |
| **Reserves** | | |
| Retained profits | 20 000 | 30 000 |
| Dividend reserve | 150 000 | 100 000 |
| General reserve | 0 | 20 000 |
| Asset revaluation reserve | 400 000 | 600 000 |

Analysis of these statements reveals the following information.

**The statement of changes in equity includes:**
- dividends declared during the year consisting of interim dividends of $80 000 and final dividends of $120 000; and
- reserve transfers from the dividend reserve and to the general reserve.

**The statement of financial position discloses:**
- dividends payable at the start of the year of $110 000;
- share capital increasing by $100 000 from $500 000 to $600 000; and
- numerous reserve account movements.

Reconstruction of the dividends payable account to reveal the amounts paid in cash would be as follows:

| Date | Details | Dr $ | Cr $ | Balance $ |
|---|---|---|---|---|
| **Dividends payable** | | | | |
| 1 July | Balance | | 110 000 | 110 000  Cr |
|  | Bank | 110 000 | | Nil |
|  | Interim dividends | | 80 000 | 80 000  Cr |
|  | Bank | 80 000 | | Nil |
| 30 June | Final dividends | | 120 000 | 120 000  Cr |

Hence the amount paid in the current year consists of dividends payable at the start of the year plus interim dividends paid in the current year.

**Dividends paid in current year**

|  | $ |
|---|---|
| Dividends payable (previous year) | 110 000 |
| Interim dividends (this year) | 80 000 |
| Dividends paid | 190 000 |

he amounts received from the share issue and the dividends paid would be reported in the statement of cash flows as follows:

**Harrap Ltd**
**Cash flow statement for the year ended 30 June**

|  | $ | $ |
|---|---|---|
| Cash flows related to financing activities |  |  |
| Cash proceeds from shares issued | 100 000 |  |
| Dividends paid | (190 000) |  |
| Net financing cash flows |  | (90 000) |

# Question 9.20

Using the following information of Tara Ltd, you are required to prepare the financing activities section of the statement of cash flows.

**Statement of changes in equity (extract)**

|  | $ |
|---|---|
| Retained profits at 1 July | 50 000 |
| Profit (after tax) | 250 000 |
| Interim dividends | (100 000) |
| Final dividends | (200 000) |
| Transfer from dividend reserve | 40 000 |
| Transfer to general reserve | (10 000) |
| Retained profits at 30 June | 30 000 |

**Statement of financial position (extract)**

|  | 1 July | 30 June |
|---|---|---|
|  | $ | $ |
| Current liabilities |  |  |
| Dividends payable | 150 000 | 200 000 |
| Shareholders' equity |  |  |
| Share capital ($1.00 each) | 400 000 | 800 000 |
| Reserves |  |  |
| Retained profits | 50 000 | 30 000 |
| Dividend reserve | 200 000 | 160 000 |
| General reserve | 50 000 | 60 000 |
| Asset revaluation reserve | 500 000 | 750 000 |

*Additional information*
- On 1 January a bonus share issue was made of one ordinary share for every two shares held.
- On 1 March ordinary shares were issued via a prospectus.

## Question 9.21

From the following information provided by Karp Ltd, you are required to prepare a statement of cash flows using the direct method of reporting cash flows from operating activities.

### Income statement for year ended 30 June

| | $ |
|---|---|
| Fees income | 800 000 |
| Operating expenses | (500 000) |
| Wages | (200 000) |
| Profit (before tax) | 100 000 |
| Less income tax expense | (30 000) |
| Profit (after tax) | 70 000 |

### Retained profits for year ended 30 June

| | $ |
|---|---|
| Retained profits (1 July) | 130 000 |
| Profit (after tax) | 70 000 |
| Transfer from general reserve | 50 000 |
| Transfer to dividend reserve | (40 000) |
| Interim dividends | (60 000) |
| Final dividends | (100 000) |
| Retained profits (30 June) | 50 000 |

**GST information:**

| | $ |
|---|---|
| GST received in cash | 80 000 |
| GST paid in cash | (75 000) |

### Statement of financial position

| | 1 July | 30 June |
|---|---|---|
| | $ | $ |
| **Current assets** | | |
| Cash at bank | 50 000 | 70 000 |
| Non-current assets | | |
| Land and buildings | 750 000 | 1 000 000 |
| | 800 000 | 1 070 000 |
| **Current liabilities** | | |
| GST payable | 5 000 | 10 000 |
| Income tax payable | 35 000 | 20 000 |
| Dividend payable | 80 000 | 100 000 |
| **Non-current liabilities** | | |
| Term loan | 100 000 | 50 000 |
| Debenture loan | 200 000 | 400 000 |
| | 420 000 | 580 000 |
| **Shareholders' equity** | | |
| Share capital ($1.00 each) | 200 000 | 400 000 |
| Retained profits | 130 000 | 50 000 |
| Dividend reserve | 0 | 40 000 |
| General reserve | 50 000 | 0 |
| | 380 000 | 490 000 |

*Additional information*

- On 1 November additional buildings were acquired.
- On 1 May ordinary shares were issued via a prospectus.

## 9.9 PROCEDURES FOR COMPLETING A COMPREHENSIVE CASH FLOW STATEMENT

To complete a comprehensive cash flow statement that includes operating, investing and financing cash flows, the following procedures are recommended:

1   Read through the income statement, statement of financial position and additional information to gain an insight into the complexities within the question. Identify accounts that may need reconstructing as evidenced by the following:
- accrual items such as debtors, creditors, inventory, prepayments and accrued expenses shown in the statement of financial position;
- asset disposals identified by 'profits' or 'losses' in the income statement;
- non-cash transactions in the income statement;
- movements in non-current assets and non-current liabilities; and
- movement in share capital and dividends paid during the year (final and interim).

2   Working with the income statement and current assets and current liabilities sections of the statement of financial position, reconstruct appropriate accounts and complete the cash flows from the operating activities section of the cash flow statement.

3 Working from the non-current assets section of the statement of financial position (and additional information), complete the cash flow from investing activities section of the cash flow statement.

4 Working from the non-current liabilities and shareholder's equity sections of the statement of financial position, complete the cash flow from financing activities section of the cash flow statement.

5 Complete the cash flow statement by calculating the movement in cash during the year, entering the cash account balance at the start and calculating the cash balance at the end of the year.

6 Prepare the reconciliation of cash account balances at the start and end of the year and reconcile with the statement of cash flows.

## Question 9.22

From the following information provided by Gilly Ltd, you are required to prepare a statement of cash flows reporting operating flows using both the direct and indirect methods.

### Income statement for year ended 30 June

| | $ |
|---|---|
| Credit sales | 600 000 |
| Cost of goods sold | (275 000) |
| Gross profit | 325 000 |
| Interest received | 25 000 |
| Wages | (100 000) |
| Leave expense | (10 000) |
| Advertising | (42 000) |
| Impairment loss – goodwill | (15 000) |
| Doubtful debts | (5 000) |
| Depreciation on vehicles | (1 000) |
| Other expenses | (31 000) |
| Profit (before tax) | 146 000 |
| Less income tax expense | (48 300) |
| Profit (after tax) | 97 700 |

### Retained profits for year ended 30 June

| | |
|---|---|
| Retained profits (1 July) | 45 000 |
| Profit (after tax) | 97 700 |
| Transfer from general reserve | 10 000 |
| | 152 700 |
| Interim dividends | (50 000) |
| Final dividends | (30 000) |
| Retained profits (30 June) | 72 700 |

### GST information:

| | |
|---|---|
| GST paid in cash | (27 800) |

### Statement of financial position

| | 1 July | 30 June |
|---|---|---|
| | $ | $ |
| **Current assets** | | |
| Cash at bank | 39 000 | 10 700 |
| Debtors | 40 000 | 70 000 |
| Allowance for doubtful debts | (4 000) | (9 000) |
| Stock on hand | 103 000 | 130 000 |
| Prepaid advertising | 5 000 | 3 000 |
| **Non-current assets** | | |
| Land and buildings | 300 000 | 590 000 |
| Vehicles | 25 000 | 25 000 |
| Less accumulated depreciation | (4 000) | (5 000) |
| Goodwill (less impairment) | 32 000 | 17 000 |
| | 536 000 | 831 700 |
| **Current liabilities** | | |
| Creditors | 80 000 | 90 000 |
| GST payable | 4 000 | 6 000 |
| Income tax payable | 15 000 | 20 000 |
| Leave payable | 2 000 | 3 000 |
| Dividend payable | 40 000 | 30 000 |
| **Non-current liabilities** | | |
| Term loan | 50 000 | 30 000 |
| Debenture loan | 0 | 140 000 |
| | 191 000 | 319 000 |
| **Shareholders' equity** | | |
| Ordinary shares ($1.00 each) | 100 000 | 200 000 |
| Retained profits | 45 000 | 72 700 |
| General reserve | 50 000 | 40 000 |
| Asset revaluation reserve | 150 000 | 200 000 |
| | 345 000 | 512 700 |

*Additional information*
- Land was revalued upwards on 1 August by $100 000.
- Additional land was purchased on 30 September.
- A bonus share dividend of one for two ordinary shares was made on 1 December.
- Shares were issued via a prospectus on 1 June.

# Question 9.23

The following data relates to Video Ltd. You are required to prepare a statement of cash flow for the year ended 30 June using both the direct and indirect methods.

### Income statement for year ended 30 June

| | $ |
|---|---|
| Rental revenue | 420 000 |
| Interest received | 30 000 |
| Profit on land sale | 80 000 |
| | 530 000 |
| Interest expense | (7 000) |
| Wages | (240 000) |
| Rent | (54 000) |
| Operating expenses | (70 000) |
| Discount expense | (1 000) |
| Depreciation on vehicles | (27 000) |
| Loss on sale of vehicle | (2 000) |
| Profit (before tax) | 129 000 |
| Less income tax expense | (14 700) |
| Profit (after tax) | 114 300 |

### Retained profits for year ended 30 June

| | $ |
|---|---|
| Retained profits (1 July) | 40 000 |
| Profit (after tax) | 114 300 |
| | 154 300 |
| Transfer to general reserve | (15 000) |
| Interim dividends | (14 000) |
| Final dividends | (25 000) |
| Retained profits (30 June) | 100 300 |

### Statement of financial position

| | 1 July $ | 30 June $ |
|---|---|---|
| **Current assets** | | |
| Cash at bank | 43 000 | 29 300 |
| Accounts receivable | 46 000 | 57 000 |
| Prepaid rent | 6 000 | 4 000 |
| **Non-current assets** | | |
| Land and buildings | 180 000 | 380 000 |
| Vehicles | 236 000 | 247 000 |
| Less accumulated depreciation | (41 000) | (62 000) |
| | 470 000 | 655 300 |
| **Current liabilities** | | |
| GST payable | 5 000 | 4 000 |
| Income tax payable | 10 000 | 5 000 |
| Dividend payable | 20 000 | 25 000 |
| **Non-current liabilities** | | |
| Term loan | 75 000 | 71 000 |
| Debenture loan | 90 000 | 120 000 |
| | 200 000 | 225 000 |
| **Shareholders' equity** | | |
| Ordinary shares ($1.00 each) | 130 000 | 185 000 |
| Retained profits | 40 000 | 100 300 |
| General reserve | 30 000 | 45 000 |
| Asset revaluation reserve | 70 000 | 100 000 |
| | 270 000 | 430 300 |

*Additional information*

**GST information:**

- GST received in cash $73 850.
- GST paid in cash ($78 300).

**Assets:**

- A motor vehicle costing $20 000 was sold on 30 April and a new vehicle purchased.
- Land and buildings were revalued upwards by $60 000 on 1 September.
- Land costing $100 000 was sold on 1 June and additional land purchased.

**Shareholder's equity:**

- The bonus issue of $30 000 shares was made on 1 November.
- In March ordinary shares were issued to the public.

# Comprehensive Assessment Activity

The information presented below relates to Grand Ltd. You are required to prepare a statement cash flow for the year ended 30 June in accordance with the Australian Accounting Standards, using both the direct and indirect methods of reporting cash flows from operating activities.

### Income statement for year ended 30 June

| | $ |
|---|---|
| Cash sales | 172 000 |
| Credit sales | 400 000 |
| | 572 000 |
| Less cost of goods sold | (312 000) |
| Gross profit | 260 000 |
| Discount received | 9 000 |
| Dividends received | 4 000 |
| | 273 000 |
| Discount expense | (5 000) |
| Bad debts | (6 000) |
| Interest expense | (12 000) |
| Wages | (145 000) |
| Leave expense | (36 000) |
| Depreciation of vehicle | (50 000) |
| Loss on sale of vehicle | (4 000) |
| Impairment loss – goodwill | (10 000) |
| Profit (before tax) | 5 000 |
| Less income tax expense | 4 500 |
| Profit (after tax) | 500 |

### Retained profits for year ended 30 June

| | |
|---|---|
| Retained profits (1 July) | 52 200 |
| Loss (after tax) | 500 |
| Transfer from general reserve | 5 000 |
| | 57 700 |
| Interim dividends | (15 000) |
| Final dividends | (30 000) |
| Retained profits (30 June) | 12 700 |

### Statement of financial position

| | 1 July | 30 June |
|---|---|---|
| | $ | $ |
| **Current assets** | | |
| Cash at bank | 122 450 | (157 800) |
| Debtors' control | 9 000 | 21 000 |
| Stock control | 5 000 | 16 500 |
| Prepaid interest expense | 250 | 500 |
| **Non-current assets** | | |
| Land and buildings | 600 000 | 1 550 000 |
| Vehicles | 210 000 | 225 000 |
| Less accumulated depreciation | (68 500) | (107 500) |
| Goodwill | 10 000 | 0 |
| Investments in shares | 320 000 | 700 000 |
| | 1 208 200 | 2 247 700 |
| **Current liabilities** | | |
| Creditors' control | 60 000 | 54 000 |
| Leave payable. | 35 000 | 40 000 |
| GST payable | 10 000 | 13 000 |
| Income tax payable | 6 000 | 8 000 |
| Dividend payable | 10 000 | 30 000 |
| **Non-current liabilities** | | |
| Term loan | 400 000 | 450 000 |
| | 521 000 | 595 000 |
| **Shareholders' equity** | | |
| Ordinary shares | 500 000 | 1 560 000 |
| Less calls in arrears | 0 | (50 000) |
| Retained profits | 52 200 | 12 700 |
| General reserve | 35 000 | 30 000 |
| Asset revaluation reserve | 100 000 | 100 000 |
| | 687 200 | 1 652 700 |

## Additional information

**GST information:**
a  GST received in cash $17 500
b  GST paid in cash ($21 950).

**Assets:**

a   A vehicle costing $18 000 was sold on 30 March and a new vehicle purchased.

b   Buildings were revalued upwards by $200 000 on 1 September and additional buildings acquired.

**Shareholder's equity:**

a   At 1 July ordinary shares consisted of 1 000 000 $1.00 ordinary shares paid to $0.50 each.

b   On 1 August a final call was made. At 30 June calls were outstanding on 100 000 shares.

c   The bonus share issue of $200 000 shares was made on 1 November.

d   In June ordinary shares were issued to the public.

# Assessment Checklist

Complete the following checklist to identify if you consider yourself capable of being assessed against each of the following outcomes.

| I can: | Chapter reference | Check ✓ |
|---|---|---|
| explain the purpose of a statement of cash flows | 9.1 | |
| identify and categorise differences in cash flows | 9.2 | |
| prepare a statement of cash flows from the cash records | 9.3 | |
| prepare a statement of cash flows using the direct and indirect methods of reporting operating activities | 9.5 9.6 9.7 9.8 9.9 | |

# CHAPTER 10

## CONSOLIDATED FINANCIAL STATEMENTS

## WHAT YOU WILL LEARN IN THIS CHAPTER?

Upon satisfactory completion of this chapter you should be able to:
- explain when corporate reporting entities need to present consolidated financial statements;
- consolidate the accounts of a parent entity and a wholly owned subsidiary for reporting purposes; and
- prepare consolidated financial statements.

**Are you already competent at these tasks?**

If you have already accomplished these tasks as a result of your recent workplace or training experiences you may wish to proceed to the Comprehensive Assessment Activity at the end of this chapter to assess your skills in these areas.

## 10.1    INTRODUCTION

A company may purchase shares in another company to obtain control over the resources held by that company, thereby creating an economic entity comprising the investing company (parent entity) and the controlled company (subsidiary company).

Where a parent entity has control over a subsidiary entity the parent entity, in addition to preparing its own financial statements, must also prepare consolidated financial statements showing the financial affairs of the economic entity as a whole.

## 10.2    CONSOLIDATED FINANCIAL STATEMENTS

When an entity has control over another entity, the controlling entity should ensure compliance with AASB10: Consolidated Financial Statements. This standard establishes the principles for the presentation and preparation of consolidated financial statements.

The purpose of the standard is to:

* define the meaning of 'control' that brings about the recognition of a parent entity (controlling entity) and subsidiary (controlled entity);
* prescribe the circumstances in which consolidated accounts are to be prepared; and
* describe the accounting requirements for consolidated financial statements.

The determination as to whether a company is required to prepare consolidated financial statements is based on the ability of an entity to control another entity. If control can be established then AASB10: Consolidated Financial Statements is relevant to the parent (controlling) entity.

The standard provides definitions which assist in clarifying terms applicable to the determination of control and the preparation of financial statements. These terms include the following:

* **Parent entity** means an entity that has control over one or more other entities.
* **Subsidiary** means an entity that is controlled by another entity.
* **Group** means a parent and its subsidiaries.
* **Consolidated financial statements** means financial statements of a group of companies presented as a single economic entity.

Companies that are both reporting entities and parent entities are required to consolidate the accounts of the parent and its subsidiaries. Consolidated reporting is prepared by combining the accounts of each of the entities comprising the economic entity and presenting the financial statements as one set of accounts.

When a company purchases shares in another company the following possibilities may arise:

1    The company **acquires all** of the shares in the acquired company and:
   **a**    gains control; or
   **b**    does not exercise control.
2    The company **does not acquire all** of the shares in the acquired company and:
   **a**    gains control; or
   **b**    does not gain control.

Where the purchasing company gains control as described in 1(a) and 2(a) above, the company must prepare consolidated financial statements in accordance with AASB10. However, if the company does not have control over the entity as described in 1(b) and 2(b) above, it is not required to prepare consolidated financial statements.

Where a company does not have control over an investment in another company it may need to ensure that it complies with the reporting requirements of AASB12: Disclosure of Investments in Other Entities.

This chapter examines the accounting requirements relating to a parent entity that has acquired **all** of the share capital of a subsidiary company and has **control** over that company; that is, the investment is a wholly owned and controlled subsidiary company.

## 10.3    CAPACITY TO CONTROL

AASB10: Consolidated Financial Statements explores the concept of control to assist parent entities in determining if they have control over a subsidiary and therefore need to issue consolidated statements.

The standard indicates that control will be evident when an investee (parent) meets all of the following criteria in relation to subsidiary investment:

a power over the subsidiary;

b exposure, or rights, to variable returns from its involvement with the subsidiary; and

c the ability to use its power over the subsidiary to affect the amount of the parent's returns.

These criteria link the power exercised by the parent entity in obtaining returns from the subsidiary to the benefit of the parent entity. The relationship between power and return are described in the following terms:

1 **Power:** may be evident when the parent entity has the ability to direct the subsidiary's activities to the benefit of the returns of the parent. Power may be exercised by having the right to control the votes on a board of directors, having the power to dictate the outcomes at meetings of shareholders, or holding a contract over the subsidiary.

2 **Returns:** relates to the parent entity's returns varying directly as a result of the performance of the subsidiary. The parent's profits or losses will be influenced directly by the profits or losses generated by the subsidiary.

Where a parent entity has the power or right to control the activities and performance of a subsidiary entity to the direct benefit of the parent entity's profits control may be apparent, in which case AASB10 requires the parent entity to issue consolidated financial statements that provide a true and fair view of the earnings and position of a single economic entity; that is, a group.

## Question 10.1

In each of the following scenarios identify whether a relationship exists that requires the preparation of consolidated financial statements. In each case justify your answer.

| | |
|---|---|
| Scenario 1 | Jag Ltd has acquired all of the share capital of Nutt Ltd |
| Scenario 2 | Host Ltd has acquired 25% of the share capital of Visit Ltd |
| Scenario 3 | Trans Ltd owns 51% of the shares of West Ltd and holds the balance of power on West Ltd's board of directors |
| Scenario 4 | Fed Ltd is the biggest shareholder of State Ltd, holding 51% of State's share capital and contractual obligations with State Ltd to receive 90% of its production |

## 10.4 PREPARING CONSOLIDATED ACCOUNTS

When a parent entity needs to issue consolidated financial statements it will have to bring together or consolidate the account balances of the parent and its subsidiaries to derive a single set of account balances that reflect the group.

This can be achieved by aggregating the accounts of the parent and subsidiaries on a worksheet, from which consolidated financial statements can be prepared.

When preparing the group accounts to reflect the activities of a single reporting entity AASB10: Consolidated Financial Statements requires the following consolidation procedures:

a combine assets, liabilities, equity, income, expenses and cash flows of the parent and its subsidiaries;

b eliminate the parent entity's investment in each subsidiary against the parent's portion of each subsidiary's equity; and

c eliminate intragroup transactions between entities in the group.

When preparing consolidated accounts that eliminate the parent's investment and intragroup transactions it is important to remember the following:

• each entity's account balances must be recorded on a consolidation worksheet each time consolidated financial statements are required;

• elimination entries are made on the consolidation worksheet. The elimination entries **are not** made in the accounts of any members of the group as each entity in the group is a separate entity that prepares its own accounts independent of consolidation accounting techniques; and

• where elimination entries made on past consolidation worksheets have an influence on current consolidation worksheets, the elimination entry will need to be repeated as worksheets have no impact on the actual account balances of entities in the group.

Once the account balances of the parent entity and each subsidiary are entered on the consolidation worksheet the following recording procedures are recommended:

**Step 1**  eliminate the parent's investment in the subsidiary's equity;

**Step 2**  eliminate intragroup (intercompany) transactions; and

**Step 3**  eliminate dividends paid by the subsidiary to the parent.

## 10.5  ELIMINATING THE PARENT'S INVESTMENT IN A SUBSIDIARY'S EQUITY

When a company purchases a controlling interest in another entity by purchasing its share capital the investment will be recorded in the parent entity's accounts at cost price.

The subsidiary entity would not record any accounting entries but would adjust its Register of Members to show that the parent entity owns the subsidiary's shares.

The journal entries to record the investment on the date of acquisition in the accounts of the parent and subsidiary would be as follows:

**Parent entity – general journal**

| Details | Dr | Cr |
|---|---|---|
| Investment in subsidiary | XX | |
|     Bank | | XX |
| *Purchased shares in subsidiary* | | |

**Subsidiary entity – general journal**

| Details | Dr | Cr |
|---|---|---|
| No entry | | |

By purchasing the subsidiary's share capital and gaining control of the subsidiary the parent entity has control over its assets and liabilities (net assets). Thus the parent entity's investment in the subsidiary equates to the net assets held by the subsidiary entity.

The consolidation process requires the accounts of the parent and subsidiary entities to be brought together to reveal the balances for economic entity as a single group. Hence the group accounts must eliminate the investment in the subsidiary against the subsidiary's equity accounts, thereby allowing the assets and liabilities of the parent and subsidiary to be reported as a single economic entity.

When eliminating an investment in a subsidiary, the elimination values of the subsidiary's equity must be consistent with the amounts at the date of acquisition of the subsidiary, not the date of preparing the group accounts. This will allow the group accounts to show the increase in wealth contributed to the group by the subsidiary since the date it was purchased.

Where the purchase price paid for the investment in the subsidiary is greater than the fair values of the net assets acquired at the date of acquisition, the entry to eliminate the investment at the date of preparing the accounts for consolidation will show goodwill on consolidation in the group accounts.

The consolidation journal entry to combine the accounts of the parent and subsidiary where the investment paid exceeds the fair value of the subsidiary would be as follows:

**Consolidation journal**

| Details | Dr | Cr |
|---|---|---|
| Share capital – subsidiary | XX | |
| Retained profits – subsidiary | XX | |
| Reserves – subsidiary | XX | |
| Goodwill on consolidation | XX | |
|     Investment in subsidiary | | XX |
| *Elimination of investment in subsidiary* | | |

**Note**: The elimination entry of the investment in a subsidiary must be recorded at the values at the **date of acquisition of the subsidiary** as these values represent the historical value of the investment in the subsidiary.

## Illustration

On 1 July 2010, Take Ltd purchased a 100% controlling interest in Over Ltd at a cost of $200 000. On this date the statement of financial position of Over Ltd was as follows:

**Over Ltd**
**Statement of financial position at 1 July 2010**

| Assets | $000's | Shareholders' equity | $000's |
|---|---|---|---|
| Bank | 50 | Ordinary shares | 100 |
| Debtors | 20 | Retained profits | 40 |
| Stock | 60 | Reserves | 30 |
| Equipment | 40 | | |
| | 170 | | 170 |

As the amount paid for the investment of $200 000 exceeds the value of shareholders' equity of $170 000 by $30 000, goodwill on consolidation will need to be brought to account whenever the accounts are prepared for consolidation.

The consolidation journal entry to eliminate the investment by Take Ltd in the future year would be as follows:

**Consolidation journal**

| Elimination reference | Details | Dr | Cr |
|---|---|---|---|
| | | $000's | $000's |
| (1) | Share capital – ordinary shares | 100 | |
| | Retained profits | 40 | |
| | Reserves | 30 | |
| | Goodwill on consolidation | 30 | |
| | Investment in subsidiary | | 200 |
| | *Elimination of investment in subsidiary* | | |

On 30 June 2015 the accounts of the parent entity (Take Ltd) and its subsidiary (Over Ltd) need to be consolidated for the purpose of issuing consolidated financial statements.

The respective financial statements of these entities on the date of reporting (30 June 2015) are as follows:

**Take Ltd – account balances 30 June 2015**

| Shareholders' equity | $000's | $000's |
|---|---|---|
| Ordinary shares | 20 | |
| Retained profits (at end) | 80 | |
| Reserves | 10 | 110 |
| **Assets** | | |
| Bank | 80 | |
| Debtors | 20 | |
| Stock | 30 | |
| Equipment | 300 | |
| Investment in Over Ltd | 200 | 630 |
| **Liabilities** | | |
| Loans | | 520 |
| **Net assets** | | 110 |

**Over Ltd – account balances 30 June 2015**

| Shareholders' equity | $000's | $000's |
|---|---|---|
| Ordinary shares | 100 | |
| Retained profits (at end) | 120 | |
| Reserves | 280 | 500 |
| **Assets** | | |
| Bank | 10 | |
| Debtors | 40 | |
| Stock | 50 | |
| Equipment | 300 | |
| Buildings | 200 | 600 |
| **Liabilities** | | |
| Loans | | 100 |
| **Net assets** | | 500 |

An evaluation of the account balances of the subsidiary Over Ltd from the date of acquisition (1 July 2010) to the date of reporting (30 June 2015) indicates an increase in wealth over the five-year period of $330 000 as shown in the following table:

**Over Ltd – account balance comparison**

| | 1 July 2010 | 30 June 2015 | Change in value |
|---|---|---|---|
| **Shareholders' equity** | **$000's** | **$000's** | **$000's** |
| Ordinary shares | 100 | 100 | 0 |
| Retained profits | 40 | 120 | 80 |
| Reserves | 30 | 280 | 250 |
| Total equity | 170 | 500 | 330 |
| **Assets** | | | |
| Bank | 50 | 10 | (40) |
| Debtors | 20 | 40 | 20 |
| Stock | 60 | 50 | (10) |
| Equipment | 40 | 300 | 260 |
| Buildings | 0 | 200 | 200 |
| | 170 | 600 | 430 |
| **Liabilities** | | | |
| Loans | 0 | 100 | 100 |
| Net assets | 170 | 500 | 330 |

This increase in wealth of Over Ltd as reflected in its asset and liability amounts would be reported in the group accounts on 30 June 2015 by:

1 including the account balances of each entity;
2 recording the elimination of the investment; and
3 aggregating the accounts to derive the group accounts.

The group accounts can be prepared in a consolidated worksheet as follows:

**Consolidated worksheet at 30 June**

| Accounts | Take Ltd | Over Ltd | Eliminations | | | | Group accounts |
|---|---|---|---|---|---|---|---|
| | | | Debit | | Credit | | |
| | **$000's** | **$000's** | **$000's** | Ref | **$000's** | Ref | **$000's** |
| **Shareholders' equity** | | | | | | | |
| Ordinary shares | 20 | 100 | 100 | (1) | | | 20 |
| Retained profits | 80 | 120 | 40 | (1) | | | 160 |
| Reserves | 10 | 280 | 30 | (1) | | | 260 |
| | 110 | 500 | | | | | 440 |
| **Assets** | | | | | | | |
| Bank | 80 | 10 | | | | | 90 |
| Debtors | 20 | 40 | | | | | 60 |
| Stock | 30 | 50 | | | | | 80 |
| Equipment | 300 | 300 | | | | | 600 |
| Investment in Over Ltd | 200 | | | | 200 | (1) | 0 |
| Buildings | | 200 | | | | | 200 |
| Goodwill on consolidation | | | 30 | (1) | | | 30 |
| | | 600 | | | | | 1 060 |
| **Liabilities** | | | | | | | |
| Loans | 520 | 100 | | | | | 620 |
| Net assets | 110 | 500 | 200 | | 200 | | 440 |

The consolidated financial statements for the year ended 30 June arising from the consolidated worksheet would be presented as follows:

**Take Ltd**
**Statement of financial position at 30 June 2015**

| Shareholders' equity | Group accounts $000's |
|---|---|
| Ordinary shares | 20 |
| Retained profits | 160 |
| Reserves | 260 |
| Total shareholders' equity | 440 |
| Assets: | |
| Bank | 90 |
| Debtors | 60 |
| Stock | 80 |
| Equipment | 600 |
| Buildings | 200 |
| Goodwill on consolidation | 30 |
| Total assets | 1 060 |
| Liabilities: | |
| Loans | 620 |
| Net assets | 440 |

## Question 10.2

From the following information you are required to prepare:

a  the consolidation journal entry to eliminate the investment in the subsidiary;

b  the consolidated worksheet at 30 June 2015; and

c  the consolidated statement of financial position at 30 June 2015.

Big Ltd purchased a 100% controlling interest in Little Ltd on 1 July 2012 for $500 000. On this date Little Ltd's accounts were as follows:

**Little Ltd**
**Statement of financial position at 1 July 2012**

| Assets | $000's | Shareholders' equity | $000's |
|---|---|---|---|
| Bank | 250 | Ordinary shares | 200 |
| Equipment | 150 | Retained profits | 200 |
| Stock | 100 | Reserves | 100 |
| | 500 | | 500 |

The financial statements of the parent and subsidiary at the date of consolidation at 30 June 2015 are as follows:

**Big Ltd – account balances 30 June 2015**

| Shareholders' equity | $000's | $000's |
|---|---|---|
| Ordinary shares | 250 | |
| Retained profits (at end) | 1 000 | |
| Reserves | 300 | 1 550 |
| **Assets** | | |
| Bank | 600 | |
| Debtors | 100 | |
| Stock | 400 | |
| Equipment | 50 | |
| Investment in Little Ltd | 500 | 1 650 |
| **Liabilities** | | |
| Loans | | 100 |
| **Net assets** | | 1 550 |

**Little Ltd – account balances 30 June 2015**

| Shareholders' equity | $000's | $000's |
|---|---|---|
| Ordinary shares | 200 | |
| Retained profits (at end) | 50 | |
| Reserves | 300 | 550 |
| **Assets** | | |
| Bank | 300 | |
| Debtors | 30 | |
| Stock | 120 | |
| Equipment | 150 | |
| | | 600 |
| **Liabilities** | | |
| Loans | | 50 |
| **Net assets** | | 550 |

## Question 10.3

On 1 July 2011, Low Ltd acquired a 100% controlling interest in High Ltd for $1 000 000. On this date High Ltd's account balances were as follows:

**High Ltd**
**Statement of financial position at 1 July 2011**

| Assets | $000's | Shareholders' equity | $000's |
|---|---|---|---|
| Bank | 20 | Ordinary shares | 300 |
| Debtors | 50 | Retained profits | 400 |
| Stock | 30 | Reserves | 200 |
| Equipment | 800 | | |
| | 900 | | 900 |

The accounts of Low Ltd and High Ltd on 30 June 2015 have been entered into the consolidated worksheet in your workbook.

You are required to complete the consolidation worksheet by:

a  preparing the consolidation journal entry to eliminate Low Ltd's investment in High Ltd;

b  complete the worksheet; and

c  prepare the consolidated statement of financial position at 30 June 2015.

## 10.6  ELIMINATION OF INTRAGROUP TRANSACTIONS

The purpose of consolidated financial statements is to present the combined activities of the parent entity and its subsidiaries (the group) as one economic unit with entities outside the group.

Where companies within the group transact with each other these transactions are called 'intragroup transactions'. These transactions do not alter the overall financial position of the group.

AASB10: Consolidated Financial Statements requires transactions between entities within the group to be eliminated when preparing consolidated financial statements.

Intragroup transactions that require annual elimination and adjustment on consolidation include:

- impairment of goodwill on consolidation;
- intercompany indebtedness and servicing;
- intercompany stock transactions;
- intercompany disposal of non-current assets; and
- intercompany dividends.

When eliminating transactions that have an impact on income tax AASB10 also requires adjustments to be made as a result of AASB112: Income Taxes.

Elimination transactions to derive the group accounts can be recorded on the consolidation worksheet. When using the worksheet it is important to remember that the worksheet does not reflect the general ledger of a single set of accounts, but the combination of a set of independent accounts; that is, the parent and its subsidiaries.

Hence elimination entries have no effect on the actual accounts of the entities in the group; they are only entries on a worksheet. Consequently elimination entries made from year to year are not recorded in a general ledger and are not cumulative. As a result, elimination entries made since the date of acquisition of a subsidiary in previous years may need to be repeated in following years where the transaction has not yet involved an entity outside the group.

## Eliminating goodwill on consolidation

Where the preparation of group accounts recognises goodwill on consolidation as a result of the value of the parent entity's investments exceeding the shareholders' equity of the subsidiary acquired, AASB136: Impairment of Assets requires the amount to be tested for impairment.

Where goodwill has been impaired the consolidated accounts must be adjusted to include the impairment loss for the current year and previous years as follows:

a the impairment amount relating to the period covering the *date of acquisition to the beginning of the current reporting period* must be recorded against retained profits as the cost relates to previous periods; and

b the impairment amount relating to the *current period* which is treated as an expense in the current year.

As impairment losses of goodwill are non-deductible for taxation purposes no taxation adjustment is required.

### Goodwill impairment

| From date of acquisition to start of current year | For the current year |
|---|---|
| Written off against previous year retained profits | Expensed against current year profits |

The consolidation journal entry to eliminate goodwill on consolidation over a number of years is as follows:

### Consolidation journal

| Details | Dr | Cr |
|---|---|---|
| Retained profits (1 July) | XX | |
| Impairment loss – goodwill (expense) | XX | |
| Goodwill on consolidation | | XX |
| *Elimination of goodwill on consolidation* | | |

## Illustration

On 1 January 2011, Banana Ltd purchased a 100% controlling interest in Republic Ltd by paying $300 000 for the fair value of assets totalling $200 000, resulting in $100 000 in goodwill on consolidation. The accounts of Republic Ltd on the date of acquisition were as follows:

**Republic Ltd**
**Statement of financial position at 1 July 2011**

| Assets | $000's | Shareholders' equity | $000's |
|---|---|---|---|
| Bank | 20 | Ordinary shares | 100 |
| Buildings | 180 | Retained profits | 80 |
| | | Reserves | 20 |
| | 200 | | 200 |

For the period 1 January 2011 to the start of the current reporting year 1 July 2014, goodwill had been tested and impaired by $50 000. In the current year the asset was tested for impairment and reduced by an additional $20 000.

**Goodwill impairment**

| From date of acquisition to start of current year | For the current year |
|---|---|
| $50 000 | $20 000 |

For the year ended 30 June 2015 the journal entries to eliminate the investment in the subsidiary and the goodwill on consolidation would be as follows:

**Consolidation journal**

| Elimination reference | Details | Dr | Cr |
|---|---|---|---|
| | | $000's | $000's |
| (1) | Share capital – ordinary shares | 100 | |
| | Retained profits (1 July) | 80 | |
| | Reserves | 20 | |
| | Goodwill on consolidation | 100 | |
| | Investment in Republic Ltd | | 300 |
| | *Elimination of investment in subsidiary* | | |
| (2) | Retained profits (1 July) | 50 | |
| | Impairment loss – goodwill (expenses) | 20 | |
| | Goodwill on consolidation | | 70 |
| | *Elimination of goodwill on consolidation* | | |

The account balances of Banana Ltd and Republic Ltd for the year ended 30 June 2015 and these elimination entries are shown in the following consolidated worksheet.

## Consolidated worksheet at 30 June 2015

| Accounts | Banana Ltd | Republic Ltd | Eliminations Debit | | Eliminations Credit | | Group accounts |
|---|---|---|---|---|---|---|---|
| | $000's | $000's | $000's | Ref | $000's | Ref | $000's |
| Fees revenue | 240 | 140 | | | | | 380 |
| Less expenses | 220 | 70 | 20 | (2) | | | 310 |
| Profit before tax | 20 | 70 | | | | | 70 |
| Less income tax expense | 6 | 21 | | | | | 27 |
| Profit after tax | 14 | 49 | | | | | 43 |
| Retained profits (1 July) | 80 | 150 | 80 | (1) | | | |
| | | | 50 | (2) | | | 100 |
| Shareholders' equity | | | | | | | |
| Retained profits (30 June) | 94 | 199 | | | | | 143 |
| Ordinary shares | 500 | 100 | 100 | (1) | | | 500 |
| Reserves | 80 | 50 | 20 | (1) | | | 110 |
| Total equity | 674 | 349 | | | | | 753 |
| Assets | | | | | | | |
| Current assets | 50 | 20 | | | | | 70 |
| Fixed assets | 344 | 350 | | | | | 694 |
| Investment in Republic Ltd | 300 | | | | 300 | (1) | 0 |
| Goodwill on consolidation | | | 100 | (1) | 70 | (2) | 30 |
| Total assets | 694 | 370 | | | | | 794 |
| Liabilities | | | | | | | |
| Loans | 20 | 21 | | | | | 41 |
| Net assets | 674 | 349 | 370 | | 370 | | 753 |

The consolidated financial statements for the year ended 30 June 2015 could be presented as follows:

**Banana Republic Group**
**Income statement**
**for year ended 30 June 2015**

| | Group accounts |
|---|---|
| | $000's |
| Fees revenue | 380 |
| Less expenses | 310 |
| Profit before tax | 70 |
| Income tax expense | 27 |
| Profit after tax | 43 |

**Banana Republic Group**
**Statement of financial position**
**at 30 June 2015**

| Shareholders' equity | Group accounts |
|---|---|
| | $000's |
| Ordinary shares | 500 |
| Retained profits | 143 |
| Reserves | 110 |
| Total equity | 753 |
| Assets | |
| Current assets | 70 |
| Fixed assets | 694 |
| Goodwill on consolidation | 30 |
| Total assets | 794 |
| Liabilities | |
| Loans | 41 |
| Net assets | 753 |

## Intercompany indebtedness and servicing

Entities in a group often make loans with each other and make interest charges on the loan which appear in the accounts of the respective entities.

The following journal entries provide a comparison of how a loan given by a parent entity to a subsidiary with associated interest charges would appear in the respective accounts.

**Parent entity – general journal**

| Details | Dr | Cr |
|---|---|---|
| Loan to subsidiary | XX | |
|     Bank | | XX |
| *Provided loan to subsidiary* | | |
| Bank | XX | |
|     Interest revenue | | XX |
| *Received interest on loan* | | |

**Subsidiary entity – general journal**

| Details | Dr | Cr |
|---|---|---|
| Bank | XX | |
|     Loan from parent | | XX |
| *Received loan from parent* | | |
| Interest expense | XX | |
|     Bank | | XX |
| *Paid interest on loan* | | |

These transactions do not alter the overall financial position of the group and if adjustments are not made assets, liabilities, income and expenses would be overstated and the consolidated financial statements would not provide a true and fair view of the group accounts.

The entries to eliminate intercompany debts and debt servicing in the journals above would be as follows:

**Consolidation journal**

| Details | Dr | Cr |
|---|---|---|
| Loan from parent | XX | |
|     Loan to subsidiary | | XX |
| *Elimination of intragroup debt* | | |
| Interest revenue | XX | |
|     Interest expense | | XX |
| *Elimination of intragroup debt servicing* | | |

In addition, where entities within the group make payment to another group entity for expenses, this will also need to be eliminated. This may occur where a company pays rent or management fees.

The entries to eliminate intercompany expenses and revenues would be as follows:

**Consolidation journal**

| Details | Dr | Cr |
|---|---|---|
| Rent revenue | XX | |
|     Rent expense | | XX |
| *Elimination of intragroup rent* | | |
| Management fees income | XX | |
|     Management fees expense | | XX |
| *Elimination of intragroup management fees* | | |

These adjustments have no effect on overall group profit and therefore do not attract income tax adjustments.

 **Illustration**

On 1 July 2011, Far Ltd purchased all of the issued capital of Away Ltd for $300 000. Away Ltd's shareholders' equity on this date consisted of:

|  | $000's |
|---|---|
| Ordinary shares | 200 |
| Retained profits | 100 |

*Additional information*

During the year ended 30 June 2015 the following intercompany transactions occurred:
- Far Ltd borrowed $100 000 from Away Ltd.
- Far Ltd paid interest of $8000 to Away Ltd on the loan.
- Away Ltd paid Far Ltd $10 000 for factory rental.

These transactions would appear as elimination entries in the consolidation journal as follows:

**Consolidation journal**

| Elimination reference | Details | Dr | Cr |
|---|---|---|---|
|  |  | $000's | $000's |
| (1) | Share capital – ordinary shares | 200 | |
|  | Retained profits (1 July) | 100 | |
|  | Investment in Away Ltd | | 300 |
|  | *Elimination of investment in subsidiary* | | |
| (2) | Loan liabilities | 100 | |
|  | Loan assets | | 100 |
|  | *Elimination of intercompany loan* | | |
| (3) | Interest revenue | 8 | |
|  | Interest expense | | 8 |
|  | *Elimination of intercompany interest* | | |
| (4) | Rent revenue | 10 | |
|  | Rent expense | | 10 |
|  | *Elimination of intercompany rent* | | |

The account balances of Far Ltd and Away Ltd for the year ended 30 June 2015 and these elimination entries are shown in the following consolidated worksheet.

**Consolidated worksheet at 30 June 2015**

| Accounts | Far Ltd | Away Ltd | Eliminations Debit | Ref | Eliminations Credit | Ref | Group accounts |
|---|---|---|---|---|---|---|---|
| | $000's | $000's | $000's | Ref | $000's | Ref | $000's |
| Service income | 162 | 58 | | | | | 220 |
| Interest revenue | 8 | 0 | 8 | (3) | | | 0 |
| Rent revenue | 10 | 0 | 10 | (4) | | | 0 |
| | 180 | 58 | | | | | 220 |
| Less expenses | | | | | | | |
| Interest expense | 30 | 8 | | | 8 | (3) | 30 |
| Other expenses | 100 | 20 | | | 10 | (4) | 110 |
| Profit before tax | 50 | 30 | | | | | 80 |
| Income tax expense | 15 | 9 | | | | | 24 |
| Profit after tax | 35 | 21 | | | | | 56 |
| Retained profits (1 July) | 80 | 300 | 100 | (1) | | | 280 |
| Equity | | | | | | | |
| Retained profits (30 June) | 115 | 321 | | | | | 336 |
| Ordinary shares | 800 | 200 | 200 | (1) | | | 800 |
| Total equity | 915 | 521 | | | | | 1 136 |
| Assets | | | | | | | |
| Loan assets | 100 | 0 | | | 100 | (2) | 0 |
| Current assets | 200 | 100 | | | | | 300 |
| Non-current assets | 715 | 521 | | | | | 1236 |
| Investment in Away Ltd | 300 | | | | 300 | (1) | 0 |
| Total assets | 1 315 | 621 | | | | | 1536 |
| Liabilities | | | | | | | |
| Loan liabilities | 400 | 100 | 100 | (2) | | | 400 |
| Net assets | 915 | 521 | 418 | | 418 | | 1 136 |

The consolidated financial statements resulting from the group accounts would be as follows:

**Far Away Group**
**Income statement**
**for year ended 30 June 2015**

| | Group accounts |
|---|---|
| | $000's |
| Service income | 220 |
| Less expenses | |
| Interest expense | 30 |
| Other expenses | 110 |
| Profit before tax | 80 |
| Income tax expense | 24 |
| Profit after tax | 56 |

**Far Away Group**
**Statement of financial position**
**at 30 June 2015**

| Shareholders' equity | Group accounts |
|---|---|
| | $000's |
| Ordinary shares | 800 |
| Retained profits | 336 |
| Total equity | 1 136 |
| Assets | |
| Current assets | 300 |
| Non-current assets | 1 236 |
| Total assets | 1 536 |
| Liabilities | |
| Loan liabilities | 400 |
| Net assets | 1 136 |

## Question 10.4

On 1 July 2012, James Ltd purchased all of the issued capital of Bond Ltd for $300 000 to gain control. On this date, Bond Ltd's shareholders' equity consisted of:

|  | $000's |
|---|---|
| Ordinary shares | 200 |
| Retained profits | 20 |
| Reserves | 50 |

### Additional information

Goodwill resulting from the investment in Bond Ltd is tested for impairment each year. The total amount of impairment losses for goodwill on consolidation is $18 000 consisting of $1000 for the current year and $17 000 for previous years.

For the year ended 30 June 2015:

- James Ltd owes Bond Ltd $100 000 for a long-term loan;
- James Ltd paid $10 000 interest on the loan from Bond Ltd; and
- Bond Ltd paid James Ltd $40 000 for management services provided during the year.

The accounts for each entity have been included in your workbook in the consolidated worksheet. For the year ended 30 June 2015 you are required to:

a   record the elimination entries in the consolidation journal;

b   enter the elimination entries into the consolidated worksheet; and

c   prepare consolidated financial statements for the year ended 30 June 2015.

## Question 10.5

Just Ltd purchased all of the share capital in Right Ltd on 1 July 2013 for $500 000 and gained control of the subsidiary. On this date Right Ltd's shareholders' equity consisted of:

|  | $000's |
|---|---|
| Ordinary shares | 250 |
| Retained profits | 50 |
| Reserves | 100 |

### Additional information

- For the year ended 30 June 2014 goodwill on consolidation was tested for impairment and an impairment loss of $30 000 recognised in the group consolidated financial statements.
- For the year ended 30 June 2015 further testing of goodwill determined an impairment loss of $20 000.
- Right Ltd has provided a long-term loan of $250 000 to Just Ltd.
- Right Ltd received $50 000 interest on the loan from Just Ltd.
- Right Ltd received $200 000 in rental income on a building used by Just Ltd.

Using the consolidated worksheet included in the workbook you are required to:

a   record appropriate elimination entries into the consolidated worksheet; and

b   prepare consolidated financial statements for the year ended 30 June 2015.

## Intercompany stock transactions

Sales reported in the consolidated financial statements should reflect sales made by the group to entities outside the group. Where entities within the group have engaged in intercompany stock transactions, sales figures will not reflect sales to third parties.

When preparing the accounts for consolidation, stock-related transactions made within the group must be eliminated to ensure that the consolidated financial statements represent a true and fair view of a single economic entity with third parties.

Intercompany stock transactions requiring elimination include:

- intercompany sales and purchases;
- unrealised profits in closing stocks; and
- unrealised profits in opening stocks.

## Intercompany sales and purchases

Intercompany sales and purchases are eliminated to avoid 'double counting'. This elimination is necessary as it is only the profit (loss) made between the economic entity and external parties that alters the financial status of the economic entity, not sales and purchases between economic entity members.

When sales are made within a group the transactions would be recorded as follows:

**Selling entity – general journal**

| Details | Dr | Cr |
|---|---|---|
| Accounts receivable | XX | |
|     Sales revenue | | XX |
| *Sales to group entity* | | |
| Cost of sales | XX | |
|     Stock | | XX |
| *Cost of sales to group entity* | | |

**Purchasing entity – general journal**

| Details | Dr | Cr |
|---|---|---|
| Stock | XX | |
|     Accounts payable | | XX |
| *Purchases from group entity* | | |

The journal entry to eliminate an intercompany sale made on credit would be as follows:

**Consolidation journal**

| Details | Dr | Cr |
|---|---|---|
| Sales revenue | XX | |
|     Cost of sales | | XX |
| *Elimination of intragroup sales* | | |
| Accounts payable | XX | |
|     Accounts receivable | | XX |
| *Elimination of intragroup debt* | | |

## Unrealised profits in closing stock

Where an entity in the group has purchased stock from another group entity and that stock has not been sold to an entity outside the group, an elimination entry is required to remove any unrealised profit in closing stock.

The elimination entry removes the profit made on the intragroup transaction and revalues stock at cost price.

When eliminating the amount of unrealised profit in closing stock an additional adjustment is required to account for income tax. If the adjustment reduces profit, income tax expense will fall and a deferred tax asset will be brought to account.

The journal entry to eliminate unrealised profit in closing stock is as follows:

**Consolidation journal**

| Details | Dr | Cr |
|---|---|---|
| Cost of sales | XX | |
|     Stock on hand | | XX |
| *Elimination of unrealised profit in closing stock* | | |
| Deferred tax asset | XX | |
|     Income tax expense | | XX |
| *Tax adjustment on unrealised profit in closing stock* | | |

## Unrealised profits in opening stock

Accounting principles require stock at the end of a reporting period to become the opening stock in the next reporting period. When preparing consolidated accounts an elimination entry will be required to adjust the value of opening stock where the closing stock in the previous year included unrealised profits. An adjustment will also be required to account for income tax on the unrealised profit.

The elimination entry to account for unrealised profits in the closing stock of the previous year and to account for income tax on the amount requires an adjustment to retained profits (at the start of the year), as the amount reported in the accounts of the holder of the stock will be overstated. (*Remember that an elimination entry only occurs on a worksheet and is not recorded in the accounts of an entity in the group; hence the entity's account balances do not include consolidation entries which eliminate unrealised profits in closing stocks made in the previous year.*)

As retained profits include profits (after tax) an entry to eliminate unrealised profits in opening stocks must be made net of tax (that is, profit less tax).

In addition the income tax on the unrealised profit in the opening stock must be brought to account in the current period on the presumption that the stock will be sold in the current year.

For example, an entity identified an unrealised profit in its opening stock of $3000. Tax on this profit at 30% amounts to $900, resulting in a profit after tax of $2100 which is the amount required to adjust retained profits at the start of the year.

The journal entry to eliminate unrealised profit in opening stock is as follows:

### Consolidation journal

| Details | Dr | Cr |
|---|---|---|
| Retained profits (at start of year) | XX | |
| Income tax expense | XX | |
| Cost of sales | | XX |
| *Elimination of unrealised profit in opening stock* | | |

## Illustration

On 1 July 2013, Aim Ltd purchased all of the issued capital of Hire Ltd for $400 000. Hire Ltd's shareholders' equity on this date consisted of:

| | $000's |
|---|---|
| Ordinary shares | 300 |
| Retained profits | 100 |

### Additional information

During the year ended 30 June 2015 the following intercompany transactions occurred:
- Hire Ltd sold stock to Aim Ltd valued at $800 000.
- Aim Ltd's stock at the start of the year included $50 000 in unrealised profit (before tax).
- Aim Ltd's stock at the end of the year includes $40 000 in unrealised profit (before tax).
- The tax rate is 30%.
  The journal entries to eliminate these intercompany transactions would be as follows:

## Consolidation journal

| Elimination reference | Details | Dr $000's | Cr $000's |
|---|---|---|---|
| (1) | Share capital – ordinary shares | 300 | |
| | Retained profits (1 July) | 100 | |
| |    Investment in Hire Ltd | | 400 |
| | *Elimination of investment in subsidiary* | | |
| (2) | Sales | 800 | |
| |    Cost of sales | | 800 |
| | *Elimination of intercompany sales* | | |
| (3) | Retained profits (1 July) | 35 | |
| | Income tax expense | 15 | |
| |    Cost of sales | | 50 |
| | *Elimination of unrealised profit in opening stock* | | |
| (4) | Cost of sales | 40 | |
| |    Stock (on hand) | | 40 |
| | *Elimination of unrealised profit in closing stock* | | |
| | Deferred tax asset | 12 | |
| |    Income tax expense | | 12 |
| | *Tax adjustment on unrealised profit in closing stock* | | |

The consolidated worksheet containing the group accounts and these eliminations follows:

## Consolidated worksheet at 30 June 2015

| Accounts | Aim Ltd $000's | Hire Ltd $000's | Eliminations Debit $000's | Ref | Eliminations Credit $000's | Ref | Group accounts $000's |
|---|---|---|---|---|---|---|---|
| Sales | 1 200 | 800 | 800 | (2) | | | 1 200 |
| Cost of sales | 660 | 480 | 40 | (4) | 800 | (2) | |
| | | | | | 50 | (3) | 330 |
| Gross profit | 540 | 320 | | | | | 870 |
| Other expenses | 50 | 20 | | | | | 70 |
| Profit before tax | 490 | 300 | | | | | 800 |
| Income tax expense | 147 | 90 | 15 | (3) | 12 | (5) | 240 |
| Profit after tax | 343 | 210 | | | | | 560 |
| Retained profits (1 July) | 100 | 200 | 100 | (1) | | | |
| | | | 35 | (3) | | | 165 |
| Equity | | | | | | | |
| Retained profits (30 June) | 443 | 410 | | | | | 725 |
| Ordinary shares | 500 | 300 | 300 | (1) | | | 500 |
| Total equity | 943 | 710 | | | | | 1 225 |
| Assets | | | | | | | |
| Stock (on hand) | 200 | 180 | | | 40 | (4) | 340 |
| Deferred tax asset | | | 12 | (5) | | | 12 |
| Non-current assets | 343 | 530 | | | | | 873 |
| Investment in Hire Ltd | 400 | | | | 400 | (1) | 0 |
| Total assets | 943 | 710 | 1 302 | | 1 302 | | 1 225 |

The consolidated financial statements resulting from the group accounts would be as follows:

**Aim Hire Group**
**Income statement**
**for year ended 30 June 2015**

|  | Group accounts |
| --- | --- |
|  | **$000's** |
| Sales | 1 200 |
| Less cost of sales | 330 |
| Gross profit | 870 |
| Less other expenses | 70 |
| Profit before tax | 800 |
| Income tax expense | 240 |
| Profit after tax | 560 |

**Aim Hire Group**
**Statement of financial position**
**at 30 June 2015**

| Shareholders' equity | Group accounts |
| --- | --- |
|  | **$000's** |
| Ordinary shares | 500 |
| Retained profits | 725 |
| Total equity | 1 225 |
| Assets |  |
| Stock on hand | 340 |
| Deferred tax asset | 12 |
| Non-current assets | 873 |
| Total assets | 1 225 |

# Question 10.6

Using the accounts shown in the workbook for the parent entity, Chocka Ltd and its wholly owned and controlled subsidiary Block Ltd, you are required to:

**a** prepare elimination entries for the consolidated worksheet;

**b** record the elimination entries into the consolidated worksheet; and

**c** prepare consolidated financial statements for the year ended 30 June 2015.

*Additional information*

On the date of acquisition Block Ltd's shareholders' equity consisted of:

|  | $000's |
| --- | --- |
| Ordinary shares | 200 |
| Retained profits | 20 |
| Reserves | 30 |

For the year ended 30 June 2015 the following intercompany transactions were identified:

- Chocka Ltd's opening stock includes an unrealised profit of $80 000;
- Block Ltd's sales include $600 000 made to Chocka Ltd;
- an unrealised profit of $60 000 is included in Chocka Ltd's closing stock; and
- the tax rate is 30%.

# Question 10.7

The accounts of Hill Ltd and Dale Ltd are shown in the consolidation worksheet in the workbook.

You are required to complete the worksheet using the following information.

On 1 July 2010, Hill Ltd purchased all of the issued capital of Dale Ltd and gained control. At this date Dale Ltd held the following shareholders' equity:

|  | $000's |
| --- | --- |
| Ordinary shares | 100 |
| Retained profits | 10 |
| Reserves | 25 |

Additional information for the year ended 30 June 2015:
- goodwill on consolidation has been tested and is to be impaired by $4000, consisting of $2000 for past consolidation periods and $2000 for the current year;
- Hill Ltd's opening stock includes $10 000 in unrealised profits;
- intercompany sales totalled $300 000 for the year;
- Dale Ltd's closing stock includes an unrealised profit of $20 000;
- Dale Ltd owes Hill Ltd $40 000 for stock purchased during the year; and
- the tax rate is 30%.

## Intercompany disposal of non-current assets

When preparing the accounts for consolidated reporting, adjustments are required to eliminate transactions associated with the disposal of assets to entities in the group where a profit or loss has occurred.

### Profit on disposal of an asset

If an entity in the group disposes of an asset to another group entity at a profit the asset remains in the group; however, the asset's values reported in the accounts of each entity are overstated and require adjustment.

When eliminating an unrealised profit on the sale of an asset in the consolidated accounts the following adjusting entries are required:
- elimination of the unrealised profit;
- elimination of overstated depreciation; and
- adjustment to income tax.

## Illustration

On 1 July 2015, YZ Ltd sold equipment costing $500 000 to its subsidiary AD Ltd for $600 000 and brought to account a profit of $100 000. Assets are depreciated at 10% p.a.

For the year ended 30 June 2016, the respective companies would have recorded the sale and depreciation transactions as follows:

**YZ Ltd – general journal**

| Details | Dr | Cr |
|---|---|---|
| | $000's | $000's |
| Bank | 600 | |
| Equipment | | 500 |
| Profit on sale of asset | | 100 |
| *Sale of asset* | | |

**AD Ltd – general journal**

| Details | Dr | Cr |
|---|---|---|
| | $000's | $000's |
| Equipment | 600 | |
| Bank | | 600 |
| *Purchase of asset* | | |
| Depreciation expense | 60 | |
| Accumulated depreciation | | 60 |
| *Annual depreciation* | | |

These entries reveal the following:
- AD Ltd has recorded the equipment at a new cost price of $600 000, being $100 000 above its original cost price of $500 000; and
- AD Ltd has included depreciation expense of $60 000 based on the $600 000 inflated cost price. This amount is $10 000 higher than the amount of $50 000, had depreciation been calculated on its original cost of $500 000.

The entries to eliminate the profit on the sale and overstated depreciation would be as follows:

**Consolidation journal**

| Details | Dr | Cr |
|---|---|---|
| | $000's | $000's |
| Profit on sale of asset | 100 | |
|     Equipment | | 100 |
| *Elimination of intragroup profit on asset sale* | | |
| Accumulated depreciation | 10 | |
|     Depreciation expense | | 10 |
| *Depreciation on equipment adjustment* | | |

In addition, an adjustment is required to income tax expense as a result of the elimination of the profit on the sale of the asset and the adjustment to depreciation expense.

The net effect of eliminating a $100 000 profit on asset sale and reducing depreciation expense by $10 000 has resulted in group profit falling by $90 000. At a tax rate of 30% income tax expense is overstated by $27 000.

The entry to adjust overstated income tax expense would be:

**Consolidation journal**

| Details | Dr | Cr |
|---|---|---|
| | $000's | $000's |
| Deferred tax asset | 27 | |
|     Income tax expense | | 27 |
| *Adjustment to income tax on asset disposal* | | |

In the following year, if the asset remains in the group, the consolidation entry to eliminate the unrealised profit in the previous year would be as follows:

**Consolidation journal**

| Details | Dr | Cr |
|---|---|---|
| | $000's | $000's |
| Retained profits (at 1 July) | 63 | |
| Income tax expense | 27 | |
| Accumulated depreciation | 10 | |
|     Equipment | | 100 |
| *Elimination of asset profit from previous year* | | |

# Question 10.8

On 1 July 2014, Growth Ltd purchased a vehicle from its controlled subsidiary Hall Ltd at a cost price of $800 000. Hall Ltd purchased the asset in a previous year for $600 000. Depreciation is charged at 10% p.a. on the straight-line method and the income tax rate is 30%.

You are required to prepare the elimination entries for the consolidated accounts at 30 June 2015.

## Loss on asset disposal

A loss on the disposal of an asset resulting from an intercompany transaction must be eliminated from the consolidated accounts and adjustments made to depreciation and taxation expense arising from the loss.

## Illustration

On 1 April 2015, Ago Ltd sold machinery costing $800 000 to its parent Long Ltd for $600 000 and brought to account a loss of $200 000. Assets are depreciated at 20% p.a.

For the year ended 30 June 2015 the respective companies would have recorded the sale and depreciation transactions as follows:

**Long Ltd – general journal**

| Details | Dr | Cr |
|---|---|---|
| | $000's | $000's |
| Machinery | 600 | |
|    Bank | | 600 |
| *Purchase of asset* | | |
| Depreciation expense | 30 | |
|    Accumulated depreciation | | 30 |
| *Depreciation for 6 months* | | |

**AD Ltd – general journal**

| Details | Dr | Cr |
|---|---|---|
| | $000's | $000's |
| Bank | 600 | |
| Loss on sale of asset | 200 | |
|    Machinery | | 800 |
| *Sale of asset* | | |

These entries reveal the following:
- Ago Ltd is carrying machinery at a new cost price of $600 000, being $200 000 below its original cost price of $800 000; and
- Ago Ltd has recorded depreciation expense for three months of $30 000 ($600 000 × 20% p.a. × 3 months) based on the lower cost price, which is $10 000 lower than the amount of $40 000, had depreciation been calculated on its original cost of $800 000.

The entries to eliminate the loss on the sale and adjust the understated depreciation would be as follows:

**Consolidation journal**

| Details | Dr | Cr |
|---|---|---|
| | $000's | $000's |
| Machinery | 200 | |
|    Loss on sale of asset | | 200 |
| *Elimination of intragroup loss on asset sale* | | |
| Depreciation expense | 10 | |
|    Accumulated depreciation | | 10 |
| *Depreciation on machinery adjustment* | | |

The combined effect of these entries increases profit by $190 000 (that is, eliminating the loss on asset sale of $200 000 and increasing depreciation by $10 000) which will increase income tax expense by $57 000.

The entry to adjust understated income tax expense would be:

**Consolidation journal**

| Details | Dr | Cr |
|---|---|---|
| | $000's | $000's |
| Income tax expense | 57 | |
|    Deferred tax liability | | 57 |
| *Adjustment to income tax on asset disposal* | | |

In the following year, if the asset remains in the group, the consolidation entry to eliminate the unrealised loss in the previous year would be as follows:

**Consolidation journal**

| Details | Dr | Cr |
|---|---|---|
| | $000's | $000's |
| Machinery | 200 | |
| Retained profits (at 1 July) | | 133 |
| Income tax expense | | 57 |
| Accumulated depreciation | | 10 |
| Elimination of asset loss from previous year | | |

## Question 10.9

Rocket Ltd sold equipment to its parent company Mars Ltd on 1 January 2014 for $750 000. The original cost of the asset was $1 000 000. Depreciation is charged at 20% on the straight-line method and the income tax rate is 30%.

You are required to prepare the elimination entries for the consolidated accounts at 30 June 2015.

## Question 10.10

Star Ltd purchased all of the issued capital of Trek Ltd on 1 July 2012 and gained control. On this date Trek Ltd held $200 000 in ordinary shares, $100 000 in retained profits and $50 000 in reserves.

On 1 July 2014, Trek Ltd sold a machinery that had a historical cost of $200 000 to Star Ltd for $300 000 and brought to account a profit on sale of asset of $100 000.

On 1 January 2015, Star Ltd brought to account a $100 000 loss on the disposal of equipment, which it had sold to Trek Ltd. The equipment originally cost $500 000.

All assets are depreciated at 20% p.a. and the rate of income tax is 30%.

You are required to complete the consolidated worksheet for the year ended 30 June 2015.

## Question 10.11

From the following information you are required to complete the consolidated worksheet for the Future Past group for the year ended 30 June 2015 shown in the workbook.

On 1 July 2012, Future Ltd purchased all the shares in Past Ltd which became a controlled subsidiary.

Past Ltd's shareholders' equity included the following amounts at the date of acquisition:

| | $ |
|---|---|
| Ordinary shares | 250 000 |
| Retained profits | 10 000 |
| Reserves | 40 000 |

*Additional information*

During the year ended 30 June 2015, the following intercompany transactions occurred:
- Future Ltd paid interest of $10 000 to Past Ltd on its $100 000 long-term loan.
- The opening stock of Future Ltd included $30 000 in unrealised profit.
- Intercompany sales total $600 000.

- The closing stock of Past Ltd includes an unrealised profit of $20 000.
- On 1 April, Future Ltd sold machinery with a cost price of $220 000 to Past Ltd for $120 000.
- Assets are depreciated at 40% p.a. using the straight-line method.
- The tax rate is 30%.

## Intercompany dividends

When a wholly owned subsidiary appropriates dividends to its parent entity from retained profits, this does not constitute a flow of funds to an external party and must be eliminated when preparing the group accounts.

The only dividend amounts that should be reported in the consolidated financial statements are the dividends paid by the parent entity to its shareholders.

### Interim dividends

When a subsidiary pays an interim dividend during the current period the amount will be taken from its retained profits account as an appropriation. The parent entity on receipt of the dividend will record the amount as income.

The journal entries for appropriation of the interim dividend by the subsidiary and the receipt by the parent entity are as follows:

**Parent Ltd – general journal**

| Details | Dr | Cr |
|---|---|---|
| | $000's | $000's |
| Bank | XX | |
| Dividends income | | XX |
| *Receipt of interim dividend* | | |

**Subsidiary Ltd – general journal**

| Details | Dr | Cr |
|---|---|---|
| | $000's | $000's |
| Retained profits (interim dividend) | XX | |
| Bank | | XX |
| *Payment of dividend* | | |

The elimination entry on consolidation to return the dividend to retained profits is as follows:

**Consolidation journal**

| Details | Dr | Cr |
|---|---|---|
| | $000's | $000's |
| Dividends income | XX | |
| Retained profits (interim dividend) | | XX |
| *Elimination of intercompany dividend* | | |

### Final dividends

The declaration of a final dividend at the end of the current reporting period by the subsidiary reduces the subsidiary's retained profits and creates a liability to the parent entity for the dividends payable in the following year. The parent entity may bring the dividend to account by recognising the dividend as income and recording the dividend as receivable.

The appropriation of the final dividend by the subsidiary and the recognition by the parent entity may be recorded as follows:

**Parent Ltd – general journal**

| Details | Dr | Cr |
|---|---|---|
| | $000's | $000's |
| Dividend receivable | XX | |
| Dividends income | | XX |
| *Receipt of interim dividend* | | |

**Subsidiary Ltd – general journal**

| Details | Dr | Cr |
|---|---|---|
| | $000's | $000's |
| Retained profits (interim dividend) | XX | |
| Dividend payable | | XX |
| *Payment of dividend* | | |

The elimination entries on consolidation to return the dividend to retained profits and remove intercompany debt are as follows:

**Consolidation journal**

| Details | Dr | Cr |
|---|---|---|
| | **$000's** | **$000's** |
| Dividends income | XX | |
|     Retained profits (final dividend) | | XX |
| *Elimination of intercompany dividend* | | |
| Dividend payable | XX | |
|     Dividend receivable | | XX |
| *Elimination of intercompany debt* | | |

## Illustration

On 1 July 2014, Big Ltd purchased a 100% controlling interest in Apple Ltd for $300 000. On this date Apple Ltd's shareholders' equity consisted of:

| | $ |
|---|---|
| Ordinary shares | 200 000 |
| Retained profits | 100 000 |

During the year ended 30 June 2015, Apple Ltd paid an interim dividend of $50 000 and declared a final dividend of $80 000.

The elimination entries for the consolidated accounts would be as follows:

**Consolidation journal**

| Elimination reference | Details | Dr | Cr |
|---|---|---|---|
| | | **$000's** | **$000's** |
| (1) | Share capital – ordinary shares | 200 | |
| | Retained profits (1 July) | 100 | |
| |     Investment in Apple Ltd | | 300 |
| | *Elimination of investment in subsidiary* | | |
| (2) | Dividends income | 130 | |
| |     Retained profits (interim dividends) | | 50 |
| |     Retained profits (final dividends) | | 80 |
| | *Elimination of intercompany dividends* | | |
| (3) | Dividends payable | 80 | |
| |     Dividends receivable | | 80 |
| | *Elimination of intercompany debt* | | |

The consolidation worksheet for the year showing these eliminations would be as follows:

### Consolidated worksheet at 30 June 2015

| Accounts | Big Ltd | Apple Ltd | Debit | Ref | Credit | Ref | Group accounts |
|---|---|---|---|---|---|---|---|
| | $000's | $000's | $000's | Ref | $000's | Ref | $000's |
| Fees income | 200 | 140 | | | | | 340 |
| Dividends income | 130 | 0 | 130 | (2) | | | 0 |
| | 330 | 140 | | | | | 340 |
| Operating expenses | 180 | 100 | | | | | 280 |
| Profit before tax | 150 | 40 | | | | | 60 |
| Income tax expense | 45 | 12 | | | | | 57 |
| Profit after tax | 105 | 28 | | | | | 3 |
| Retained profits (1 July) | 80 | 150 | 100 | (1) | | | 130 |
| | 185 | 178 | | | | | 133 |
| Less interim dividend | 60 | 50 | | | 50 | (2) | 60 |
| Final dividend | 60 | 80 | | | 80 | (2) | 60 |
| Shareholders' equity | | | | | | | |
| Retained profits (30 June) | 65 | 48 | | | | | 13 |
| Ordinary shares | 500 | 200 | 200 | (1) | | | 500 |
| Total equity | 565 | 248 | | | | | 513 |
| Assets | | | | | | | |
| Current assets | 50 | 20 | | | | | 70 |
| Dividends receivable | 80 | 0 | | | 80 | (3) | 0 |
| Non-current assets | 195 | 308 | | | | | 503 |
| Investment in Apple Ltd | 300 | – | | | 300 | (1) | 0 |
| Total assets | 625 | 328 | | | | | 573 |
| Liabilities | | | | | | | |
| Dividends payable | 60 | 80 | 80 | (3) | | | 60 |
| Net assets | 565 | 248 | 510 | | 510 | | 513 |

The consolidated financial statements would be presented as follows:

**Big Apple Group**
**Income statement**
**for year ended 30 June 2015**

| | Group accounts |
|---|---|
| | $000's |
| Fees income | 340 |
| Less operating expenses | 280 |
| Profit before tax | 60 |
| Income tax expense | 57 |
| Profit after tax | 3 |

**Big Apple Group**
**Statement of changes in equity**
**at 30 June 2015**

| Retained profits | Group accounts |
|---|---|
| | $000's |
| Balance at 1 June | 130 |
| Profit (after tax) | 3 |
| Total funds for appropriation | 133 |
| Less dividends paid | |
| Interim dividends | 60 |
| Final dividends | 60 |
| Balance at 30 June | 13 |

**Big Apple Group**
**Statement of financial position**
**at 30 June 2015**

|  | Group accounts |
|---|---|
| **Shareholders' equity** | **$000's** |
| Ordinary shares | 500 |
| Retained profits | 13 |
| **Total equity** | 513 |
| **Assets** | |
| Current assets | 70 |
| Non-current assets | 503 |
| **Total assets** | 573 |
| Less liabilities – dividends payable | 60 |
| **Net assets** | 513 |

# Question 10.12

The workbook contains a consolidated worksheet showing the accounts for Bag Ltd and Limit Ltd. You are required to:

a   prepare consolidation journal entries to eliminate the following transactions;

b   complete the worksheet; and

c   prepare consolidated financial statements at 30 June 2015.

### Additional information

- On 1 June 2012, Bag Ltd purchased all of the issued capital of Limit Ltd and took control of the subsidiary. At this date Limit Ltd held the following shareholders' equity:

|  | $ |
|---|---|
| Ordinary shares | 200 000 |
| Retained profits | 60 000 |
| Reserves | 40 000 |

- During the year Limit Ltd paid an interim dividend of $70 000.
- On 30 June Limit Ltd declared a final dividend of $130 000.

# Question 10.13

Trade Ltd purchased all the shares in Winds Ltd on 1 July 2011 and gained control. Using the information below and the consolidated worksheet in the workbook for the year ended 30 June 2015, you are required to:

a   prepare consolidation journal entries to eliminate and adjust the accounts;

b   complete the worksheet; and

c   prepare consolidated financial statements at 30 June 2015.

### Additional information

- On 1 July 2011, Winds Ltd's shareholders' equity included the following:

|  | $ |
|---|---|
| Ordinary shares | 40 000 |
| Retained profits | 80 000 |
| Reserves | 120 000 |

- Intercompany sales totalled $300 000.
- An unrealised profit of $50 000 is included in opening inventory.
- Closing inventory includes an unrealised profit of $30 000.
- Winds Ltd paid an interim dividend during the year and declared a final dividend at 30 June.
- The tax rate is 30%.

## 10.7 SUMMARY OF ELIMINATION ENTRIES ON CONSOLIDATION

The elimination and adjusting entries used in this chapter to prepare the accounts of a parent entity and its wholly owned subsidiary for disclosure in the consolidated financial statements are as follows.

**Elimination of an investment in a subsidiary:**

#### Consolidation journal

| Details | Dr | Cr |
|---|---|---|
| Share capital – subsidiary | XX | |
| Retained profits – subsidiary | XX | |
| Reserves – subsidiary | XX | |
| Goodwill on consolidation | XX | |
|     Investment in subsidiary | | XX |

**Elimination of goodwill:**

#### Consolidation journal

| Details | Dr | Cr |
|---|---|---|
| Retained profits (1 July) | XX | |
| Impairment loss – goodwill (expense) | XX | |
|     Goodwill on consolidation | | XX |

**Elimination of intercompany loans and interest:**

#### Consolidation journal

| Details | Dr | Cr |
|---|---|---|
| Loan from parent | XX | |
|     Loan to subsidiary | | XX |
| Interest revenue | XX | |
|     Interest expense | | XX |

**Elimination of intercompany sales and indebtedness:**

#### Consolidation journal

| Details | Dr | Cr |
|---|---|---|
| Sales revenue | XX | |
|     Cost of sales | | XX |
| Accounts payable | XX | |
|     Accounts receivable | | XX |

Elimination of unrealised profit in opening stock:

**Consolidation journal**

| Details | Dr | Cr |
|---|---|---|
| Retained profits (at start of year) | XX | |
| Income tax expense | XX | |
|     Cost of sales | | XX |

Elimination of unrealised profit in closing stock:

**Consolidation journal**

| Details | Dr | Cr |
|---|---|---|
| Cost of sales | XX | |
|     Stock on hand | | XX |
| Deferred tax asset | XX | |
|     Income tax expense | | XX |

Elimination of intercompany profit on asset disposal, with depreciation and tax adjustments:

**Consolidation journal**

| Details | Dr | Cr |
|---|---|---|
| Profit on sale of asset | XX | |
|     Asset | | XX |
| Accumulated depreciation | XX | |
|     Depreciation expense | | XX |
| Deferred tax asset | XX | |
|     Income tax expense | | XX |

Elimination of intercompany loss on asset disposal, with depreciation and tax adjustments:

**Consolidation journal**

| Details | Dr | Cr |
|---|---|---|
| Asset | XX | |
|     Loss on sale of asset | | XX |
| Depreciation expense | XX | |
|     Accumulated depreciation | | XX |
| Income tax expense | XX | |
|     Deferred tax liability | | XX |

Elimination of interim and final dividends paid by the subsidiary:

**Consolidation journal**

| Details | Dr | Cr |
|---|---|---|
| Dividends income | XX | |
|     Retained profits (interim dividend) | | XX |
|     Retained profits (final dividend) | | |
| Dividend payable | XX | |
|     Dividend receivable | | XX |

# Comprehensive illustration

On 1 July 2011 Sea Ltd acquired all the share capital of Gull Ltd for $100 000. On this date Gull Ltd's account balances were as follows:

**Statement of financial position**

| Assets | $000's | Liabilities | $000's |
|---|---|---|---|
| Current assets | 50 | Current liabilities | 20 |
| Non-current assets | 190 | Non-current liabilities | 155 |
| | | Shareholders' equity | |
| | | Ordinary shares | 60 |
| | | Retained profits | 5 |
| | 240 | | 240 |

*Additional information*

1  Goodwill has been tested for impairment since the date of acquisition. For the period 1 July 2011 to 30 June 2014, $20 000 of goodwill has been impaired with an additional $5000 impairment loss for the year ended 30 June 2015.
2  For the year ended 30 June 2015 the following intercompany transactions occurred:
  – intercompany sales totalled $300 000;
  – Gull Ltd owes Sea Ltd $50 000 for stock sold during the year;
  – opening stock includes an unrealised profit of $20 000;
  – closing stock includes a $30 000 unrealised profit;
  – Gull Ltd owes Sea Ltd $200 000 for a long-term loan;
  – Gull Ltd paid $20 000 interest on the long-term loan;
  – on 1 March Sea Ltd sold an asset costing $600 000 to Gull Ltd making a profit of $120 000;
  – Gull Ltd paid and declared dividends during the year which were brought to account by Sea Ltd;
  – assets are depreciated at 25% p.a. using the straight-line method of depreciation; and
  – the tax rate is 30%.
The consolidation journal entries resulting from this information would be as follows:

**Consolidation journal**

| Elimination reference | Details | Dr $000's | Cr $000's |
|---|---|---|---|
| (1) | Share capital – ordinary shares | 60 | |
| | Retained profits (1 July) | 5 | |
| | Goodwill on consolidation | 35 | |
| | Investment in Gull Ltd | | 100 |
| | *Elimination of investment in subsidiary* | | |
| (2) | Retained profits (1 July) | 20 | |
| | Operating expenses (impairment loss – goodwill) | 5 | |
| | Goodwill on consolidation | | 25 |
| | *Elimination of goodwill on consolidation* | | |

▶

▶

| | | | |
|---|---|---|---|
| (3) | Sales | 300 | |
| | Cost of goods sold | | 300 |
| | *Elimination of intercompany sales* | | |
| (4) | Current liabilities (accounts payable) | 50 | |
| | Current assets (accounts receivable) | | 50 |
| | *Elimination of intercompany indebtedness* | | |
| (5) | Retained profits (1 July) | 14 | |
| | Income tax expense | 6 | |
| | Cost of goods sold | | 20 |
| | *Elimination of unrealised profit in opening stock* | | |
| (6) | Cost of goods sold | 30 | |
| | Current assets (stock on hand) | | 30 |
| | *Elimination of unrealised profit in closing stock* | | |
| | Non-current assets (deferred tax asset) | 9 | |
| | Income tax expense | | 9 |
| | *Tax adjustment on unrealised profit in closing stock* | | |
| (7) | Non-current liabilities (loan from Sea Ltd) | 200 | |
| | Non-current assets (loan to Gull Ltd) | | 200 |
| | *Elimination of intercompany loan* | | |
| | Interest revenue | 20 | |
| | Interest expense | | 20 |
| | *Elimination of interest on intercompany loan* | | |
| (8) | Profit on asset sale | 120 | |
| | Non-current assets (plant and equipment) | | 120 |
| | *Elimination of unrealised profit in asset sale* | | |
| | Non-current assets (plant and equipment accumulated depreciation) | 10 | |
| | Operating expenses (depreciation expense) | | 10 |
| | *Depreciation adjustment on profit asset sale* | | |
| | Non-current assets (deferred tax asset) | 33 | |
| | Income tax expense | | 33 |
| | *Tax adjustment on profit on asset sale* | | |
| (9) | Dividends income | 50 | |
| | Retained profits (interim dividends) | | 20 |
| | Retained profits (final dividends) | | 30 |
| | *Elimination of intercompany dividends* | | |
| | Current liabilities (dividends payable) | 30 | |
| | Current assets (dividends receivable) | | 30 |
| | *Elimination of intercompany debt* | | |

Consolidated worksheet at 30 June 2015

| Accounts | Sea Ltd | Gull Ltd | Eliminations | | | | Group accounts |
| | | | Debit | | Credit | | |
| | $000's | $000's | $000's | Ref | $000's | Ref | $000's |
|---|---|---|---|---|---|---|---|
| Sales | 680 | 860 | 300 | (3) | | | 1 240 |
| Less cost of goods sold | 240 | 580 | 30 | (6) | 300 | (3) | |
| | | | | | 20 | (5) | 530 |
| Gross profit | 440 | 280 | | | | | 710 |
| Interest revenue | 60 | 30 | 20 | (7) | | | 70 |
| Dividends income | 50 | 0 | 50 | (9) | | | 0 |
| Profit on asset sale | 120 | | 120 | (8) | | | 0 |
| | 670 | 310 | | | | | 780 |
| Interest expense | 25 | 30 | | | 20 | (7) | 35 |
| Operating expenses | 125 | 150 | 5 | (2) | 10 | (8) | 270 |
| Profit before tax | 520 | 130 | | | | | 475 |
| Income tax expense | 156 | 39 | 6 | (5) | 9 | (6) | |
| | | | | | 33 | (8) | 159 |
| Profit after tax | 364 | 91 | | | | | 316 |
| Retained profits (1 July) | 25 | 30 | 5 | (1) | | | |
| | | | 20 | (2) | | | |
| | | | 14 | (5) | | | 16 |
| | 389 | 121 | | | | | 332 |
| Less interim dividend | 10 | 20 | | | 20 | (9) | 10 |
| Final dividend | 50 | 30 | | | 30 | (9) | 50 |
| Shareholders' equity | | | | | | | |
| Retained profits (30 June) | 329 | 71 | | | | | 272 |
| Ordinary shares | 200 | 60 | 60 | (1) | | | 200 |
| Reserves | 25 | 120 | | | | | 145 |
| Total equity | 554 | 251 | | | | | 617 |
| Assets | | | | | | | |
| Current assets | | | | | | | |
| Bank | 80 | 50 | | | | | 130 |
| Accounts receivable | 60 | 80 | | | 50 | (4) | 90 |
| Inventory | 100 | 90 | | | 30 | (6) | 160 |
| Dividends receivable | 30 | | | | 30 | (9) | 0 |
| Non-current assets | | | | | | | |
| Loan to Gull Ltd | 200 | | | | 200 | (7) | 0 |
| Plant and equipment | 364 | 431 | 10 | (8) | 120 | (8) | 685 |
| Deferred tax asset | 20 | 10 | 9 | (6) | | | |
| | | | 33 | (8) | | | 72 |
| Investment in Gull Ltd | 100 | | | | 100 | (1) | 0 |
| Goodwill on consolidation | | | 35 | (1) | 25 | (2) | 10 |
| Total assets | 954 | 661 | | | | | 1 147 |
| Liabilities | | | | | | | |
| Current liabilities | | | | | | | |
| Accounts payable | 100 | 80 | 50 | (4) | | | 130 |
| Dividends payable | 50 | 30 | 30 | (9) | | | 50 |
| Non-current liabilities | | | | | | | |
| Loans | 250 | 300 | 200 | (7) | | | 350 |
| Total liabilities | 400 | 410 | | | | | 530 |
| Net assets | 554 | 251 | 997 | | 997 | | 617 |

### Sea Gull Group
### Income statement
### for year ended 30 June 2015

| | Group accounts $000's |
|---|---|
| Sales | 1 240 |
| Less cost of goods sold | 530 |
| Gross profit | 710 |
| Add Interest revenue | 70 |
| | 780 |
| Less interest expense | 35 |
| Other expenses | 270 |
| Profit before tax | 475 |
| Less income tax expense | 159 |
| Profit (loss) after tax | 316 |

### Sea Gull Group
### Statement of changes in equity
### at 30 June 2015

| Retained profits | Group accounts $000's |
|---|---|
| Balance at 1 June | 16 |
| Profit (after tax) | 316 |
| Total funds for appropriation | 332 |
| Less dividends paid | |
| Interim dividends | 10 |
| Final dividends | 50 |
| Balance at 30 June | 272 |

### Sea Gull Group
### Statement of financial position
### at 30 June 2015

| | Group accounts $000's |
|---|---|
| Shareholders' equity | |
| Ordinary shares | 200 |
| Retained profits | 272 |
| Reserves | 145 |
| Total equity | 617 |
| Assets | |
| Current assets | |
| Bank | 130 |
| Accounts receivable | 90 |
| Inventory | 160 |
| Non-current assets | |
| Plant and equipment | 685 |
| Deferred tax asset | 72 |
| Goodwill on consolidation | 10 |
| Total assets | 1 147 |
| Less liabilities | |
| Current liabilities | |
| Accounts payable | 130 |
| Dividends payable | 50 |
| Non-current liabilities | |
| Loans | 350 |
| Total liabilities | 530 |
| Net assets | 617 |

# Question 10.14

From the following information you are required to:

a   prepare the journal entries to eliminate and adjust the accounts for intercompany transactions;

b   complete the consolidated worksheet in the workbook at 30 June 2015; and

c   prepare the consolidated financial statements for the period ended 30 June 2015.

On 1 January 2012, Best Ltd purchased all of the issued capital of Time Ltd and obtained control. At this date Time Ltd held the following shareholders' equity:

|  | $000's |
|---|---|
| Ordinary shares | 300 |
| Retained profits | 100 |
| Reserves | 50 |

### Additional information

1   Goodwill has been tested for impairment since the date of acquisition. For the period 1 July 2012 to 30 June 2014, $30 000 of goodwill has been impaired with an additional $15 000 impairment loss for the year ended 30 June 2015.

2   For the year ended 30 June 2015 the following intercompany transactions occurred:
   - intercompany sales totalled $500 000;
   - opening stock includes an unrealised profit of $40 000;
   - closing stock includes a $20 000 unrealised profit;
   - a long-term loan intercompany loan exists of $100 000;
   - intercompany interest of $10 000 was paid on the long-term loan;
   - on 1 January Time Ltd sold an asset costing $400 000 to Best Ltd for $480 000;
   - Time Ltd paid and declared dividends during the year;
   - assets are depreciated at 25% p.a. using the straight-line method of depreciation; and
   - the tax rate is 30%.

# Question 10.15

On 1 July 2013, Gold Ltd purchased all of the issued shares of Rush Ltd and acquired the following financial position:

**Rush Ltd**
**Statement of financial position**
**at 1 July 2013**

| Assets | $000's | Liabilities | $000's |
|---|---|---|---|
| Current assets | 200 | Current liabilities | 100 |
| Non-current assets | 800 | Non-current liabilities | 200 |
|  |  | Shareholders' equity |  |
|  |  | Ordinary shares | 500 |
|  |  | Retained profits | 50 |
|  |  | Reserves | 150 |
|  | 1 000 |  | 1 000 |

Using this information and that presented below, you are required to:

a   prepare the consolidated worksheet in the workbook at 30 June 2015; and

b   prepare consolidated financial statements for the year ended 30 June 2015

*Additional information*

- Gold Ltd's opening stock includes $50 000 in unrealised profit.
- Intercompany sales: Rush Ltd sold Gold Ltd stock valued at $200 000.
- Gold Ltd's closing stock includes stock from Rush Ltd at a mark-up of $10 000.
- Rush Ltd paid Gold Ltd $100 000 in management fees.
- Rush Ltd has brought to account a loss on sale of an asset as a result of selling Gold Ltd an asset on 1 January which had an original cost of $800 000.
- Assets are depreciated at 20% p.a. using the straight-line method.
- The tax rate is 30%.

# Comprehensive Assessment Activity

Twin Ltd is the parent entity of Waters Ltd, a wholly owned subsidiary.

Using the following account balances and additional information you are required to prepare the consolidated financial statements for the Twin Waters group for the year ended 30 June 2015.

Twin Ltd acquired the share capital of Waters Ltd on 1 July 2013. On this date Waters Ltd's account balances included the following equity account balances:

|  | $000's |
|---|---|
| Ordinary shares | 250 |
| Retained profits | 100 |
| Reserves | 50 |

The account balances of Twin Ltd and Waters Ltd on 30 June 2015 were as follows:

| Income statement | | |
|---|---|---|
|  | **Twin Ltd** $000's | **Waters Ltd** $000's |
| Sales | 700 | 900 |
| Less cost of goods sold | 300 | 600 |
| Gross profit | 400 | 300 |
| Interest received | 120 | |
| Dividends income | 100 | |
|  | 620 | 300 |
| Loss on asset sale | | 100 |
| Interest on loans | 25 | 40 |
| Operating expenses | 315 | 280 |
| Profit (loss) before tax | 280 | (120) |
| Income tax expense | 84 | (36) |
| Profit (loss) after tax | 196 | (84) |
| Retained profits (1 July) | 200 | 200 |
|  | 396 | 116 |
| Less interim dividend | 100 | 50 |
| Final dividend | 60 | 50 |
| Retained profits (30 July) | 236 | 16 |

| Statement of financial position | | |
|---|---|---|
|  | **Twin Ltd** $000's | **Waters Ltd** $000's |
| **Shareholders' equity** | | |
| Ordinary shares | 500 | 250 |
| Retained profits | 236 | 16 |
| Reserves | 400 | 250 |
| Total equity | 1 136 | 516 |
| **Assets** | | |
| **Current assets** | | |
| Bank | 40 | 20 |
| Inventory | 60 | 70 |
| Dividends receivable | 50 | 0 |
| **Non-current assets** | | |
| Plant and equipment | 741 | 866 |
| Deferred tax asset | 20 | 15 |
| Loan to Waters Ltd | 50 | 0 |
| Investment in Waters Ltd | 500 | 0 |
| Total assets | 1 461 | 971 |
| **Liabilities** | | |
| **Current liabilities** | | |
| Dividends payable | 60 | 50 |
| **Non-current liabilities** | | |
| Deferred tax liability | 15 | 5 |
| Loans | 250 | 400 |
| Total liabilities | 325 | 455 |

## Additional information

1   Goodwill has been tested for impairment since the date of acquisition. For the period 1 July 2013 to 30 June 2014, $50 000 of goodwill has been impaired with an additional $20 000 impairment loss for the year ended 30 June 2015.

2   For the year ended 30 June 2015 the following intercompany transactions occurred:
    - Opening stock includes an unrealised profit of $30 000.
    - Intercompany sales totalled $400 000.
    - Closing stock includes a $40 000 unrealised profit.
    - A long-term intercompany loan exists of $50 000.
    - Intercompany interest of $10 000 was paid on the long-term loan.
    - On 1 January Waters Ltd sold an asset costing $500 000 to Best Ltd for $400 000.
    - Assets are depreciated at 40% p.a. using the straight-line method of depreciation.
    - The tax rate is 30%.

# Assessment Checklist

Complete the following checklist to identify if you consider yourself capable of being assessed against each of the following outcomes.

| I can: | Chapter reference | Check ✓ |
|---|---|---|
| explain when a parent entity must prepare consolidated financial statements | 10.2<br>10.3 | |
| consolidate the accounts of a parent entity and a wholly owned subsidiary for reporting purposes and prepare consolidated financial statements | 10.4<br>10.5<br>10.6<br>10.7 | |

# Index